CHORAL DIRECTOR'S GUIDE

written and edited by

Kenneth L. Neidig

and

John W. Jennings

PARKER PUBLISHING COMPANY, INC.   West Nyack, N.Y.

Second Printing...August, 1967

For the

Choral Director

The director of the choral activities of young people soon finds that his college course of study has provided him with an excellent foundation on which to build a choral conducting career, but that there are a number of problems which formal classroom study alone will not solve:

- How to work with the administration, colleagues, and the public to set up a successful choral program—that will last.
- How to find appropriate music of high quality—for both training and performance—among the endless stacks of publications available.
- How to develop a rehearsal technique that will not only get the job done, making full use of every second of available time, but will provide a perpetual challenge and pleasant experience for the students as well.
- How to hold the interest of youngsters through the critical junior high years.
- How to synthesize and assimilate his background from the many required music courses into a practical guide to stylistic performance.
- How to organize a chamber ensemble.
- How to produce a public performance that is musical, educational for the students, and yet will appeal to a non-professional audience of parents, relatives, and friends.
- How to teach class voice lessons, or how to get the most out of contests and festivals, summer camps and workshops, or money spent for facilities and equipment.
- How to plan a personal curriculum, formal and informal, as a lifetime blueprint for professional development.

These problems have been solved at one time or another, at one place or another, by one person or another, through study, hard

iii   52241

work, brilliant insight, and a great deal of experimentation over long periods of time.

The school choral conductor, who may even be an instrumentalist who suddenly finds himself in charge of a chorus, will find that he may share the cumulative knowledge and experience of many extremely successful directors through the pages of this one book.

- Each has had many years in the field.
- Each is a recognized expert in his field.
- Each has produced notable, lasting results.

It is our hope that through this generous sharing of ideas, techniques, and experiences, the very important work being carried on in school systems throughout the country may be made more meaningful to the student, more satisfying for the director, and more beneficial to the community.

Kenneth L. Neidig
John W. Jennings

Contents

1

Personal and Professional Development

by Wiley L. Housewright

Florida State University

Wiley L. Housewright

is Professor of Music Education and Conductor of the University Singers, Florida State University, Tallahassee. He holds the Ed.D. from New York University, M.A. from Columbia University, and the B.S. from North Texas State College. Other studies have been at the Julliard and Eastman Schools of Music, and Texas Christian University. He has been director of music in the public schools of Forth Worth, Texas and Batavia, N.Y., lecturer in music at New York University, Associate Professor of Music Literature for the University of Texas, and Professor of Music Education at Indiana University and the University of Michigan.

He serves on the advisory boards of the Department of State's International Cultural Exchange Service, the Ford Foundation's Program in Humanities and the Arts, and the United States National Commission for UNESCO. His many talents and interests have taken him to the principal countries of Europe (he read a paper, "Music Education: Goals and Processes" at an international conference in Vienna), South America, and the Near and Far East (Fulbright teaching and research).

Dr. Housewright was named President-elect at the 1966 Convention of the Music Educators National Conference climaxing many years of professional organization activity. He has served on the Board of Directors, Executive Committee, and as President of the Southern Division. Since 1958, Dr. Housewright has been Chairman of the Editorial Board for the Music Educators Journal.

The successful completion of requirements for a degree in music should be considered only as the most basic of training for the very complicated job of directing a school's choral music program. During 4 years in college the potential instructor may have accumulated a bagfull of tricks, but has only begun to investigate the great choral literature of the world, has only partially developed his own vocal capacity, and has not yet made the transition from choral *singer* to choral *director*.

So the degree is never the *end* of anything, merely the beginning ... an obvious statement, of course, but do choral directors really believe it? Probably not—until they begin to sense the magnitude of their task, until the day they realize the value of a vast reservoir of reserve knowledge from which they can select the precise technique or the particular phrase that will provide the instantaneous solution 85 impatient teen-agers expected over 10 seconds ago (isn't that an eternity?).

What Does It Take?

The director who expects to develop personally and professionally throughout a long and successful career must never hesitate to learn anything at any time, in any place, from any one, which will add to his knowledge and skill—no matter how formidable the task may seem at the time.

A successful choral conductor must have a strong theoretical background, with the ability to analyze every aspect of the music he rehearses, down to the very finest detail. This is essential not only to conserve valuable rehearsal time, but also to assure personal understanding and subsequent communication of the composer's intention.

Ability as both pianist and singer are also necessary. The conductor should be able to demonstrate the tone he desires from the choir. I know many fine instrumentalists who have had great success with choruses because of their organizational ability, flash, and spontaneity ... yet the choral sound has never been quite satisfactory. It is a limitation no one can overcome, unless he himself has been through vocal training, or has sung with an outstanding choral organization.

The "Ideal" Choral Director

Fortunately our society has not yet progressed to the point of baby-factory produced specialists (such as those described by Huxley in *Brave New World*) who have exactly the same qualifications, but any "spec sheet" for a model choral director would have to include the following:

Enthusiasm. Every individual has what Whitehead describes as a "Romance Period," which is similar to those times throughout the history of the world when great leaps forward have been made by the enthusiastic thrusts of adventurous souls. We, as choral directors, must ourselves attempt to maintain the same joy of discovery which is so gratifying when observed in our most eager students. The things I do today in connection with my professional life are just as interesting and exciting for me as the things I did in the traditionally "idealistic" stages of my life (immediately post-college) . . . if they were not I would leave the field immediately.

Initiative. The effective director must lead the students, the school administration, and the community to an ever-expanding appreciation of choral music. More effective programs or new ways to attack the problems of the old programs often must be initiated.

Patience. Many directors start something new every day, but the really effective people have the patience to work with students until each project has reached a successful resolution—time, after time, after time. Nothing can be so deadening, however, as work which becomes drudgery because it is repetitive without being creative.

Imagination. One's only real problem is that life is too short to investigate all the wonderful aspects of choral directing. Choral repertoire, for instance, is so vast, yet there are those who continue to teach the same 6 pieces every year. The imaginative person will be able to maintain a dynamic situation which in turn can provide both himself and his students with a constant stimulus for greater achievement.

Idealism. Every director should keep in mind an ideal for which his group must strive—as vocalists, as musicians, and as human beings.

Realism. The worst kind of choir is a smug one, yet the problem is one of the most difficult to combat amongst a select group in a good choral music program. When the conductor really understands the fine work many other choirs are doing (not just those within a 50 mile radius!) he is in a much better position to control his own ego, as well as to "bat down" the smug singers who can cause such a destructive wave of unrealistic superiority.

Precision without pedantry. Every good teacher knows precisely how he will present the material to be learned. Although experienced instructors can accurately anticipate responses, the really creative person is prepared to make sensitive modifications as the exciting drama of student, teacher, ideas, learning process, action and reaction begins to evolve.

Open-mindedness. Many of the great advances in every field of human endeavor have been made because one individual not only successfully assimilated the knowledge and experience of many others, but, ironically, at the same time, raised serious questions as to its validity and refused to allow his thoughts to be restricted by current "facts." The political philosopher who said, "The tenacity of outworn creeds has tragically blocked the road of human progress," could have just as easily been talking about choral music instruction.

Emotional composure. Disappointing things happen in rehearsals, many of them unexpected. They cannot be taken personally, but must be approached merely as problems to be solved. The director's emotional makeup must be such that he is not easily thrown out of this desirable professional character.

Physical and mental energy. Every aspect of the choral director's job requires great drive to insure the successful completion of the many projects he will initiate. The person whose energy is sapped by problems of physical or mental health cannot function effectively in this demanding atmosphere.

Introspection. Choral directors, traditionally, have been ready to fly into action. The question, "Will you conduct?" is often interrupted by a fast "yes" skimming off the top of a breeze on its way to the podium. It is dangerously easy to think of students as trained seals and to teach them a few tricks which will stand them in good stead for the next 20 minutes . . . but how about the next 50 (plus) years of their lives? . . . or the future of what you hope will become a permanent, successful choral music program?

Regular, sometimes long, but always thoughtful, periods must be spent in contemplation—assessing both present and past efforts, re-evaluating basic philosophy and methods of implementation, and making dynamic plans for the future based on the conclusions reached.

SELF EVALUATION—THE BEGINNING

One must take into account those things he seems to do best as well as to realistically face his limitations. I have very little confidence in scientific tests of musical talent, but I do feel that one should compare everything he does with what others do, in the context of accepted requirements for a successful choral director. Director "A" may be much better at achieving a good choral sound, but Director "B" may be more effective musically. One may emphasize diction, while the other is a master of phrasing. Neither can afford to neglect his role as a human being in constant personal relationship with other human beings, of course.

While contest ratings may bear some relationship to the ability of the conductor, the system tends to provide security for the technician as it neglects the thoughtful teacher of musical values, and I hesitate to use ratings at the state festival as a reliable measuring device.

Those personal and professional deficiencies which can be corrected should be attended to immediately. Others which may be impossible to bring up to a satisfactory level, we must be prepared to accomodate and to somehow live with them. For instance, I usually decline when asked to direct community singing, since I am just not as good at it as a lot of people I know. It is unfortunate that we must accept any limitations at all. Most of us would like to be able to do everything well, but it seems to be impossible at this stage of mankind's development.

The Personal Study Plan

The thoughtful choral director who has honestly investigated his personal and professional qualifications must then fashion some plan of lifetime personal study which will not only nourish steady growth, but also provide the periodic revitalization so necessary in any process of development.

There are various study techniques available, even for the full time choral director who may already feel overworked.

College courses. Many excellent classes are offered during the summer, and some on Saturdays throughout the school year. The name of the instructor (rather than the course title) is most useful when picking those which will be of the greatest value to you.

Workshops. A well organized, serious workshop, set up on a regular academic plan (although accelerated), can provide an opportunity to observe the choral techniques of outstanding conductors, expose a lot of interesting literature, and give the director just the change of pace he may need at that point. Workshops must be chosen carefully, however. Some confused conductors, loaded down with compositions of questionable value, have been seen returning from sessions designed only to promote the sale of music by the clinician or his associates.

Hero worship. This practice, so common among the teen-agers we teach, is a legitimate technique for the choral director—if used with discretion. In our profession there are many who display those personal and professional qualities which are so admirable as to be worthy of emulation. By examining their sense of values, observing their relationships with other human beings, and analyzing their choral techniques, our own lives may be enriched and our professional progress somewhat accelerated.

"Bull sessions." Informal conversations with others in the profession can be a fine source of useful ideas and information. By developing the maturity to ask and listen, rather than the inclination always to tell, and the technique to shift a conversation from the weather or the latest gossip to something more significant, every choral director can *learn* as he enjoys the fellowship of good company.

Broadcast and recorded music. Time spent traveling in a car or in moments of relaxation at home can often serve a dual purpose, if good music is sought out on the radio dial, or put on the phonograph. The concept of style—so important to the success of a choral conductor—can be helped by surrounding oneself with an atmosphere of the best performances available.

Visits. When they can be arranged, visits to other schools can be of great value. Joint concerts often provide a fresh point of view. Obviously, personal visiting time is limited, but there are other opportunities such as during holidays *not* common to all schools, or on a choir tour, en route to music contests, festivals, conventions, and professional meetings. Some schools provide the teacher with "Professional" or "in-service training" days for this purpose.

Applied music. There is never an end to the progress which can be made through the study of voice or piano, both of which are valuable to the choral director. Even though formal lessons are not scheduled, a regular practice plan should be maintained, though the individual sessions may be shortened by the pressures of your teaching schedule.

Reading. Developments in the music profession, as in the entire world, have become so rapid that merely "keeping up" is a prodigious undertaking, yet the choral director must try. Articles and reviews of new books and records in magazines, journals, and research bulletins, are often the best quick sources of the greatest amount of information. One of the great fallacies of public thinking about musicians in the 20th century is that they are artists who are out of touch with everything except their own specialized world. While there is some element of truth in this, I have found the more mature musicians to be quite capable of exchanging information or debating other subjects as well.

Rapid, selective reading—with a purpose—helps one to be well-informed on both the personal and the professional level.

The professional library. By making wise, and regular, purchases over a period of time, a very useful professional library can be accumulated. The following lists of books and records contain many items around which libraries may be built. Other items of special interest can be added to these suggestions (not intended to be comprehensive) by the individual collector, so that his library will carry the stamp of his own preferences.

BOOKS

Davison, Archibald T. *Choral Conducting.* Cambridge: Harvard University Press, 1945.

Davison, Archibald T. *Techniques of Choral Composition.* Cambridge: Harvard University Press, 1945.

Ehret, Walter. *The Choral Conductor's Handbook.* New York: Edward B. Marks Music Co., 1959.

Howerton, George. *Technique and Style in Choral Singing.* New York: Carl Fischer, 1958.

Jacobs, Arthur, ed. *Choral Music.* Baltimore: Penguin Books, 1963.

Krone, Max. *The Chorus and its Conductor.* Chicago: Neil A Kjos, 1945.

RECORDS

BACH, JOHANN SEBESTIAN
 Cantatas (your choice)
 Magnificat
 Mass in B Minor
 St. Matthew Passion
BEETHOVEN, LUDWIG VAN
 Missa Solemnis
BERLIOZ, HECTOR
 L'Enfance du Christ
 Requiem
BLOCH, ERNEST
 Sacred Service

 (Avodath Hakodesh)
BRAHMS, JOHANNES
 Alto Rhapsody
 German Requiem
 Liebeslieder Waltzes, Op. 52
 Part Songs and Motets
BRITTEN, BENJAMIN
 Ceremony of Carols
 War Requiem
BRUCKNER, ANTON
 Mass in D Minor
 Motets

RECORDS *(cont.)*
Te Deum
BUXTEHUDE, DIETRICH
Cantatas
BYRD, WILLIAM
Masses and Motets
CHERUBINI, LUIGI
Requiem in C Minor
DEBUSSY, CLAUDE
La Damoiselle élue
Le Martyre de St. Sébastien
DES PREZ, JOSQUIN
Missa Pange lingua
Motets
FAURE, GABRIEL
Requiem
GESUALDO, DON CARLO
Madrigals
GIBBONS, ORLANDO
Madrigals, Anthems
HANDEL, GEORGE FRIDERICK
Israel in Egypt
Messiah
HAYDN, FRANZ JOSEPH
Creation
Mass No. 7 in C "Paukenmesse"
(Missa in Tempore Belli)
Mass No. 9, "Nelson Mass"
HONNEGER, ARTHUR
Christmas Cantata
Jeanne d'Arc au bûcher
Roi David
JANNEQUIN, CLEMENT
Chansons
KODALY, ZOLTAN
Psalmus Hungaricus
LASSUS, ORLANDUS
Motets and Madrigals
LULLY, JEAN BAPTISTE
Miserere
MENDELSSOHN, FELIX
Elijah
MONTEVERDI, CLAUDIO
Madrigals
MORLEY, THOMAS
Madrigals

MOZART, WOLFGANG AMADEUS
Mass in C "Coronation," K. 317
Mass in c "The Great," K. 427
Requiem in d minor, K. 626
ORFF, CARL
Carmina Burana
PALESTRINA, GIOVANNI DA
Motets
Missa Papae Marcelli
PERGOLESI, GIOVANNI
Stabat Mater
POULENC, FRANCIS
Gloria
Stabat Mater
PROKOFIEV, SERGEI
Alexander Nevsky
PURCELL, HENRY
Hail, Bright Cecilia
SAINT SAENS, CAMILLE
Christmas Oratorio
SCHUBERT, FRANZ
Mass in G
SCHÜTZ, HEINRICH
Motets
Psalms
St. Matthew Passion
STRAVINSKY, IGOR
Symphony of Psalms
TALLIS, THOMAS
Lamentations of Jeremiah
THOMPSON, RANDALL
Alleluia
Testament of Freedom
VAUGHAN WILLIAMS, RALPH
Mass
Sea Symphony
Serenade to Music
VERDI, GIUSEPPE
Requiem Mass
Te Deum
VICTORIA, TOMAS LUIS DE
Messa da Requiem
WALTON, WILLIAM
Belshazzar's Feast

PROFESSIONAL SINGING ENGAGEMENTS

Since the rehearsal time of professional groups, where members are paid by the hour, in much more limited than that of school groups, who have only the end-of-period bell (not the cash register) to restrict them, great lessons in the principle of *economy through maximum effort* can be learned by the school director who works professionally.

Probably the most valuable experience I ever had was as a member of a small group within the *Collegiate Chorale,* when Robert Shaw was making the transition in his career from popular to serious music.[1] But experience with a top-notch choral organization is very difficult for most teachers with a full time position to acquire. Many summer jobs either have so little to do with real music (resort waiters and waitresses who sing), or are so demanding vocally (singing one show in the evening while rehearsing next week's production during the day) that they are of questionable value.

PROFESSIONAL ORGANIZATIONS

Membership in the Music Educators National Conference, for the broad picture, or smaller groups like the American Choral Directors Association, the American Choral Foundation, and the National Association of Teachers of Singing, for more specialized areas, should be considered as a necessity of professional life. One may not have time to be active in each, but their regular magazines, journals, research bulletins, supplemental publications, clinics, workshops, and other worthwhile projects, are excellent sources of valuable information.

Many other groups may be of special value, according to one's own tastes and instincts. For example, I belong to the College Music Society because I find their interesting controversies to be at the very heart of the best thinking in the profession. As a member of the American Musicological Society and the Music Library Association, I have been able to keep in touch with invaluable publications in these fields over a period of many years.

---

[1] *Editor's note*: Professional requirements were extremely demanding. The first time through a new piece (Hindemith, Milhaud, Schuman, etc.) was for over-all familiarization; the second time was to correct all mistakes; the third time was to memorize. The size of the group was reduced until every member in it was able to deliver . . . now!

THE LADDER OF SUCCESS

Good teaching—the most professional performance of the duties for which one is hired—is the first way attention is centered on a choral director "on the way up." The director who not only can present an outstanding choir today, but who has been able to set up a school program which will insure outstanding concerts and musically educated students in years to come, gains the respect of musicians and educators, the admiration of parents, and the attention of administrators.

Those who make themselves available for assignments which are important to the academic community (committees, offices) and who participate in civic affairs (service clubs, churches) demonstrate their willingness to help others and, in the process, become more aware of the problems others face.

Music educators are often criticized for being so preoccupied with their own concerns that they ignore the rest of the school. Even though most are so over scheduled that they have very little time, it is important to work on school committees. If the music program falls out of balance with the rest of the school, we should be the first to know. Also, musicians can present an artistic, sensitive, point of view which is often badly needed, but seldom occurs to others because their particular academic discipline is different.

In addition to good teaching and service to the broader spectrum, one of the things which makes a most attractive candidate for greater professional opportunities is personal creation—composition, arranging, or editing of choral music, personal performance, research and publication of articles in professional magazines.

CHANGING JOBS—GRACEFULLY

Care must be taken when a possible move is being considered. Immediate comfort and security often cause choral directors to pass up what could be a great professional opportunity. Others, in almost frantic search for financial success, move every time they can get a $300 increase in pay.

No job is without problems. Unless one is prepared to accept a new set of difficulties in exchange for those he wishes to escape, he should not consider a change of positions, but, rather, stay on to face *and solve* the small problems. Continuity is a great element in eventual success. However, if personality conflicts or other seemingly irresolvable impasses occur, it is in the best interests of all concerned for the director to seek a more compatible situation elsewhere.

True success comes from the wisdom to recognize and take advantage of opportunities which fit into a career plan that is "tailor-made" for the particular personal qualities and professional qualifications of the individual.

THE PERSONAL DATA SHEET

Every choral director should prepare a brief resumé covering both educational background and professional experience. At the end of each school year appropriate items can be added. In this way, material is always immediately available when you receive requests for personal information. The following suggested form may be helpful in preparing your own personal data sheet.

Full name	photo	Present employment
Birthplace - date		Home address

Married? - wife's maiden name - date   City - State

Children? - year of birth   Type teaching certificate - State - no.

- -

EDUCATION

                                    (Score)   (Percentile)
Nationally recognized tests: Graduate Record Exam
                               National Teachers Exam
                               Others
              (School)   (Years attended)   (Name of degree - date)
Doctoral level
   major areas and number of hours in each - activities - honors
Master's level
   major areas and number of hours in each - activities - honors
Bachelor's level
   major areas and number of hours in each - activities - honors
High School level
   major areas and number of credits in each - activities - honors

PROFESSIONAL ACTIVITIES

Personal performance   Civic organizations
Professional associations   Personal activities
Record of employment (date-employer-duties-accomplishments)
Publications (national-state-local)

THE EMPLOYMENT PICTURE

According to a very fine publication designed to acquaint high school students with "A Career in Music Education,"[2] music teachers may be either men or women who have a deep love for a wide variety of music, are interested in helping others, and have made better than average grades in high school. They are in good health (including adequate energy and emotional stability), blessed with a lively imagination and a pleasant sense of humor. They have developed the ability to work with other people, to communicate effectively, and to organize detail. For this, yearly salaries ranging from $4,000 for beginning instructors to $18,000 for supervisors or college professors can be anticipated.

While it is extremely difficult to determine an exact formula for success because many people with what might seem to be the most *un*-likely of qualifications have gained great personal and professional standing, there do seem to be certain basic requirements which are generally desired at the various levels of music education.

The following chart is intended only as a guide. The duties of several positions are often combined, especially in the smaller schools. Since complete personal and professional competency is assumed as a requirement for every music education position, only those qualities which seem to demand extra emphasis have been listed.

THE EMPLOYMENT PICTURE
For the Vocal/Choral Musician/Teacher

ELEMENTARY: Methodical, Thorough, Patient

(Professional title and description of duties)	*(Special personal qualities and skills required for each position)*
SPECIAL MUSIC TEACHER – visits each room on a regular schedule, working directly with the students.	Solo singing usually unaccompanied. Children's song repertoire. Clear presentation of all fundamentals.

---

[2] Music Educators National Conference, Washington, D.C., 1962.

ELEMENTARY: *Methodical, Thorough, Patient (cont.)*

MUSIC CONSULTANT (SUPERVISOR) – assists the classroom teacher (who actually does the teaching) with procedures and materials.

Rapport with classroom teachers. Wealth of usable materials. Understanding of good teachers who have limited music education. Clear presentation of sequence of learning and aims of music teaching.

CHORUS DIRECTOR – conducts performing groups (2 and 3 part) of selected students.

Piano. Children's chorus repertoire. Knowledge of and techniques for development of the child's voice.

JUNIOR HIGH: Psychologist, Optimistic, Magnetic

GENERAL MUSIC TEACHER – required music for every student, with emphasis on music fundamentals, singing, appreciation.

Ability to cope with Jr. High age behavior and emotional problems. Voice production fundamentals. Rapport with boys.

CHORUS DIRECTOR – s e l e c t e d mixed chorus, boys and girls choruses, small ensembles, feeder system, high school assistance.

Rapid part singing rehearsal technique. Great knowledge of changing voice.

SENIOR HIGH: Competitive, Challenging, Cooperative

CHORUS DIRECTOR – organize and conduct mixed chorus, boys and girls groups, feeder choruses, small ensembles.

Organizational ability. Competitive spirit, energy and enthusiasm compatible with students of this age group.

MUSIC CLASS TEACHER – voice, theory, appreciation, history.

Logical sequence of presentation, realistic assessment of high school level, voice fundamentals.

COLLEGE: Outstanding, Unique, Inspiring

VOICE TEACHER – studio lessons, voice major guidance, recital preparation.

Solo work, recitals, repertoire, voice production fundamentals, remedial techniques.

CHORAL DIRECTOR—mixed chorus, male and female choruses, select choir, madrigal and other small ensembles.

Marked success with Sr. High performing groups or apprenticeship to college conductor.

COLLEGE: *Outstanding, Unique, Inspiring (cont.)*

MUSIC EDUCATION – classes in materials, methods, philosophy, history; personal guidance for prospective teachers.

Instrumental, as well as vocal/choral experience. Awareness of entire musical scene. Realistic, but inspirational approach to training of future teachers.

MUSIC LITERATURE INSTRUCTOR – classes covering the significant music throughout the long development of the art.

Cultured, "arts-oriented" person who also has knowledge of the relationship of music to history, philosophy, politics, etc.

ADMINISTRATIVE: Efficient, Perceptive, Mature

MUSIC SUPERVISOR – (large city or county system) and COLLEGE MUSIC DEPARTMENT HEAD – equipment purchases, curriculum, teaching methods, personnel management.

"Idea" person who can utilize the talents of all to best advantage. Efficient organizer. Public relations. Mature sense of balance—within music as well as in relation to other educational areas.

BUILDING A FUTURE

For those who can qualify, the future is always bright. But it is brightest for those who are able to display their unique qualifications in an area which will show them off to their best advantage.

For example, a lot of what has and is being written about the voice change is absolute nonsense. It has no scientific or psychological basis, but is merely the *opinion* of teachers who have spent a lot of time working with junior high students, and who may be quite fallable, though verbose.

It seems almost unbelievable to me that even with the invention of ingenious measuring devices, we now have little scientifically corroborated evidence to support any side of the argument which continues to rage about the development of the adolescent male voice. A bright young person could create a great career for himself by doing systematic studies of this entire area.

There are equally fertile fields for those who can apply their talent to the exact place it is needed.

DEVELOPMENT—A LIFE-LONG PROCESS

Some of the most wonderful moments in my life have happened quite unexpectedly, but almost always as a direct result of something else which I *had* planned: even though improvisation can be one of the most interesting processes of music, there must always be an underlying structure on which to base the imaginative variations.

And so the lifetime developmental process cannot be planned in fine detail, but evolves naturally as one finds a set of principles he can "live with" today, but may modify in any one of several directions tomorrow.

I have found it best to first determine the most desirable atmosphere for the development of your own particular talents, abilities, and interests, and then to thrive as well as you can during a period of growth and maturation. The opportunities which present themselves during the course of a professional lifetime cannot always be anticipated, but the important thing is to *be prepared to deliver* when opportunity does come your way.

2

Public Relations

by Louis H. Diercks

Ohio State University

Louis H. Diercks

now teaches at the University of New Mexico, following his retirement from a career full of innovation and truly significant professional contribution as head of the Ohio State University School of Music's Division of Choral and Church Music, where he directed the Symphonic Choir and the 375-voice University Chorus. He received the B.A. degree from Bradley Polytechnic College in 1926, the B.M. from Mac Phail School of Music the same year, and the M.A. from the University of Iowa in 1932.

Prof. Diercks joined the Ohio State faculty in 1933, and in 1937 founded the Symphonic Choir, which won the 1938 CBS network's "Choral Quest" competition. Yearly American tours have resulted in great critical acclaim, including Detroit, Washington, D.C., and New York's Town Hall. In 1955 the choir sang before some 485,000 people of at least 53 nationalities, and took second place in an international competition while on a tour of Europe. In 1960, Prof. Diercks conducted a 7 month choral research project in Germany and the British Isles. He has written a cantata, "The Prodigal Son," several choral works, and numerous articles on choral problems and techniques. Outstanding leadership of the Symphonic Choir has earned Prof. Diercks a reputation as one of the country's foremost figures in college choral work, but the regular rehearsal period of the same choir—at noon, 5 days a week—has also earned "Pappy" Diercks the title, "The only man at Ohio State who hasn't had lunch since 1937."

An effective public relations program is based primarily upon the projection, in every direction, of the truest possible image of the school's choral music offerings. While the director's main objective should be to develop the best system of music education possible in a given situation, it is also important that he keep the public informed of systematic progress toward that goal. News of accomplishments, presented as a statement of fact, without boasting, can help to keep both the music program and the entire school system in the best possible light. Even though professional advertising men, with seemingly unlimited "sales gimmicks" may cause some temporary excitement, *honesty* and *integrity* are necessary when establishing a permanently successful relationship with the public. Never let the public down.

Circles of Public Relations

Just as a rock tossed into a very placid pool will create a seemingly endless series of concentric circles, the *self image*, when tossed into the pool of public opinion, will send out seemingly endless waves of influence to every portion of the population. (*see* Fig. 2-1)

The Nucleus—The Self Image

The director and his students must first develop a firm concept of what it is they are trying to accomplish, and then make constant objective evaluations of efforts toward this goal. This is by far the most important part of the entire public relations effort, since the size, shape and quality of the self image so directly determines the form of the image projected to each segment of the public. A nucleus which is well-rounded will produce a regular, smooth effect, clearly defined in each outer circle; but a distorted center will create an eccentric system of jagged lines serving only as a source of confusion to everyone.

Music has never been merely a "science of sound," but is virtually a way of life. Choral music, especially, is concerned with ideas— from every philosophical background and of every theological persuasion—because of the unbreakable bond between text and musical line. This marvelous quality must be conveyed to each student as his individual development is strongly encouraged and carefully guided by the director, who, himself, must constantly grow in understanding.

There is also the necessity for mature cooperation between all

members, even as they develop individually. Whereas it is possible
for members of a prominent orchestra's woodwind section, for instance, to produce flawless ensemble sounds (when not even on
speaking terms), singers, whose instrument is literally their own
flesh and blood, must "get along" or the quality of the sound will
change. They must not only like each other—they must like themselves.

The Director's Image

Those who teach have been entrusted with the responsibility of
guiding young people to a greater musical and personal maturity.
Fortunately, the experience will be one of growth and development for the instructor as well, if he is willing to experiment. He
must be sure that the youngsters always recognize the day to day
and always look for fresh opportunities to expand his intellectual
horizons. For instance, in 1937, experiments with a synthesis of media we called "Choral-Dance-Theatre" were started. By 1948 it has
become so exciting for us that we shared the form with MENC,
meeting in Detroit. In addition to the stimulation provided to both
the singers and director by the excitement of probing into a fresh
area, we discovered that dancing and singing are very closely related in that (1) both are expressed by the entire body, and (2)
a musical phrase can actually be a thrilling kinesthetic experience.

Adults must realize that even though concert performances of the
pupils may fall far short of a teacher's aspirations (which have
been developing through many seasons of personal dreams, growth,
and experimentation), standards must be kept high so that students,
being forced to *reach* for success, have the best opportunity to
develop their talents. But, most important to the teen-ager, adults
progress they are making.

Choral directors must remember, and demonstrate to their students, that the process is more important than the product. Those
ethereal peaks, those great moments of insight, seldom come during
a concert performance (except possibly with a professional group
which has not been over rehearsed), but a great rehearsal can be
the most moving experience of an entire musical life.

During the same Choral-Dance-Theatre experimental period, we
were singing Luis Sandi's Mexican Indian lullaby, "Yaqui Cradle
Song" as the dancers were extemporizing movement and pattern.
Suddenly one of the dancers interrupted us and said, "I believe this

baby is dead!" Without comment, the singers evoked tone colors more sombre than before, the tempo changed, and the dancers became weeping mothers and spirits leaping above the dead child. Such events of discovery we have come to call "Ah ha! moments"— those split seconds when this whole crazy world suddenly seems to make sense, sometimes only for an instant when measured by the clock, but often amounting to a lifetime when measured by its influence on the spirit. Out of such stuff is made the image of the choir's meaning to its members. This is a "felt" thing which can be transmitted excitingly to audiences at concerts.

THE STUDENT'S IMAGE

Each succeeding group must be indoctrinated with the aim, purpose, and heritage of the organization, as molded by the director. Every new member of each group must realize that the fame or image of the choir has been passed on to him by those who have come before . . . and he must struggle not only to maintain this position of honor, but also to grow, both as an individual and as a group member. In order to help instill the proper attitude—an expanded capacity for loyalty—in each prospective Symphonic Choir member at Ohio State University, we have developed an induction ceremony which is presented early in the students' choir experience and administered formally at the end of his first year, with all members present.

THE SYMPHONIC CHOIR

Aims

Symphonic Choir is primarily a musical organization. Its ideals are the musical expression of that which is highest, greatest, and most valuable in choral art. However, the achievement of perfection in any field depends on more than mere technical proficiency. To feel sincerely and vividly is the lot of many. It is the strength of emotion. But appreciation belongs to the few. Only those who blend passion with understanding can realize the essence of performance.

Music is one of the most universal expressions of living. Its power is derived from its ability to portray as physical sound all the joys and sorrows of both the musician and his audience. Skill alone produces only the hollow rattling of emotional skeletons. Symphonic Choir strives to develop upon such a skeleton the depths of spiritual perception and the resulting responsibility which together can produce sincere art. Only those who care for fundamental truth can achieve the richness of vital harmony which marks the true aristocrat and artist.

You have been selected as potential Symphonichoirs. It is your privilege and responsibility to cultivate those physical, mental, and spiritual qualities which contribute the most toward the efforts of the Choir to achieve that aristocracy.

Music as an Expression of Beauty

It has been said that music is a "picture painted on a background of silence." But, it is an ever-changing picture, whose images, shades, and tones are as infinite as the ranks of its observers. It is painted with great, raw overtones and whispered echoes; it is splashed with surf-torn dissonances, and irresistible harmonic tidal waves.

An attentive listener may see the red rush of a titanic battle, or the rending agony of a crucifixion. He may watch the delicate intricacies of a fairy ball, or the dragging stride of a chain gang. He may follow the growth of a nation or an ideal. Sometimes the picture is expressed in the simple form of a lullaby. Again it may present a complex series of orchestral variations, depicting several conflicting ideas.

Beauty is most apparent to those who share in its creation. The intimate contact of participation stimulates more sensitive evaluation and understanding. Bovee said, "The beauty seen is partly in the beholder." However, if vision is blurred by many diverging viewpoints, its effectiveness is diminished. For this reason, you, as new Symphonichoirs, must strive to achieve unity of perception, appreciation, and expression. Beauty attained by these standards is the only beauty acceptable in the aristocracy of those who care.

Music as a Means to Moral and Spiritual Growth

Music should hold a prominent position in the hearts of those who believe that all men are brothers, and that all nations are one people, with the same basic problems, the same hopes and fears, the same desires and longings, and the same weaknesses to be conquered. The evidence of history, both ancient and contemporary, presents the indisputable fact that, given equal opportunity, no scientific or technical achievement is impossible for any specific group.

Music has long held a unique place in the culture of men and of nations, in their efforts to strengthen and improve themselves. The chants of stone age warriors still echo in the Australian bush. African tribesmen still unite their voices in musical rhythms when the gods of seed-time and harvest are propitiated. The great war chants of the Norsemen brought terror to many an ancient coastal village, as the flames leaped high above some newly raided town. The invincible spirit of the Cossacks is felt again whenever their fierce choruses ring through our concert halls.

Protestantism has marched down through the centuries with the courageous faith of Luther's "Ein Festa Burg," "A Mighty Fortress Is Our God." We of this country are not yet unfamiliar with a certain little piece of musical impudence which was flaunted in the faces of the British in 1776. The songs of the colored slaves of the south still shorten weary days as they once did in endless rows of cotton. Unity of peoples has always achieved expression in music.

So today the blood of the ex-poilu surges to the strains of the Marseillaise. There are lumps in the throats of undemonstrative Englishmen when they rise to sing "God Save the Queen." Those of us who have followed the Stars and Stripes know the thrill of a common cause when Francis Scott Key's first rhetorical question breaks the silence.

And now, when the importance of world unity becomes more and more paramount, we should make use of the peculiar universality of music to the utmost limits of our ability. We do not need to understand the Russian language to appreciate the pathos, suffering, and faith which produced Tschesnokoff's "Salvation is Created." The loneliness of Schubert's "Wanderer" is felt without the translation of one German phrase. To understand the music, the art of a people, is to understand their culture, and the problems and struggles which produced it. With understanding comes tolerance and appreciation, willingness to live, and to help live. Music is one means by which this unity of spirit and effort may be more readily instigated and cultivated than by any other implement.

The mass achievement of such perception is acquired on an individual basis. Therefore, we, as individuals, must take advantage of each opportunity for refinement which is available to us. We dare not leave a single phase of our potentialities for someone else to develop or we will again diverge in our opinions and thereby lose all we have gained. The moral and spiritual strength accruing to us will be the reward we obtain, not only for ourselves, but for our children and the world community in which they will live or perish.

This individual strength and security has been exemplified by many men in many ways and in many times. However, as members of Symphonic Choir interested in its future and its effect on our own future, we will do well to follow and uphold the standards set for us by a member of this group, who followed his convictions through the last, ultimate test on a battlefield in Italy during the recent great international holocaust. I am referring to Richard DeSelm, a tenor in the Choir from 1937 to 1940.

Dick was a quiet, unassuming young man, whose fine intellectual and spiritual perceptions were stirred by the ideals and attainments of the Choir. A true musician, he realized that the accomplishments of Symphonic, ultimates in themselves, were such only because they served to

further strengthen and enrich the lives and potentialities of the participants, enabling them to go forward to newer and greater living, feeling,
understanding, and interpretation.

His faith in Symphonic Choir as a way of strengthening and furthering
his belief was such that, while recovering from wounds received in
action, he made the following written request of his mother, Mrs.
DeSelm. With her very kind permission I now quote briefly from that
letter. "If anything should happen to me, I want you to give one thousand
dollars of my money to the Music Department, to be used for the advancement of choral music."

Shortly after that he returned to active duty and was killed. The
interest from that fund is now awarded annually as the Richard DeSelm
Memorial Scholarship. This is given to the man who, during the previous
year, was considered by the Director of the Choir and the music faculty
to have been most helpful to Symphonic by his spirit, achievement, and
example. The scholarship, first awarded in 1945, has been given to Paul
Buckley, Harold Fiske, Harold Beckett, Charles Jackson, and Dane
Stoll. It is the high privilege of the Choir as a whole, and of the scholarship winners in particular, to maintain inviolate the ideals for which
Dick DeSelm gave his life.

Music and Loyalty and Responsibility

We of Symphonic feel that one of the best means of continuing the
high purpose of Dick DeSelm is the production and sincere interpretation of the very best music of which we are capable.

But great music is never produced without a sincere loyalty and sense
of responsibility towards its creation. Where individuals are concerned,
as in the case of the composer or the solo artist, the necessary devotion
is more easily achieved for the interests and desires of only one personality must be subordinated and coordinated. But the successful integra-
tion of even a small group of individual talents and ambitions is a task
which the greatest of directors cannot accomplish alone.

The most powerful aid upon which the director may rely is found in
the musician himself. Man is by nature gregarious. The desire to share
thoughts, experiences, and emotions is more easily fulfilled through
musical expression than through any other medium. Harmony and
melody are universal in their message and appeal. Conceptions may be
realized, shared, and deepened, either consecutively or simultaneously.
It is this ability of music to both emit and transmit which ultimately
molds and directs all truly great musical organizations.

Symphonic Choir is composed of individuals. Its greatest weakness,
and its greatest strength, are both found in the way each Symphonichoir
evaluates himself as a part of the whole. If you choose to regard your
place in Symphonic as merely a means of technical improvement, you

will defeat both yourself and the Choir. Such an attitude will separate you from us, and your participation will consist of mere vocal exercise. But if you sincerely aspire to the rank of true aristocracy, your abilities and experiences will blend with and multiply those of the Choir as a whole, just as each small facet of a diamond, though itself unnoticed, contributes to the fire and glory of the entire stone.

You have been selected to uphold the standards and achievements of a nationally eminent choir, the symbol of whose success is on the table before you. The future of that choir depends upon the extent to which you are willing to strive for unity of understanding, response, and creation. You must acquire sensitivity that you may add your emotions and desires to those around you. You must lose your identity as individuals and change from a group of voices to the many tones of one great voice. You must read, but do not read notes; read the impulses and passions of which they are a symbol. You must sing, but do not sing music; sing hate and love, war and peace, turmoil and tranquillity, death and life. And, as you give yourself freely to the perfecting and focusing of the great creative and interpretative power which is Symphonic Choir, you will be revitalizing and multiplying your own talents and appreciation, both now and after graduation.

You have signified your willingness to accept this great responsibility by your application for membership. We make but one demand upon you. Be loyal to the best that is within you.

(Will the Choir please stand?) "Will you be loyal to yourselves and to Symphonic Choir? If so, answer, "We will." Hear our creed.

Aristocracy

We do not seek that elevated rank
Which comes with wealth accrued; we do not crave
The royalty of monarch's high decree.
No boundary of empire can define
Or limit the nobility we seek.
We ask no crest, or banner's flaunted fame.
We do not hunger for the plaudits of
Our fellow men; their hollow shoutings bear
No glory to the seeking heart. Give us
The open mind, the ear attuned to the
Far call of songs unsung, of burdens not
Yet lifted from the shoulders of the world,
And let us join, with earnest heartfelt prayer,
The aristocracy of those who care.

I now propose a toast: Mr. President, Professor Diercks, Symphonichoirs—to Symphonic Choir.

Carmen Ohio

The First Circle

Public relations effort in the first circle has as its primary concern the projection of a *curricular* image. Music is an integral part of life. Rather than merely an activity pursued during "spare time," it can be that deep aesthetic experience which gives meaning to the routine actions of daily life. Many enlightened school administrators now realize this, and support music programs as a part of the curriculum; others have come part way to the "co-curricular" concept; but some continue to treat music as an extracurricular activity.

Since most principals and superintendents are well aware that the music department can often serve as a "good right arm" in maintaining pleasant relationships between school and community, a very satisfactory understanding between choral director and administration can often be negotiated with a minimum of difficulty.

Sometimes the recruiting of faculty members for the "music team" is not so easy. The most direct, honest, and effective method I have found (it is one with many valuable by-products as well) is to explain to the other teachers, both directly and indirectly through actions, that your primary concern is for the progress and growth of each individual student to match the progress and growth of the student in other programs. Colleagues must be firmly convinced you are interested neither in exploiting students for the glory of the department, nor in satisfying your own personal aspirations at the expense of others.

The English teacher who receives a note from you telling her of the Robert Frost and T.S. Eliot texts you have programmed on a fall concert, or who sees your students (who sing *Beowulf* with pleasure) leading her class out of the boredom of unfamiliarity to the fascination of reading an ancient language, or who, at your suggestion, joins you in a Shakespeare festival, cannot fail to realize the value of choral music in the curriculum. Where is literature more avidly "consumed" than in the choral program?

Without exception, every time I have shared a bow with another department, I have strengthened my own position.

A program which integrates into the total school plan, which cooperates with other departments, which has the best interests of each individual student in proper focus, which is efficient in the use of money and conservative in the consumption of out of class time—in short, a program which gives as well as receives—can be a delight to everyone. However, too aggressive a program operated by a director who is too demanding, who conveys the impression that he is bigger than his school, can result in disaster for all. Many times a successful program with many students vying for a seat in the choir can adversely affect the ego of one who is not extremely cautious . . . keep your head.

The Second Circle

Parents and other adult members of the community will receive some general impression of the school choral music program through the random comments which adolescents seem to drop so freely, but the projection of the truest possible image cannot be left to chance. Actually teen-agers often do not communicate with their parents very well. Monthly newsletters, several phone calls each week, talks to civic clubs, and frequent press releases are valuable aids to more direct explanation of the purposes of the educational program.

Students often resent, rather than respect, the parents "interest" and "support", since they sometimes feel (correctly) that it is not sincere, that the parent is attending a concert because of a sense of duty, rather than because he is honestly interested in the same things his children enjoy. Students are also embarassed when their parents admire a director for "what he is doing for our little Jackie." John, who is 16 and feels quite mature, doesn't want to be "supported"—he wants to stand on his own and would much rather his parents respected his director for some other reason.

Public relations efforts in this second circle should concentrate, therefore, on educating the adults, so that they will support the choral music program, not merely from a hollow sense of parental obligation (because someone has told them it is "good" for their children), but rather because they, themselves, consider music a vital part of their own lives.

Early in my teaching career I found that adult music education was needed very badly in my particular community, since we seemed to have difficulty getting an audience to show much interest in music of any sort. We decided to form a Choral Union (complete with officers, by-laws, and budget!) whose members were to come from the entire central section of the state. One of the local civic clubs picked up the idea and took it to the Chamber of Commerce, who were promptly convinced that the venture would bring people, and money, to our town. They, in turn, enlisted the aid of a lovely lady, a doctor's wife, who honestly believed in our venture. Being a leader in the community, her acceptance of the presidential chair helped greatly. We began with only a chorus, but by the second year an orchestra, a drama department, and 1300 associate members had been added. We produced plays, operas, and concerts locally, and hired additional attractions from outside—we had a concert series.

Even though their original motives for joining the movement might have been more social, financial, or political than they were musical, these people became genuinely interested in the arts. Their "support" of the school choral music program took on a new honesty, which was accepted without embarrassment by their children, since both they and the youngsters now shared an interest in music for its own sake, rather than the relatively narrow "what it does for our little Jackie."

THE THIRD CIRCLE

The director of a successful school choral music program has the opportunity—in many cases, the obligation—to share his experiences with those beyond his own community. As the truest image of each outstanding program is spread by word-of-mouth, newspaper reports, guest appearances, magazine articles, and concert tours, not only is the prestige of that particular director, group of students, and school program enhanced, but choral organizations everywhere can profit from the favorable public image which develops, and from the general dissemination of fresh ideas and reliable techniques.

Articles for national publication should be prepared by choral conductors who have information and opinions which can be of value to others. Some directors, although able to do outstanding, exciting work, find that when they try to write about it, the spark cannot be recaptured and the result is rather dry and uninteresting. Therefore, one must try to discover whether one is primarily a "doer," "thinker," "speaker," or "writer." As you concentrate on your strength, try also to develop some of your lesser abilities as well. To the degree that you are able to influence the thoughts of others, to rub off a little of yourself, to that degree the mere mortal musician may even achieve a degree of immortality.

Personal advancement, which should never be the prime motivation, is nonetheless a normal result of successful public relations work in the third circle. Outstanding directors who have created outstanding programs are often asked to serve as guest conductors, judges, clinicians, and lecturers, according to their individual talents. Elementary and junior high teachers move to high schools; high school directors go into college work; college conductors become music department heads. Fortunately for our profession there are numerous teachers who resist this "normal" process of being "kicked upstairs" since they prefer to do their work at a particular level. Gradually salaries are being adjusted to reward good teaching in each category rather than to place so much emphasis on the "top" that we serious deplete the quality at the "bottom."

CONCERTS—THE BEST PUBLIC CONTACT

For a choral organization, concerts do most to project the truest possible image of the school music program to the public. Nothing can match the impact of an enthusiastic public performance of music well chosen for the occasion from a repertoire of high quality and interesting compositions. Some music which is just a step ahead of the understanding of most of the audience should always be included, since this can help to stretch the musical horizons of the public. When carried on over a period of years, great progress can be made; but, moving too fast, or attempting to force things on people without careful preparation, can result in serious problems for the program and for the director.

Audiences can grow in perception, too. The conductor who can speak to an audience in warm, very human terms, commenting on his reasons for programming a certain piece, or indicating interesting effects to expect in it, can make an important and lasting impression on the public, particularly with those rather reluctant people who may have come with friends or relatives, and who may be experiencing their first real contact with music and musicians.

THE CONCERT TOUR

While primarily a prestige builder, the choir trip cannot remain merely this, but must assist in accomplishing several other goals if the expenditure of so much time, effort, and money is to be worthwhile.

Be careful never to allow students to barge into a colleague's class and announce, "The choir is excused from your class to go on a trip." It is much better to prepare a note and give duplicated copies to students for each teacher whose class is to be missed. The note should assume an interest in culture ("Knowing that you are interested in the cultural growth of our community. . . .") and *ask*, even though it has already been approved by the principal, if the teacher will excuse the student and allow him to make up the work missed. The purpose of the intended absence should also be stated:

1. To provide a valuable educational experience for the student.
2. To provide an incentive for high achievement of all the members and potential members of the choir.
3. To aid in raising the cultural tone of the entire area by sharing with neighbors the fruits of the school music program.

I have seldom met rebuff from any colleague who has been approached in this manner. In a few cases I will even suggest leaving students at home who may have a rather unfirm standing in a class. Avoid any idea that the program is extra curricular, however. It is not.

In addition to the musical advantages provided by a repetition of material along with a realization that every repetition is a new concert for a new audience, there are several other "fringe benefits:"

1. A general educational experience is possible if the director will plan interesting side trips to factories, historical locations, concerts by other school groups, etc. Too many times a touring group sees only the inside of a bus, and the inside of numerous auditoriums.

2. Students can learn something about courtesy and manners. They should be directed to record the names and addresses of those families with whom they stay during the tour, and to write thank-you letters when they return home. Those sudents who have not developed acceptable table manners and feel awkward with the tools used in eating may be invited to the home of the director for dinner. A letter from a Defiance, Ohio mother indicates the excellent public relations value of well-mannered students:

". . . Chivalry is not dead! and I was so glad my two sons were able to observe it in the actions of the two boys from your fine choir who stayed in our home overnight. . . ."

3. There is great permanent value for both the choir and each individual student in the personal contacts with people in various sponsoring communities. Acquaintances made during the relatively brief time always aid in an exchange of ideas between communities and often develop into lasting friendships, sometimes producing later job opportunities, social advancement . . . even marriages!

4. Since it is difficult for a group to be assessed properly in the "home port," it is wise to send articles or music critics' reviews from

out-of-town newspapers directly to your administration and to the local editor for possible reprint.

5. A good musical organization should service its area with quality music. Since the music performed should neither insult nor unreasonably challenge the musical intelligence of his listeners, the wise conductor will keep a sensitive hand on the pulse of the tour area. By putting himself in the place of each audience, he will be able to program pieces which can entertain as they help to elevate the artistic taste of the listeners. To facilitate such flexibility we program our entire repertoire on tour and I act as "emcee" for each concert—custom-building every performance.

6. Because of the quasi-social elements of rehearsal and performance, music teachers possess what can be a powerful persuader in the solution of the many problems of mid-twentieth century America's social revolution. On one of our tours we gave an evening concert in a small southern town. The free afternoon which preceded the performance marked the first time in many years that Negroes (several of our choir members) had been seen in town. One woman admitted that before the concert she thought, "It is a shock to see those people on our streets!" but after the program she exclaimed, "My! Aren't they talented!" With the active pursuit of some common goal, prejudice begins to disappear. Music can provide this common activity, and thus soften the blow of social revolution even as it accelerates the process.

Where longer concert tours are an impossibility it may be valuable to arrange for exchange joint-concerts. This device, while having the disadvantage of inviting comparisons, has the advantage of assuring an audience more readily than a performance with no local participation. Many of the items on the tour check list below are equally valid for such an exchange effort.

CONCERT TOUR CHECK LIST

18 MONTHS AHEAD

Select farthest geographic point of tour. Book this spot with flexibility of dates if possible so dates can be juggled if necessary.
Clear this with your administration.
Determine length of tour in days and distance.
Determine charges for concerts (cash-meals-lodging).
Plan general contour of trip.
Contact prospective sponsors.

12 MONTHS AHEAD

Enter tour dates in school calendar.
Get O.K. on budget
Begin to choose repertoire.

MAY 15

Secure contracts from sponsors (calendars are made earlier every
  year).
Consider fund raising methods, if necessary.
Order music.
Check bus costs and get option on dates.

AT BEGINNING OF SCHOOL YEAR

Start next year's tour plans, as above.
Recheck bus arrangements.
Prepare promotional material (pictures, posters, brochures).
Prepare publicity releases.
Get promotional help from local Chamber of Commerce or other local
  civic clubs (Kiwanis, Rotary, Lions, etc.)
Carry to conclusion any of previous items not secured.
Set fund raising in operation.

3 MONTHS BEFORE TOUR

Send first news release.
Prepare detailed itinerary including roommate list for sponsors.
Keep your administration informed.
Prepare program for issue to sponsors and for printer, if you furnish
  program.

2 MONTHS BEFORE TOUR

Send news releases at shorter intervals.
Charter buses secured.
Secure public relations outlet for each community on tour.
Plan side trips of value.
Check trip insurance.
Recheck budget and financing.
Have students get permission for tour from parents.
Alert all students to rules of behavior on tour. Spell it out.

1 MONTH BEFORE TOUR

Inform colleagues of tour dates. Ask for release of students if class
  absences are involved.
Check concert attire, and props, if used.

Check with stage manager and assign riser crew, stage crew, costume managers, etc.

Continue to send out news releases.

Ask sponsors to save all news items (from local papers, etc.) for you.

Advise students on what to pack—travel light.

Prepare copy of itinerary. Include time schedule and name of contact in an emergency. Remember that State Highway Patrols will always cooperate in contacting en route. Send copies to parents and school administration.

1 WEEK BEFORE TOUR

Secure cash and travelers checks.

Give students some form of tour schedule on which they may insert names and addresses of hosts in order to send "thank you" notes.

Review all duties of committees and crews.

Help students with packing hints.

Recheck with faculty.

Final check with administration.

Review students' obligations (1) behavior - courtesy - image of school (2) purpose of tour - professional.

WITHIN 1 WEEK AFTER RETURN FROM TOUR

Letters from director - thanks to sponsors, newspapers.

"Thank you" notes from students.

"Thank you" note from student president or secretary to sponsor.

Check condition of costume and stage equipment.

Prepare final financial summary and evaluation of tour to be given to administration during a verbal discussion of same, including plans for next tour.

Release post tour publicity.

THE MECHANICS OF PUBLIC RELATIONS

Efforts to influence the opinions of the public have probably been carried on since the beginnings of man, but ever since World War II there has been such a tremendous increase in the number of professional public relations experts that a multimillion dollar industry, requiring the services of tens of thousands of persons, has been created. The choral director can, and must, learn a great deal from these professionals.

Word-of-mouth advertising is the least expensive and the most effective form, but other techniques must be used to "prime the pump" of public persuasiveness.

The press release is the most important single physical item in all public relations work. News media, particularly local outlets, do not have a staff large enough to gather all of the news, therefore you must make it available, well in advance of publication deadlines, in a form which can be used with a minimum of effort on their part. Follow this guide:

1. Use one side of an 8½ x 11 inch piece of plain white paper.
2. The organization, name of director, and telephone number is placed in the upper left hand corner. Indicate the type of release in the upper right hand corner (*Immediate, Exclusive, Delayed*). Give the release date.
3. Type the story, double spaced, beginning 3 inches from the top. Leave 1½ inch margins at right and left.
4. Cover *Who, What, When, Where,* and *Why* in a direct style: simple sentences, few modifiers, no "$1.25 words." All essential facts are placed in the first paragraph and developed later in order of importance so that the newspaper editor can cut the release anywhere to fit his available space, and still have a complete article.
5. Check thoroughly for accuracy. Do not use nicknames of students. Keep a carbon copy.
6. Develop a list of outlets for your area: downtown newspapers, community newspapers, industrial and commercial newspapers, local radio and television stations, newsletters (the weekly "throwaway").

Feature articles may be prepared by the director or he can alert local writers to interesting situations—the unusual attracts attention.[1] Stories on the track meet winners in the chorus, an anniversary concert featuring alumni, pre-season camps and rehearsals all make good topics. The possibilities are almost limitless for one with imagination, but remember a key phrase, *human interest without banality.*

Posters do not normally sell anything, but merely remind people of something they already find interesting. Those printed on shiny (filled) light weight paper are best for photo reproduction, and are less expensive than the cardboard type. Because they will not stand

---

[1] *Editor's note:* Prof. Diercks conducts the very unusual *Ohio Conference Methodist Ministers Choir,* made up entirely of ordained ministers. The average travel per member is 190 miles per rehearsal, and attendance records show an average of 48 out of 51 members present for rehearsals. The most frequent reason for absence is the death of a parishioner.

up by themselves, they are likely to be placed in a more prominent display space by the downtown merchants, rather than leaned against the back of a window and forgotten. A good poster *demands* attention.

An identity (some unique feature, or "signature") should be developed for use on posters, handbills, concert programs, record jackets, stationery, and other printed matter connected with the choral music program. A particular color or color combination, distinctive style of type, an eye catching design which may even be a little confusing at first glance (*see* Fig. 2-2)— something which will reflect the dignity and quality of the group—can be used for many years to establish an identity with the public.

Recordings of choral performances will be enjoyed now and cherished years later, even if the quality is considerably less than professional. There are many firms, advertising regularly in music magazines, which will supervise the recording of the group, press the discs, prepare attractive jackets, and deliver a finished product. If the school owns very high quality recording equipment, the director may prefer to send tapes directly to a commercial processor, and have the jackets printed locally.

A *Choir booklet* may be prepared to stimulate interest among potential choir tour sponsors, to promote a general feeling of good will toward the choir, and to serve as a memento for each member. Photographs, repertoire lists, and feature articles related to the history, purpose, and current activities of the organization should be included.

Photographs must always be chosen carefully both for their news or promotional value and for their eye appeal. Since both the printing process and the coarse stock used by newspapers greatly reduce the sharpness of a photo, even greater care must be taken when submitting pictures for this type of publication. Prints should have a glossy surface, and must be sharp and clear with marked contrast. Large group photos are not desirable for newspaper use since the reduction in size, coarse screen, and rough newsprint will all but obliterate the faces. Only the size of the group is indicated by such a picture, and that could be better told in words. Groups of 3–7, with some identifying feature (piano, choir robes, concert poster in the background, initialed blazer) are best.

A knowledge of the signs and symbols used by professional proofreaders to indicate mistakes in copy will aid the choral director in his role as public relations man. Since editors do not mind a few handwritten corrections on material, time may be saved (and a professional impression made at the same time) through the use of proofreader's marks. (*see* Fig. 2-3)

Budget Your Time

Since the development of a desirable *self-image* is accomplished through recurring cycles of (1) determination of goals, and (2) periodic objective examination of accomplishments (an acceptable process no matter what the subject), it is reasonable to expect this part of public relations work to permeate the choral director's every thought, every decision, every action and reaction. However, this is not to say that public relations, as a whole, should so completely dominate the scene. Development of a worthwhile program is the primary goal; the time to be spent in telling the public about the progress toward that goal must be very carefully budgeted.

Over the years I have found that as the capability of the conductor and the excellence of his product becomes known, the requests for his services increase, often to the point that some firm policy must be set in order to avoid misunderstandings and hurt feel-

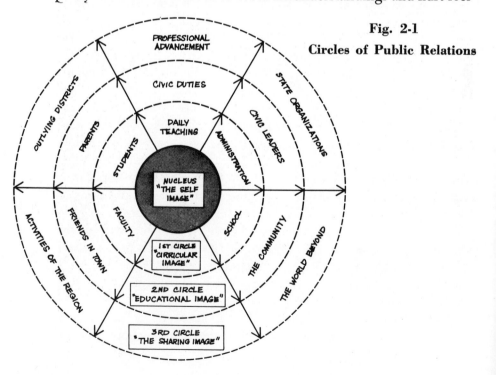

Fig. 2-1

Circles of Public Relations

ings. I have set 20 hours outside of class periods, with one day of classes per quarter as the maximum which Ohio State University Symphonic Choir members will be involved in activities of the

Fig. 2-2

Publicity Poster

(Department of Photography, Ohio State University)

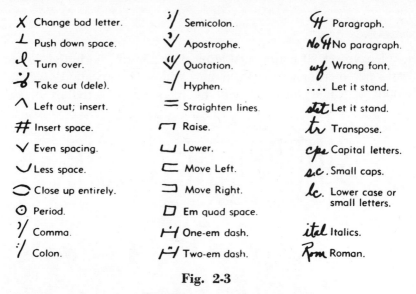

Fig. 2-3

Proofreader's Marks

choir, and one festival or workshop per quarter as the maximum for myself. When our commitments reach these figures, all other requests are graciously, but firmly, refused.[2] Our extended tours are between quarters with no absence from classes.

Each choral director should survey his program carefully and set up a performance quota which is in balance with sound educational objectives. Too many conductors have discovered too late that an organization so solidly "booked up" for concerts and other activities lacks not only the necessary time for a worthwhile educational program, but even must get by on less than an adequate number of rehearsals for the many performances. The program soon either crumbles completely or degenerates into an exclusive presentation of a very light, easy to learn, and perhaps musically worthless, repertoire. On the other hand, a firm policy including an out-of-class quota can help the director to answer requests for services with the world which logic tells him to pronounce "no," but because of the reasonableness of requests, potential prestige to be gained, his honest desire for beautiful music to be performed everywhere (plus a small pinch of ego thrown in), always seems to come out "yes."

[2] *Editor's note*: A man of principle, who practices what he "preaches," Professor Diercks turned down a request to conduct the Ohio All-State Chorus (his own state!) one year, because only the previous week he had filled his outside-of-class quota as a result of a similar request from a neighboring state.

3

The Voice Class

by Louis Nicholas

George Peabody College for Teachers

Louis Nicholas

is Associate Professor of Music at George Peabody College for Teachers in Nashville, Tennessee. He has served in many responsible positions for the National Association of Teachers of Singing (NATS), including the presidency. The members of both the Vine Street Christian Church and The Temple, Congregation Ohabai Sholom enjoy his services as Director of Music. As Music Editor (and critic) for The Nashville Tennessean his leadership and good taste have been important factors in the development of Nashville's legitimate music activities.

Mr. Nicholas began his musical study with violin lessons, then continued to scholarships for piano and voice. Vocal study was pursued under the direction of Clare Elby at the Memphis College of Music, Arthur Hackett, and Edyth Walker, the great Wagnerian soprano.

The taste and artistry which characterize his singing are due also to the fine academic and cultural background of an A.B. degree from Southwestern (with Honors in English and French), the Mus.M. from the University of Michigan, and further graduate study at Teachers College, Columbia University. He has given over 30 entirely different recital programs, including a series of 8 lecture/recitals on "The Development of Solo Song" covering 7 centuries and 10 countries.

40

Vocal technique, each person singing properly, is the basic ingredient of every facet of the student's school music experience from solo singing to membership in the largest mass chorus. As obvious and readily acceptable to all as this statement may be, many choral directors simply fail to teach their students *how to sing*. Reasons for the neglect vary.

Conductors, who remember and use the rehearsal techniques of their college directors, sometimes forget that the choir was composed mainly of voice majors who were receiving expert private attention at the same time. Individual instruction during the public school day is too uneconomical to be attempted in most school districts, and the daily schedule of most directors is entirely too full to consider it anyway.

In some programs, therefore, youngsters receive only the most random, informal, and incomplete kind of voice instruction during four years which are devoted entirely to the rehearsal and performance of pieces for the annual Christmas Program, Spring Concert, State Contest, and Commencement.

Another reason for the neglect of basic vocal technique is that many choral directors are too busy with either school-related, civic, or personal activities to consider setting up a private lesson schedule on their own time. Many who do have the time, work in communities blessed with a limited number of competent voice instructors. Many school people prefer to avoid any possible conflict with those whose sole income stems from private teaching. Others prefer to avoid completely the difficulties which sometimes arise when one accepts money for instruction directly from the parents of his own choir members.

The net result, regardless of the reason, is often inadequate voice training for the student. This is unfair, not only to the individual youngster who gives so freely of his time and talent, but also to the conductor, school, and community, since it so seriously limits the level of achievement to which a choral organization can rise.

CLASS INSTRUCTION CAN BE THE ANSWER

The fundamentals of good vocal production must be taught to all students if a really first rate choral organization is desired. This can be done most efficiently when students study together, since the same basic instruction may be presented to the entire group at the same time by one qualified instructor.

Although the ideal schedule would ultimately include a combination of both class and private lessons, the voice class may be used very effectively for the students' "basic training" preceding regular choir membership.[1]

ADVANTAGES OVER PRIVATE LESSONS

Since the elements of both friendly competition and social pressure operate to stimulate learning and to raise standards, there is usually more progress during a year of class voice than can be expected with private instruction of teen-agers during the same period of time. There are numerous other advantages as well:

1. Class members see a great variety of vocal problems discovered and treated by a professional teacher.
2. A student can often recognize one of his own difficulties more clearly and correct it more rapidly when the same flaw is also pointed out in the singing of another student.
3. Superior students inspire and encourage the less gifted to more determined efforts in order to meet the higher standards.
4. Since a textbook is normally used in a voice class (but not in a private lesson), the instruction is likely to be better organized and more inclusive.
5. The constant presence of an "audience" tends to help the student overcome his fears and inhibitions more quickly. Confidence increases as he realizes that his classmates have problems too—perhaps not the same as his—but problems all the same. When the private student attends his friends' recitals he hears only the polished result, not the involved process which created it. Many times he assumes that he himself must be exceptionally *un*talented, since he is battling so many problems which the other fellow does not seem to have.
6. The class is exposed to a wider range of vocal literature than any individual could attempt.
7. In private teaching the singer is trained to project his own solo personality, which is not particularly valuable in choral work. However, in class teaching, students may be prepared equally well for both solo and ensemble singing. Thus there is virtually 100% carry over to the entire choral program.
8. For the student who one day may become a voice teacher or

---

[1] *Editor's note:* See the very effective system developed by Thomas Hilbish in Princeton, N.J. (Chapter 13)

choral director himself, there is a great opportunity to gain insight into the vocal problems of others.

Organization of Classes

Very satisfactory results can be accomplished when a one hour voice class is scheduled 3 times per week; however, since close supervision by the instructor is so necessary in the early stages, daily classes, even if shorter in length, are more valuable. Enrollment should be restricted to 25, since there is too little opportunity for attention to individual problems if the class is any larger.

In a new choral music program, the first year should be devoted primarily to class voice (even though it may say "mixed chorus" on the schedule). In a more mature program all first year choral students should be scheduled in a separate period for voice class, instead of for ensemble practice with the experienced students.

A very effective summer program of combination class voice and private lessons can often be worked out by a choral director interested in the advancement of his students, an upgrading of the quality of his work, and an addition to his summer income.

Objectives of Class Voice Training

The National Association of Teachers of Singing (NATS), in an official pronouncement[2], clearly defines the four primary objectives of any basic system of training the singing voice.

To Liberate the Voice

1. By coordinating the actions of the breath, vocal cord vibration, and the resonating parts of the body.
2. By analyzing the function of the lungs.
3. By using vowels and vowel sounds to develop a balanced and resonant tone quality throughout the entire range.
4. By learning the correct physical sensations of tone production in all parts of the body (the difference between cause and effect).
5. By eliminating muscular interference and tensions that impede complete freedom.
6. By revealing the natural beauty and expressive tone quality of the voice.

---

[2] *Editor's note*: Copies of the entire pronouncement (*Course Outline Methods of Teaching Singing*) are available for a very small fee from the national secretary of NATS.

To Strengthen the Voice

1. By learning the proper pitch attack, with correct vowel form on sustained sounds to develop the vigor and power of the voice in order to condition the entire body to endure the fatigue of constant and heavy use of the voice.
2. By exercising to equalize the voice from top to bottom and from bottom to top on all vowel sounds and vowel sound mixtures at all degrees of intensity and power.
3. By eliminating register breaks.
4. By making the voice flexible and creating an even legato.
5. By learning the correct use of the lips, tongue, palate, and other movable parts of the vocal apparatus.
6. By learning how to utilize the various resonances of the voice for full and complete freedom of vocal expression.
7. By making the voice agile, learning the techniques of staccato, martellato, trill, etc.

To Beautify the Voice

1. By acquiring aesthetic awareness and keen sensitivity toward the music and dramatic expressive qualities of the singing voice.
2. By increasing the capacity to understand and interpret beautiful music vocally.
3. By widening the range of expressiveness and control of the vocal instrument as a means to fulfill the most difficult demands of artistic expression.

To Develop a Singing Repertoire

1. By covering the entire literature of music for the voice, and by becoming proficient in interpreting the various styles (Classic, Romantic, Contemporary, etc.).
2. By covering the fields of opera, oratorio, and the song literature of the world.
3. By acquiring experience and skill in the rendition and interpretation of vocal masterpieces.
4. By learning the art of communication by practical singing experiences before the public.
5. By learning the business of professional singing (what is expected of an artist/singer).

A COURSE OF STUDY

A suitable text should be adopted which is consistent with the objectives of class voice training outlined above, and which allows the individual instructor to teach in his own "style." The following texts are suggested for examination:

Expressive Singing, by Van A. Christy, Wm. C. Brown Co., Dubuque, Iowa, 1961. In four volumes (I-text, 252 pp; I—song anthology, 45 songs; II—text, 354 pp; II—song anthology, 44 songs). Vol. I—text, the "how", contains basic principles for the student, and is arranged in a series of lessons. Volume II—text, the details of how and why, is correlated chapter by chapter with Volume I—text, and is a compendious tome of advanced theory, technic, pedagogy, and repertoire for the *teacher.* There are many lists of solo music, selected from various approaches (voice range, country, composer, etc.)

Class Method of Voice Training, by D.A. Clippinger, Oliver Ditson, pub. This is one of the older, but also one of the most sensible texts on the subject. There is an adequate supply of useful songs, along with a few which are badly "dated."

Universal Song, by Frederick H. Haywood, G. Schirmer, pub., original copyright 1917. Published in several small volumes which are convenient in format, this book has been used for many years.

The Solo Singer by Harry Robert Wilson, C. Fischer, pub. 1941, Volume I for medium-high voice; Volume II for high and low voice.

The Singing Road by Arthur E. Ward, C. Fischer, pub., paper cover, Volume I—21 songs, Volume II and III—9 songs each.

Group Voice by Bernard Taylor, G. Schirmer, pub.

The above 3 books are sound, unpretentious, inexpensive, and contain a good selection of songs.

Class Lessons in Singing, by Anne E. Pierce and Estelle Liebling, Silver Burdette and Co., pub. An elaborate, valuable, but expensive book.

Functional Lessons in Singing, by Ivan Trusler and Walter Ehret, Prentice-Hall, Inc. 1960. This book, consistent and detailed in its development of a basically sound premise, might even be a basis for some self-help. A clean and precise format, with clear illustrations make for good eye appeal, and a more modern look than some of those previously listed.

Guide for Young Singers, by Millard H. Cates, University Music Press, 1959. This guide was planned specifically for the students enrolled in class voice at the University of Michigan. It is very practical and can be used very effectively by high school teachers as well as in college.

VOICE CLASS ACTIVITIES

The best results will be achieved in a relaxed atmosphere, where humor often reduces tensions, and mistakes can be treated not as earth shaking events, but as normal steps in a pleasant course of study.

The teacher must develop a varied approach which is predominantly group centered, since young people quickly become bored, restless, and eventually a discipline problem when the class period is turned into a private lesson for one or two students.

The following activities can be employed for varying periods of time, and in a flexible sequence, in order to maintain interest, and thus achieve maximum progress.

1. Vocal exercises to "warm up" the voice and develop technique.
2. Study and singing of solos and duets as a group.
3. Solo performances of a song, or part of a song, with either verbal or written criticism offered by the other class members. Written critiques from fellow students are often the most successful teaching aids.
4. Class discussion of problems of vocal production, theory, style, interpretation, and stage deportment.
5. Part songs sung by the entire group.
6. Duets, trios, quartets, etc. from operas, operettas, and oratorios sung by solo voices.
7. Study of sight singing and general musicianship.
8. Informal recitals, with proper stage deportment required; critique sheets may be used.
9. Performances by the instructor or guest artists.
10. Listening to fine recordings to provide stimulus in the areas of style, interpretation, technique, tone, and repertoire.

THE SINGER'S INSTRUMENT

The voice—the most personal of all musical instruments because it originates within the very body of the performer—has three parts:

1. *The Motor* is the breathing apparatus, consisting of lungs, ribs, and muscles. The lungs, encased by the ribs, rest upon the muscular partition called the diaphragm and are allowed to inflate when the rib cage is expanded.
2. *The Vibrator* is the vocal cords (or folds), which are two bands of elastic tissue slung between the front and back part of the

larynx. They act somewhat like double reeds on the oboe or bassoon. When the cords, under varying conditions of tension, are set in motion by breath passing through, sound is produced.

3. *The Resonator* consists primarily of the cavities of the larynx, pharynx, mouth, nose, and sinuses. These provide spaces in which air may vibrate in sympathy with the weak impulses coming from the vocal cords. In this way the very insignificant volume of tone produced by the vocal cords alone can be amplified to the rich, resonant level of a well trained voice.

Since the instrument is a physical part of the singer himself it follows that bodily condition and mental health are much more vividly reflected in vocal performance than in the playing of any instrumentalist. It is obvious that the singer must be unusually careful to keep himself in top physical shape if his voice is to function at its best. He must regulate his diet, get plenty of rest, exercise properly, and attend to all rules of good health if he expects to avoid the colds, headaches, and other ailments which can affect the singing apparatus both directly and indirectly. Such emotional ills and strains as pessimism, jealousy, worry, distrust, and the like, militate quite as strongly against free and effetcive use of the voice as do muscular tensions brought on by bodily fatigue or physical illness.

Excessive smoking, drinking of alcoholic beverages, singing out of doors, susceptibility to head colds and laryngitis, allergic reactions of all sorts, and cheerleading all affect the voice adversely to varying degrees. For these reasons, "Plain living and positive thinking" is a very good slogan for a singer to follow in order to maintain the physical and mental health necessary for his instrument to function at maximum efficiency.

CLASSIFYING VOICES

In spite of the fact that most young students are always asking, "What am I?" the wise vocal teacher will refrain from classifying voices too soon. Many voices do not show their true, unmistakable characteristics in early stages of training. This is especially true of boys' voices, since they develop later than girls'.

It is best to work for freedom and ease of production as you allow the voice to find its own level rather than to try to force it into a mold. The same vocal exercises may be sung by all class members, but the low voices should drop out as the pattern ascends if they are unable to sing easily, and, conversely, the high voices should not sing when the pitch descends too low for comfortable production.

Some voices present no problem in classification, but others are extremely difficult to categorize, even after a considerable amount of study. *The quality of the voice within the most easily produced middle octave* will be the determining factor. The ease with which voices can sing in a certain tessitura can be of secondary help, but range itself is deceptive (particularly in the untrained voice), and should never be used as the only means of classifying voices.

Breathing Exercises

Very few beginning students have notable success developing a really efficient breathing mechanism. Both the pupil and the teacher must realize this. Keep explanations simple, and do not hesitate to use terms and techniques (which may fall in and out of good repute, according to the latest speech or published article) . . . if they work for you!

Breathing is a process of air *rushing in* to fill an empty space (the lungs) made available when the wall of the container (the ribs) is expanded. Exercises are based on this process of voluntary expansion, accompanied by an almost involuntary influx of air.

1. Practice breathing deeply in a reclining position (the chest is not so apt to sink).
2. When standing, weight should be distributed evenly between feet, spine straight, rib cage expanded, with the chest comfortably high.
3. Exhale, quickly, with a "kick" from the mid-region, several times in succession, causing expansion (and thus a breath) as an immediate reaction in order to recover the sudden loss of air.
4. Follow the "quick succession" exercise described in No. 3 with the same process performed slowly. This is more difficult because the student will be inclined to allow the chest to sink.
5. Correct "chest sinking" by breathing vigorously in the following manner: inhale as you bend over, hands extended together, with palms out (stretching the back to an open feeling), exhale as you straighten up and bring the arms out and back (stretching the chest to a high and open feeling).
6. Sing with arms raised, shoulders relaxed, to keep the chest in a high position.

7. Repeat single tones with "Hmmmm . . ." to establish vigorous use of the breathing mechanism, then progress to more sustained tones.

VOCAL EXERCISES

Only a few basic vocal exercises are necessary, although these may be varied, *ad infinitum*. They are:

1. Sustained tones.
2. Scales.
3. Arpeggios.
4. Combinations of the three above.

Each type of exercise should be sung both legato and staccato (actually these are mechanically the same, except that the former is in "slow motion"), first emphasizing the free flow of breath, and second, connecting the breath to the tone, striving for the best sound each particular voice is capable of producing.

SOME PROBLEMS AND SOLUTIONS

Students often develop certain qualities in their singing which can be corrected by various daily exercises or by a combination of explanations and remedial techniques used by the instructor. As an aid (1) to discover the undesirable trait (2) to understand its cause, and (3) to correct it, the following review of faults in tone quality and other areas is presented.

Various Tone Quality Faults

1. THROATY AND GUTTURAL Caused by tensions in tongue and throat; no forward resonance. *Solution:* Use hum, the *moo, moh, mah, may, mee,* on a single pitch; then *noo, no, nah,* etc. to establish forward resonance. *Kah, kah, kah,* etc. sung on a single pitch, with the jaw quiet and back of tongue darting freely will help to release the tensions.
2. PINCHED AND THIN, OFTEN METALLIC AND SHRILL Caused by tension. *Solution:* Vocalize on *oh, ah, aw,* constantly striving to develop a concept of spaciousness and depth, as well as freedom, in the student's mind and ear.
3. HOLLOW OR "HOOTY" Caused by lack of resonance. *Solution:* Work on hum, and on *ee* and *aye* for more concentration of tone.

4. BREATHY Caused by inefficient use of air. *Solution:* Use hum for more efficient use of air. Work on staccato for "toning up" the leaky vocal cords, and watch to be sure the student is not pushing too much air through the cords.
5. "NOSEY" Caused by blocking the head and nasal opening with the soft palate and directing the resonance forward. *Solution:* Preface the pure vowel with "g" or "k".
6. OVERLY NASAL Caused by too much nose and mask resonance for a balanced tone. *Solution:* Vocalize primarily on *oh* and *ah,* with concept of depth of tone, as well as freedom in the mind and ear.
7. TOO SOMBRE OR MUFFLED Caused by lack of forward resonance. *Solution:* Vocalize on bright vowels *ee* and *aye,* and hum. Check to be sure upper lip is not pulled down.

Other Faults

EXCESSIVE OR TREMOLO VIBRATOR Caused by tightness, forcing, muscle weakness, excessive breath pressure, insufficient breath control. *Solution:* Treat possible causes separately until the true cause is determined, then eliminate.

STRAIGHT TONE WITH NO VIBRATO Caused by tight throat. *Solution:* Trill major third, using the vowel *ah.* Make sure jaw remains quiet.

OFF PITCH (EAR OK) Caused by not listening, lack of practice. *Solution:* Make exercises on various intervals; require student to listen very carefully to himself as he sings it slowly. Instructor plays tones *after* he has sung them.

SHORT BREATH SUPPLY Caused by poor breathing routine, breath taken too late, wasted at beginning of phrase, improper concept of the phrase. *Solution:* Time for breath should be robbed from the preceding phrase. Check to be sure it is taken soon enough that it can be managed with confidence at beginning of new phrase and not wasted. Check phrase concept. If singer has a clear idea of the phrase, he will usually have sufficient breath to sing it.

LACK OF SOSTENUTO ON LONG TONES Caused by improper concept, poor breath support. *Solution:* Give the student proper concept from your own example, or from fine recordings; lead him to reduce breath energy after the tone is attacked.

LACK OF PRECISION ON STACCATO AND ACCENTED TONES Caused by poor muscle response. *Solution:* Exaggerate the muscle response.

GRUNT OR GASP AT RELEASE OF TONE Caused by improper concept, carelessness. *Solution:* Exaggerated imitation by the teacher will usually show the pupil how undesirable this is; he will need reminders from time to time to keep from these excesses.

LEGATO DESTROYED Caused by:

1. Failure to keep uniform vowel color.
2. Anticipation of consonants.
3. Wavering or jerky air supply.

Solution: Merely call No. 1 and 2 to the attention of the student. For No. 3, practice deep breathing, sustained tones. Build the students self-confidence and sense of well being.

Many faults of diction can be cured merely if the teacher recognizes them and brings them to the attention of the pupil. Check these causes:

1. Improper vowel color.
2. Lingering on the vanishing point of diphthongs.
3. Making dark vowels too breathy and bright vowels too thin and shrill.
4. Habitually too white or too dark tone color.
5. Radical change of vowel quality at various points in the scale due to failure to adjust gradually to ease tension.
6. Incorrect pronunciation.
7. Careless or inaudible articulation.
8. Omission of some consonants.
9. Substitution of one vowel or consonant sound for another.
10. Prolonged or exaggerated consonants.
11. Insertion of extraneous sounds, such as the aspirate "h" before attacks and *ah* after and between words.

GOOD TEACHING SONGS

Although some individual members of the voice class may meet personal problems in some of the songs recommended here, most will be able to profit from their use, and all may enjoy music of quality in the process.

TITLE	COMPOSER	PUBLISHER
First Year Songs		
Alleluia	O'Connor-Morris	Boosey
Bendemeer's Stream	Gatty	Boosey
Cargoes	Dobson	G. Schirmer

TITLE	COMPOSER	PUBLISHER
First Year Songs		
Caro Mio Ben	Giordani	G. Schirmer
Cherry Ripe	Horn	G. Schirmer
Clorinda	Morgan	Boosey
Come, Let's Be Merry	Old English	Boosey
Come to the Fair	Martin	Boosey
Cradle Song (Lullaby)	Mozart	G. Schirmer
Cradle Song	Schubert	C. Fischer
Drink to Me Only With Thine Eyes	Quilter	Boosey
Florian's Song	Godard	G. Schirmer
Go Lovely Rose	Quilter	Chappell
Green Pastures	Sanderson	Boosey
Heart Worships, The	Holst	Galaxy
Hedge Roses	Schubert	G. Schirmer
If Thou Lovest Me	Pergolesi	G. Schirmer
I Know A Hill	Whelpley	Boston
I Know Where I'm Going	Hughes	Boosey
In Questa Tomba	Beethoven	G. Schirmer
In the Time of Roses	Reichardt	Presser
I Love Thee	Beethoven	G. Schirmer
I've Been Roaming	Horn	G. Schirmer
It Was A Lover and His Lass	Morley	Ditson
Linden Lea	R. V. Williams	Boosey
Mamselle Maria	Guion	G. Schirmer
My Lord What A Morning	Burleigh	Ricordi
My Master Hath A Garden	R. Thompson	E. C. Schirmer
My Mother Bids Me Bind My Hair	Haydn	C. Fischer
O Mistress Mine	Quilter	Boosey
Passing By	Purcell	Presser
Prayer of the Norwegian Child	Kountz	G. Schirmer
Rose of Tralee, The		
Sandy River	Russell	G. Schirmer
Simple Gifts	Copland	Boosey
Sylvelin	Sinding	G. Schirmer
Think On Me	Scott-Perrenot	Galaxy
This Lovely Rose	Roy	G. Schirmer
To Anthea	Hatton	Oxford
Velvet Shoes	R. Thompson	E. C. Schirmer
Vergin, tutta amor	Durante	G. Schirmer
Wayfarer's Night Song	Martin	Boosey
When Love Is Kind	A.L.	Boosey

TITLE	COMPOSER	PUBLISHER

Second Year Songs

TITLE	COMPOSER	PUBLISHER
Après un Rêve	Fauré	G. Schirmer
As Ever I Saw	Warlock	Boosey
Blow Ye Winds	Dougherty	G. Schirmer
Bois Epais	Lully	Boosey
But The Lord Is Mindful Of His Own	Mendelssohn	Presser
Cloths Of Heaven, The	Dunhill	Galaxy
Come and Trip I	Carmichael	Boosey
Deep River	Burleigh	Ricordi
Du bist wie eine Blume	Schumann	G. Schirmer
Go Way From My Window	Niles	G. Schirmer
Hist! Hist!	Arnold	Galaxy
Ich grolle nicht	Schumann	G. Schirmer
I Want Jesus To Walk With Me	Boatner	Galaxy
Jesus, The Very Thought Of Thee	Thiman	Novello
Lilacs	Rachmaninoff	G. Schirmer
Linden Tree, The	Schubert	G. Schirmer
Mary of Allendale	Wilson	Boosey
Memory, A	Ganz	G. Schirmer
My Lovely Celia	Munro	Boosey
Myself When Young	Lehmann	Boston
No Candle Was There	Lehmann	Chappell
Nymphs and Shepherds	Purcell	G. Schirmer
O Rest In the Lord	Mendelssohn	Presser
Page's Road Song, The	Novello	Boosey
Palisir d'Armour	Martini	Presser
Rolling Down to Rio	German	Gray
Sea Fever	Ireland	Augener
She Never Told Her Love	Haydn	G. Schirmer
Sleep That Flits, The	Carpenter	G. Schirmer
Star Vicino	Rosa	G. Schirmer
Sweet Chance That Led My Steps	Head	Boosey
Tally Ho!	Leoni	G. Schirmer
Thou Art Like A Flower *Du bist . .)*	Schumann	G. Schirmer
Tu lo sai	Torelli	Witmark
Verborgenheit	Wolf	G. Schirmer
Virgin's Slumber Song	Reger	Associated
Water Mill, The	R. V. Williams	Oxford
When I Bring You Colored Toys	Carpenter	G. Schirmer
Where'er You Walk	Handel	Presser

TITLE	COMPOSER	PUBLISHER

Second Year Songs

| Who Is Sylvia | Schubert | G. Schirmer |
| Yarmouth Fair | Warlock | Oxford |

Collections

Those songs from the class voice methods recommended on page 45, plus:

The Arnold Book of Old Songs	Quilter	Boosey
Old English Melodies, Vol. I and II	H. Lane Wilson	Boosey
Pathways of Song	Earhart-LaForge	Witmark
Reliquary of English Songs	Potter	G. Schirmer

THE GOAL—INFINITE BEAUTY

The director who undertakes to teach class voice lessons should have as his goal the development, within the capability of each student, of the fundamentals of good singing:

Posture adjustment that provides for
Breathing apparatus of such sufficient action that the singer can produce, with a minimum of apparent effort,
Tone of good quality throughout a
Range sufficient for the performance of the major portion of the literature appropriate to one's voice, calling on
Dynamics from the *pp* to *ff* levels, and
Variety of tone from a seamless legato to the most flute-like staccato at all pitch and dynamic levels, plus
Enunciation and projection required to convey texts clearly and understandably with the tone quality suggested by the mood of the song and the meaning of the words, all coupled with an
Understanding of text and the ability to utilize color, accent, and varieties of emphases to make each performance most meaningful and of infinite beauty.

4

The Chamber Ensemble

by Rose Marie Grentzer

University of Maryland

Rose Marie Grentzer

is Professor of Music, Chairman of the Music Education Division, and Director of the Madrigal Singers at the University of Maryland. She has formerly been Professor of Music and Chairman of the Music Education Department at Oberlin Conservatory of Music; Head of the Music Education Department at the Julliard School of Music; Instructor in Music and Music Education at the University of Michigan; Director of Vocal Music, Ann Arbor (Michigan) High School; and Supervisor of Music, Braddock (Pennsylvania) Schools.

Miss Grentzer has conducted choral groups of all ages and ability levels, acted as adjudicator, worskhop clinician, music and curriculum consultant, visiting professor and lecturer, and has served professional organizations at both state and national levels. She is coauthor of the Birchard Music Series, as well as the writer of numerous articles and book reviews.

The University of Maryland Madrigal Singers, which she organized in 1958, have distinguished themselves through outstanding concerts and radio-TV broadcasts, appearances for the Secretary of State, Folger Shakespeare Library, Kennedy Cultural Center, MENC, ACDA, and a tour of the Near East, North Africa, Great Britain and Ireland as part of the Cultural Presentations Program under the auspices of the United States Department of State.

A small ensemble of select singers performing the best chamber music from all periods can provide a deep musical experience for students, an image-building performance group for the school, encouragement and inspiration for greater musical activity in the community, and a source of the most profound educational and musical compensations a director can ever hope to experience in all choral music.

Students develop a very wonderful personal relationship with other members of the ensemble. The tremendous self-discipline required to sing independent parts in what is often a polyphonic style, and the complete cooperation demanded by both the music and the intimate nature of the group, work to establish a unity of purpose which binds students together in a way that is second to no other musical experience. (We have had several "Madrigal Marriages" at the University of Maryland, although I can't quite recommend this for high school students.)

School administrators—including not only those who possess great aesthetic sensitivity, but also the ones who seem to delight in telling you they are "tone deaf"—can see and appreciate an audience's response to quality performance, and can sense the great enthusiasm of ensemble members. Since the group needs a relatively small performance area and is more mobile than a large chorus, it is more suited for appearances at civic and professional meetings. Students, who have a chance to mingle with community leaders at these affairs, both in and out of town, can build a very good and lasting image of the high type of individual your school is producing.

The Community benefits not only from having a top quality performing group available for programs, but in a much larger sense, all cultural pursuits are aided by this tangible evidence of the high level achievement possible with talent, effort, and professional direction.[1]

Choral Directors find both challenge and satisfaction in directing the efforts of selected students toward an understanding of some of the world's greatest choral literature. Most of the school choral director's day is spent in pursuit of the goal to which we are all

---

[1] *Editor's note:* High School directors and students throughout the area served by the University of Maryland have been motivated to organize successful chamber music groups, purchase harpsichords, etc., as a direct result of the popularity of Miss Grentzer's groups which are heard in concerts and over radio and television. Many of their students come to the University (not necessarily as music majors) and become members of the Madrigal group. In this way, the even larger "community" of music education is served and musical standards of performance reach even greater heights.

sincerely dedicated: music education *for all.* While we, as educators, would not want to change this situation, our own musical souls often need to be nurtured. The choral director who organizes a group of chamber music singers can provide the challenge his most talented students need as he satisfies his own soul: the performance of a small selected group of singers reflects the conductor's concept of choral tone, his acuity of hearing in the intonation of the group, his sense of dynamics, his sensitivity and understanding of the musical phrase (particularly in music of contrapuntal texture), and his interpretation of the performance practices of the period, including nuances, accents, stresses, dissonances, verbal phrasing, and relation of words to notes.

"Madrigal" vs. "Chamber"

A madrigal group in today's high school is a "prestige item" just as the *a cappella* choir was at one time. And, just as "a cappella" (unaccompanied) often lost its original meaning when used in the name of a group, "madrigal" seems also to be undergoing a change. The term is now being used loosely to designate a group of select voices from 5 to 25 singers. The repertoire of the groups seems to include music from every historical period (including folk music) and is not limited to the "madrigal" alone.

The University of Maryland Madrigal Singers evolved from a class in choral conducting I taught in 1958. It has numbered from 12 to 15 singers and has included instrumentalists who play recorders, harpsichord, rebec, lute, guitar, gamba — depending on the performers available. Students come from a variety of academic fields in addition to music. The original impetus of the group remains: a deep interest in vocal and instrumental works of the Renaissance period . . . particularly in the madrigal as a musical form.

In formal concerts the first part of the program consists of a variety of music from the Renaissance period, including vocal and instrumental solos, duets, trios, quartets, and other small ensembles. After intermission the singers perform a program consisting of early American music (including fuging tunes), contemporary American music with its interesting contrapuntal texture, and American folk songs.

So, even though the name "Madrigal Singers" indicates a more limited scope and is technically incorrect for the group, it has nonetheless been retained. The largest part of the repertoire still consists of madrigals and the instrumentalists play music of the Renaissance period only. This seems to be true of many such groups, although others are using the term "chamber" in some way ("Chamber Singers," "Chamber Ensemble"). After all, to perform the repertoire of this group musically calls for a minimum number of voices —otherwise the musical texture suffers and the compositions lose their charm.

For all practical purposes, then, "Madrigal" when used in the name of a small ensemble does not necessarily limit the group to the singing of music of the Renaissance period, but it does limit, to some extent, the repertoire which a group of this size can perform.

How to Organize the Group

The best size for a chamber ensemble depends on the voices which are available and the choral literature to be performed. If the membership becomes too large, obviously it is no longer a chamber ensemble, although if the purpose is to sing Bach cantatas, then as many as 25 could be used. Three factors seem to lead to the conclusion that for most purposes 15 singers are ideal:

1. The core of the group's repertoire remains the 5 part 16th Century madrigal: the usual S A (counter-tenor) T B B or the more practical S S A T B or S A T B B).
2. Only experienced professionals can meet the demands of one singer to one part; therefore it is desirable to double the basic voicing.
3. It is easier *vocally* (not necessarily always better *musically*) for 3 people to achieve a good blend on the same part, rather than just 2.

Rehearsals in most schools are held outside of regular class hours, although credit, with full curriculum acceptance, can be justified, and is being offered in some school systems. Directors who have originally scheduled only 1 or 2 rehearsals per week have found that the students enjoy the group so much that they also rehearse outside of school time. As with any closely-knit ensemble, based on an almost automatic give-and-take understanding between the members, daily sessions are most desirable.

Student Officers, elected by the members, can contribute a great deal to the efficiency of the operation. Our officers were able to

organize the group so well that on an overseas tour everything —
harpsichord, costumes, evening clothes, and other equipment — was
packed and ready to load on the bus in 7 minutes! But the really
important thing, of course, is the valuable experience the officers
receive in practical self-government.

Rules and Regulations are valuable, but they must be reevaluated
and changed when necessary as the group matures and acquires
certain traditional practices. Standards of behavior and dress should
be prescribed and followed; but while it may be essential in the
beginning to "have a rule" that no matter where they go for an
appearance with the group, members must dress up — girls in heels
and hose, boys in dark suits, white shirts and tie — once a tradition
of dignity and graciousness is established, it may no longer be necessary to spell it out so clearly. Based on the principle *with privilege
comes responsibility*, rules can be drawn up by the officers, with
your guidance. With a group of selected students it is often possible
to work close to the ideal of "he who governs least governs best."

Formal Auditions should be held. If students have studied voice
(this practice is becoming more common with high school students)
they are asked to perform a prepared vocal solo. Others are asked
to sing (artistically) one of the patriotic songs. Transposition to the
key best suited for the voice is permitted. Range is tested through
a series of vocalises. They are asked to sight read; intonation is
checked specifically as they sing a major third from notes sounded
at random on the piano. I insist on (and respect) the recommendations of previous teachers on matters of personality, dependability,
and general intelligence. Adequate time should be allowed for each
applicant's audition.

Changes in Personnel must be made when absolutely necessary
for the well being of the group, but once I have chosen the members, I become dedicated to them and I try to help them correct
musical or personal difficulties which may develop, rather than to
replace an erring member with cold-blooded and professional-style
efficiency. The students realize this and respect the interest in their
development. We are primarily educators. Students are dropped
only if they are tardy, undependable, uncooperative.

How to Choose the Members

The ideal chamber ensemble member must be a "good sport" as
well as a good musician. Avoid the complainer or the reformer, but
seek those with an intellectual curiosity and a positive attitude (in

other words a good healthy teenager)—and there are plenty of them around today! Look for the following specific qualities:

1. *Interest*. The student must be particularly interested in music of this type, and in singing with a small group.
2. *Adaptability*. Even the world's best musician is out of place in a chamber ensemble if he cannot conform to the collective wishes of the group.
3. *Alertness*. The ability to learn quickly, to react instantly, to enjoy the association with other intelligent, alert young people is essential.
4. *Keen Ear*. Members must have a well developed sense of pitch. There are no large sections in which to hide the insecure ear.
5. *Good Voice*. Not necessarily a "great" voice. Blend is extremely important, therefore the voice must be very flexible, even if not of outstanding solo quality (I reject the great soloist who cannot, or will not, blend).
6. *Style*. The ability to imitate, to respond, to react to the spoken, sung, or even *felt*, suggestions of the director and the other members.

COSTUMING THE ENSEMBLE

The only purpose of costuming is to establish a mood and to suggest an authentic atmosphere for the music being sung. It must tastefully enhance, never distract. The University of Maryland Madrigal Singers perform Renaissance music and the programs of Nöels in richly colored costumes of the Elizabethan period. Other repertoires are presented in contemporary formal dress. (*see* Fig. 4-1).

I have found that although we get many requests for our patterns (which we do not have), most groups enjoy doing historical research into the Elizabethan period in order to design an authentic costume (many times in cooperation with the home economics department) which will be practical, economical, and uniquely *their own*. I have yet to find a group of students who really like the costumes of another school. They always think they can do something better (and often do!).

Colorfast, easily washable materials are best. Colors should be chosen with care after consideration of all performing situations. Television producers can advise you on what is best for both black and white, and color TV transmission.

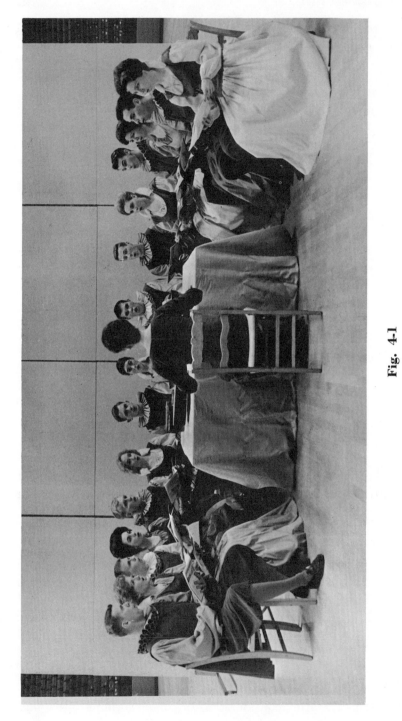

Fig. 4-1

Costuming the Chamber Ensemble: Elizabethan
for Madrigals, Formal for Modern

Fig. 4-1 (*cont.*)

It has been our experience that it is best for the school to pay for the costumes or for the money to be raised by an interested group, rather than to try to keep up with the bookkeeping necessary for individual ownership and subsequent resale. The care and maintenance should also be conducted on a group (rather than personal) basis, since even colorfast materials will lose their uniformity when washed at different times in different detergents. Incidentally, even your best friend, in a chamber ensemble, *will* tell you that the use of deodorants is essential when performing in costume under lights.

FINDING MUSIC

Music of the 15th and 16th Centuries can be found in many catalogs; however, contemporary music written within the vocal range, and which will be effective when sung by a small group, is hard to find. Folk songs, are in most instances over-arranged, in bad taste, or conceived for massed festival chorus. For obvious economic reasons, publishers are not inclined to concentrate on music for *small* ensembles; however, with the growing interetst in the chamber group, the situation is improving. Publisher's catalogs are an invaluable source of reference.[2] Reference collections are available in many libraries, or the librarian can advise you how to get some of these materials on loan from other libraries.

I believe in *applied* musicology, and always encourage my college students to seek out good chamber music and submit it for publication. Some have sold pieces unearthed by their research. There are only so many hours in the day, however, and most school choral directors simply do not have the time to devote to this sort of searching.

I can recommend the following list of pieces (used by the University of Maryland Madrigal Singers on a U. S. State Department sponsored tour) as some of the best material available:

TITLE	COMPOSER	EDITOR	PUBLISHER
	15th and 16th Centuries		
ENGLISH SACRED			
Call to Remembrance	Farrant	Greyson	Bourne
Gabriel's Message			
(Book of Carols)	anonymous	G. Shaw	Oxford
Non Nobis Domine	Byrd		Ditson

[7] *Editor's note:* See Chapter 5 for a list of publishers and procedures for secuing music "on approval."

TITLE	COMPOSER	EDITOR	PUBLISHER

15th and 16th Centuries

ENGLISH SECULAR

TITLE	COMPOSER	EDITOR	PUBLISHER
All Creatures Now Are Merry Minded	Bennet	Zanzig	Ditson
All Ye Who Music Love	Donato	Zanzig	Ditson
April Is In My Mistress' Face	Morley		E. C. Schirmer
Come Again, Sweet Love	Dowland	Lincoln	G. Schirmer
Flora Gave Me Fairest Flowers	Wilbye	H. C. Leighter	E. C. Schirmer
Flow My Tears (solo)	Dowland	C. Scott	Oxford
Go Ye, My Canzonets (duet)	Morley		Ditson
It Was A Frog in the Well	Ravenscroft		manuscript
It Was A Lover And His Lass (solo)	Morley		Boston
John Come Kisse Me Now (solo)	folk		manuscript
Messenger of Spring	Pilkington	Fellows	Stainer
Mother I Will Have A Husband	Vautor	Fellows	Galaxy
Rest, Sweet Nymphs	Pilkington	H. C. Leighter	E. C. Schirmer
Silver Swan	Gibbons	H. C. Leighter	E. C. Schirmer
Sing We And Chant It	Morley	H. C. Leighter	E. C. Schirmer
Weep 'O Mine Eyes	Bennet	Greyson	Bourne
Wooing Song, A	Ravenscroft		manuscript

FRENCH SACRED

TITLE	COMPOSER	EDITOR	PUBLISHER
Allon, Gay Bergeres	Costeley	Parker & Shaw	G. Schirmer
Easter Carols (Book of Carols)		M. Shaw	Oxford
Love Is Come Again	French		
The Lamb of God	folk		

FRENCH SECULAR

TITLE	COMPOSER	EDITOR	PUBLISHER
French Chansons		Seay	Summy

Title	Composer	Editor	Publisher
15th and 16th Centuries			
Amours ont Change de facon	Mahiet		
C'est Grand Pitie	Certon		
Pour ung Plaisir	Sermisy		
Il e Bel e Bon	Passereau	Greyson	Bourne
La Tete Mi Fait Si Grande Mal	anonymous	Seay	G. Schirmer
Mon Coeur Se Recommende A Vous	di Lasso		Ditson
Troubadour Songs (solo)	Ventadorn	Wellescz	Oxford
Maintenant conseillez-moi			
Quand je vois les feuilles			
Quand parfois je vois l'alouette			

ITALIAN AND FLEMISH SECULAR

Contrapunto Bestiale Alle Mente	Banchieri	Greyson	Bourne
El Grillo	Dascanio		manuscript
Fa Una Canzone	Vecchi		Lawson-Gould
Matona, Mia Cara	di Lasso	H. C. Leighter	E. C. Schirmer
O Occhi, Manza Mia	di Lasso	H. C. Leighter	E. C. Schirmer
Se Ben or Non Scopro (solo)	Tromboncino		manuscript
So Well I Know Who's Happy	Vecchi	H. C. Leighter	E. C. Schirmer

ITALIAN SACRED

Adoramus Te Christe	Palestrina	Deis	Ditson
Caligaverunt Oculi Mei	Victoria		G. Schirmer
Bone Jesu	Palestrina		E. C. Schirmer

GERMAN SACRED

Christ ist Erstanden	Hassler		Marks
Lamb of God	German	Christiansen	Augsburg
O Welt Ich Muss Dich Lassen	Isaac		G. Schirmer
Psallite	Praetorius	Greyson	Bourne

TITLE	COMPOSER	EDITOR	PUBLISHER

15th and 16th Centuries

GERMAN SECULAR

Nun Fanget An	Hassler	Geiringer	G. Schirmer
Sei ist Mir Lieb'	Praetorius		Ditson
Tanzen und Springen	Hassler	Greyson	Bourne
With Love My Heart			
Is Ringing	Hassler		Ditson

SPANISH SACRED

Dadme Albricias,			
Hijos d'Eva	anonymous	Greenberg	Associated
E la don don,			
Verges María	anonymous	Greenberg	Associated
Ríu, Ríu, Chíu	anonymous	Greenberg	Associated

17th Century

Ardo e Scoprir	Monteverdi		manuscript
(duet)			
Cantata—Passion of			
Our Lord			
Jesus Christ			
(St. John)	Schütz	Klein	Boosey
Cantate Domine	Pitoni	Greyson	Bourne
Easter Carols (Book			
of Carols)	anonymous	M. Shaw	Oxford
Hilariter			
My Dancing Day			
Exultate Deo	A. Scarlatti	Rekko	Marks
Komm Süsser Tod	Bach	K. Davis (arr.)	G. Schirmer
Ye Watchers And Ye			
Holy Ones	German	Fischer (arr.)	Ditson

18th Century

EUROPEAN

Adoramus Te, Christe	Mozart	Zanzig	Ditson
O Vos Omnes	Perti		E. C. Schirmer
Solo und Mehrstim-			
mige Gesänge	Haydn	Grentzer	manuscript
Abendlied zu Gott			
An der Vetter (trio)			
Die Beredsamkeit			
Eine Sehr Gewohn-			

Title	Composer	Editor	Publisher

18th Century

liche Geschichte
  (solo)
Fuhl hieher du
  wust es fuhlen
  (duet)
Sympathie

AMERICAN

Title	Composer	Editor	Publisher
Dormant	French	Lowens	G. Schirmer
Geneva	Cole	Grentzer	manuscript
Modern Music	Billings	David	Mercury
Salisbury	Brownson	Lowens	Marks
When Jesus Wept	Billings		Mercury

19th Century

EUROPEAN

Title	Composer	Editor	Publisher
In Monte Oliveti	Schubert	Granville	Choral Art

AMERICAN

Title	Composer	Editor	Publisher
Boatman's Dance, The	minstrel song	Copland (adapt.)	Boosey
Wondrous Love	anonymous	from "Southern Harmony"	

20th Century

Title	Composer	Editor	Publisher
Crossing the Han River	Mennin		C. Fischer
Fable, A	Dello Joio		C. Fischer
Four Canonic Choruses Epitaph Epitaph for Joseph Conrad Night Stuff Come Not	Schuman		G. Schirmer
Geographical Fugue	Toch		Mills
Jesus Christ Is Risen Today (from "Easter Cantata")	Hovhannes		Peters
Lark, The	Copland		E. C. Schirmer
Musicians Wrestle Everywhere	Carter		Music Press
Reincarnations	Barber		G. Schirmer

TITLE	COMPOSER	EDITOR	PUBLISHER

20th Century

Title	Composer	Editor	Publisher
Mary Hynes			
Anthony O Daly			
The Coolin			
This Is A Garden (Women's Chorus)	Persichetti		C. Fischer
Three Way Canon			
Blues	Brant		Mercury
To All, To Each	Schuman		G. Schirmer
What Will Love Do (Women's Chorus)	Phillips		C. Fischer

AMERICAN FOLK MUSIC

Title	Composer	Editor	Publisher
Bold Fisherman		Siegmeister	Presser
Bought Me A Cat		Copland (arr.)	Boosey
Boys Can Whistle		Wilson	Presser
Coffee Grows On White Oak Trees			
Creole Slumber Song			
If I Had A Ribbon Bow (solo)		Niles	G. Schirmer
I'll Not Marry (Women's Chorus)			manuscript
Let Us Break Bread Together		Ryder (arr.)	J. Fischer
Lolly Tu-Dum		Churchill (arr.)	Belwin
Mary Wore Three Links			manuscript
Mousie's Courting Song			manuscript
Riddle Song			manuscript
Shenandoah		Hartley (arr.)	C. Fischer
Sourwood Mountain			
Story of Noah			manuscript
This Lonesome Valley		Zanzig	Birchard
Wayfaring Stranger			

Harpsichord Solos

16TH CENTURY

Title	Composer	Editor	Publisher
Alman	John Bull		
Coranto			
Duchess of Brunswicks Toye			

TITLE	COMPOSER	EDITOR	PUBLISHER

Harpsichord Solos

Duke of Brunswicks Alman
John Come Kisse Me Now — William Byrd
Variationen uber das Lied "Est-ce-Mars" — Jan P. Sweelinck

18TH CENTURY

La Poule — J. Ph. Rameau
Le Coucou — Louis C. Daquin
Suite — Gottlieb Muffat
  Overture — Sarabande
  Vivace — Rigaudon
  Allemande — Menuet II, Trio
  Courante — Gigue

Recorder and Harpsichord Music

16TH CENTURY

Music From Shakespeare's Plays — anonymous, ed. Carl Dolmetsch
  La Volta — The Sick Tune — Heartease
  English Jig — Light O' Love — Morisco
  The Measure — Fortune My Foe — Corranto

18TH CENTURY

Partita in E minor — Georg P. Telemann
  Andante, Aria I, Vivace, Aria II, Presto,
  Aria III, Vivace, Aria VI, Siciliana, Aria V,
  Vivace, Aria VI, Presto
Sonata in G major — Willem de Fesch
  Largo, Allemande, Aria, Gavotta
Sonata in F major — Jean B. Loeillet
  Adagio, Allegro, Adagio, Gigue

RECORDINGS — FOR STYLE REFERENCE

There are many first rate professional groups and conductors who have made outstanding recordings of the chamber repertoire, as well as increasing numbers of college and university groups which are excellent. Since recording companies change their catalog every month it is best to consult the following guides to recordings, which are available at local dealers: W. Schwann Inc. (137 Newbury Street, Boston, Mass.) L.P. Record Catalog, Phonolog, and for foreign publications, Gramaphone Classical L.P. Record Catalog, and Bielefelder Katalog.

The outstanding ensembles are the New York Pro Musica and the Abbey Singers, both directed by Noah Greenberg and available on Decca and Columbia labels; the Deller Consort, recorded on Vanguard and other labels; Pro Musica Antiqua of Brussels, Sir Safford Cape director; the Luca Marenzio Singers from Italy. Other excellent ensembles to be found on less familiar labels are The Roger Blanchard Ensemble with Poulteau Consort, Jean-Paul Kreder Ensemble, and the Budapest Madrigal Ensemble—to name only a few.

The group best known in the United States and the one which undoubtedly has had the greatest influence on setting standards of musical performance in this country is the New York Pro Musica. Noah Greenberg was an outstanding musician, and has made available some of the obscure literature of the early Renaissance.

An English group which has a wonderful feeling for the madrigal style is the Deller Consort. This is one of the most magnificent groups ever assembled. It is conducted by Alfred Deller, a countertenor, scholar, and teacher. All of his performances are outstanding.[3]

SPECIAL REHEARSAL TECHNIQUES

Because you are working with a small, select group, progress can be much faster than with a full choir, even though your basic technique may not change. In exchange for this pleasure, there is increased obligation, of course.

Always start on time, developing the idea that the job must be done in the period allotted, with no extra rehearsals. Every practice session should be demanding, but also full of fun and relaxation. The group must be able to laugh a little, and then get right back to serious work.

Even though there is more room for give-and-take in a group like this, it actually demands a stricter musical and personal discipline. You cannot waste the time and talents of these outstanding youngsters, but must always be ready with the next logical step in preparing a piece, based on your background, concept of style, and intense study of the pieces.

Sometimes musical decisions must be tempered by visual and psychological considerations. While professional groups such as those conducted by Alfred Deller or Noah Greenberg can use only those

---

[3] *Editor's note:* Many high school and college groups have recordings available, some of which are excellent. The University of Maryland Madrigal Singers have produced a series of recordings of the music of the Renaissance period published by the Bourne Company.

singers needed for perfect balance of certain works, while others remain silent on stage, this is sometimes difficult to do with an amateur group. Even though students try to conceal their feelings, it is usually obvious from their hurt expressions that they want to sing *all* the time and that they feel their silence indicates a lack of competence on their part. It is difficult to convince them that they have been asked *not* to sing purely for reasons of balance.

INSTRUMENTAL ACCOMPANIMENT

Various instruments can be used to add variety, color, and authenticity to the repertoire of a chamber ensemble. (*see* Fig. 4-2.) Since it takes so much time to learn these instruments correctly, it seems to work out best when the instrumentalists concentrate on playing, except in those very rare cases when a student both sings and plays extremely well.

Instruments which can be used include the following:

Harpsichord. The keyboard instrument in common use from the 16th through the 18th century. Strings are plucked by leather or quill points connected with the keys. There are many instruments on the market ranging in price from $700 to $3,500 and over—also a $150 kit for home workshop assembly.[4]

Lute. The sort of "pear-shaped guitar." This is the instrument probably most closely associated with Elizabethan ballads.

Rebec. A small Medieval fiddle, with pear-shaped body, vaulted back, and 3 strings. It is played with a bow.

Recorder. The vertically played, wooden, flute-like instrument, now enjoying such a revival in homes and elementary school classrooms. Most music stores stock a full range (soprano to bass) of instruments with prices ranging from $3.50 to $75.00.

Classical Guitar. Also enjoying great popularity. There are often students who can learn this style, even though they may have started with "rock 'n' roll."

A recording called "The Renaissance Band," by Noah Greenberg and the New York Pro Musica demonstrates several other instruments of the period as well. Pictures and explanatory notes are included.

---

[4] *Harpsichords (assmbled)*:Sabathil & Son, Dept. M 3911 W. 25th, Vancouver, B. C., Canada; The Cannon Guild, Inc., 5 Howard St., Cambridge, Mass. *Harpsichord (kit form)*: Zuckerman Harpsichords, Dept. L, 115 Christopher St., New York, N. Y. 10014.

Fig. 4-2
The University of Maryland Madrigal Singers Perform During a
Birthday Celebration of William Shakespeare at the Folger
Shakespeare Library in Washington, D.C.

PROGRAMMING THE SELECTIONS

With music selected from several different periods, the addition of instruments, and the inclusion of solos, duets, trios, and other small ensembles, a full concert can be presented. The programs reproduced in Figure 4–3 show how the order of various selections can be arranged to create a varied evening of listening, which is unified by the consistently "chamber" approach. Costumes are changed during intermission from Elizabethan to contemporary formal.

PERFORMING WITH THE ENSEMBLE

Perhaps both the thrill and the value of public performance can best be expressed by the short paragraphs which appeared in every printed program (in many different languages), which was distributed during a tour of the Near East, North Africa, and Western Europe.

A Message from the Secretary of State

The Cultural Presentations Program of the Department of State is an eloquent realization of the American people's wish to share with the rest of the world the best of our arts developed by academic as well as professional groups.

The program was born of our conviction that good relations among nations are rooted in mutual understanding. Since true understanding is a matter of both heart and mind, our Government attaches great importance to the sending abroad of our most representative cultural attractions. The culture of any country is the key to the hearts and minds of its people.

Dean Rusk

Chamber music is an intimate form of music. Its performance depends on the sensitivity of each individual and the interdependence of each member of the group. This quality of intimacy seems to facilitate communication between performers and the audience.

We eagerly anticipate the privilege of reaching out in friendship through this type of music, and trust that the musical sensitivity so necessary for performance will be a medium for a better understanding of the people and the culture of the countries which it will be our privilege to visit.

I

Das Herz Tut Mir Aufspringen	Hans Leo Hassler
Sie Ist Mir Lieb	Michael Praetorius
Amor in Nachen	Giovanni Gastoldi
Ein Hennlein Weiss	Antonio Scandello

Madrigal Singers

II

Nun Fanget An	Hans Leo Hassler
Dadme Albricias Hijos d'Eva	Anonymous, 16th Century
Riu, Riu, Chiu	Anonymous, 16th Century

Madrigal Singers, recorders, harpsichord
Lin Maxwell, soloist

III

Pavane, Galiarde	Claude Gervais
Barley Break	William Byrd

Recorder quartet

Amusette, No. 4	Jacques Aubert

Le Coulouin, Menuet, Le Moulinet
Robert Bonner, recorder, and harpsichord

Four Villancicos	Joan da Nola

Recorder trio

Earle of Salisbury	William Byrd

Pavane, Galliard
Christine Hagan, harpsichord

Music from Shakespeare's Plays	ed. by Carl Dolmetsch
La Volta	William Byrd
English Jig	Anonymous, 16th Century
Canaries	Anonymous, 16th Century
The Measure	Anonymous, 16th Century
Morisco	Anonymous, 16th Century

Narrator, recorders, harpsichord, percussion

IV

Though Amaryllis Dance	William Byrd
Weep O Mine Eyes	John Bennet
Echo Song	Orlando di Lasso

Madrigal Singers

INTERMISSION

V

Salisbury	Oliver Brownson
Crossing the Han River	Peter Mennin
Three Canonic Choruses	William Schuman

Epitaph
Epitaph for Joseph Conrad
Come Not

Solo Voices and Madrigal Singers

VI

Chee Malee Walee	Iraqui Folk Song
Pano St. Alonia	Greek Folk Song
Lolly Tu-Dum	American Folk Song
Three Way Canon Blues	William Brant

Madrigal Singers

Fig. 4-3

**Spring and Maryland Tour Programs of University
of Maryland Singers**

University of Maryland Madrigal Singers

ROSE MARIE GRENTZER, CONDUCTOR

I

All Ye Who Music Love	Baldassare Donato
O, Eyes of My Beloved	Orlando di Lasso
Matona, Lovely Maiden	Orlando di Lasso
So Well I Know Who's Happy	Orazio Vecchi

Madrigal Singers

II

It Was a Lover and His Lass	Thomas Morley

Nancy Matheny and harpsichord

Come Shepherd Swain	John Wilbye

Anne Carter, Sandra Higginbotham, Sharon Wilhelm

Allegro from Sonata, Bb Major	Wolfgang A. Mozart

Miss Eisenstadt

John Come Kiss Me Now	William Byrd

a. Song, Linden Maxwell
b. Harpsichord, Miss Eisenstadt

Frottola	Bartolomeo Tromboncino

Anne Carter, harpsichord and rebec

Counterpoint of the Animals	Adriano Banchieri

Madrigal Singers

INTERMISSION

III

Sing We and Chant It	Thomas Morley
Come Again Sweet Love	John Dowland
The Silver Swan	Orlando Gibbons
All Creatures Now are Merry Minded	John Bennet

Madrigal Singers

IV

Salisbury	Oliver Brownson
Geneva	John Cole
Consonance	William Billings
Modern Music	William Billings

Madrigal Singers

V

Mary Wore Three Links of Chain	Negro Spiritual

Madrigal Singers

Jesus Walked This Lonesome Valley	White Spiritual

Linden Maxwell, and guitar

It Was a Frog in the Well	Thomas Ravenscroft

Soloists, Madrigal Singers, and guitar

A Wooing Song of the Yeoman of Kent's Son	Thomas Ravenscroft

Marvin Gardner, Jr., guitar and chorus

Three Way Canon Blues	Henry Brant

Madrigal Singers

Fig. 4-3 (*cont.*)

We look forward to meeting our friends in other lands, knowing that our lives will be greatly enriched through the interchange of ideas, and we trust that music will be a vehicle for mutual understanding. It is a great honor to be chosen by the Department of State to represent the people of our country.

Rose Marie Grentzer

"Conducting" the Chamber Group

The conductor should remain as inconspicuous as possible, giving only the minimum amount of direction. Although traditionally the conductor also sings with the ensemble, this is a mistake with school groups. Singing prohibits one from hearing the overall blend, and the addition of one mature voice mars the ensemble of young singers.

If the group is small enough and secure enough to perform alone, the conductor should watch and listen from a seat in the audience. However, most conductor-less school groups tend to distort the tempo, and are unable to handle the many other unexpected problems which arise during the course of a performance.

"It's Good Stuff if You Don't Inhale It"

At the same time you are molding a chamber ensemble into the kind of high quality, closely knit group which can be an exciting example of the very best training your choral program has to offer, you must also be careful to guide the members to an honest feeling of humility. Confidence which comes from the realization that they are *the best* must be balanced by an awareness of how much *more* there is to learn. Before giving compliments I warn them: "It's good stuff if you don't inhale it."

The chamber ensemble is an excellent medium for plain old *character building*. You, as the leader, can do a great deal to train a lot of "nice people" who also sing well, but it takes time and careful planning.

Music for Teen-Agers

Each generation, with predictable regularity, seems to insist on condemning the music of the "younger generation," often failing to realize that the current "musical" favorite is simply another fad to which adolescents (and many others) have always been susceptible. The mass hysteria really has little or nothing to do with *musical* taste, but rather is more closely associated with conformity, emotional release, identity, and so on. The adoration of "musical" groups merely becomes the vehicle for these psychological gyrations. Founded on this basic confusion of *music* and *fad*, many of us then proceed to underestimate the *musical* tastes of our students. Rather than worry about "cultural degeneration," however, inspired music teachers who understand this "teen-age dichotomy"are offering their students the challenge of really great music . . . and the youngsters love it!

Teen-agers Become Adults

Since the chamber ensemble can be the most challenging and rewarding part of a fine choral music program, outstanding students with great career potential are often attracted to the group. The very nature of the ensemble, dictated by the music itself, encourages them to sing in similar groups for the rest of their lives. It is not unusual to find doctors, lawyers, engineers, and other professionals who have become so "addicted" in school that they form amateur singing groups in their own communities.

Future Music Teachers

The chamber situation because of the selectivity of membership and the intimacy of association is also excellent for recruiting the best possible future choral music teachers. Students have an unusual opportunity to learn a great deal about the duties of the director long before entering a college music department for formal study.

With this great opportunity to guide outstanding candidates into the profession comes, as usual, great obligation as well. I remember walking past the open door of a high school French class. Inside was one of my ensemble members teaching the group a French song. As I stood out of sight and listened, it was amazing to hear my own rehearsal techniques being reproduced in such complete detail. The fact that even after 4 years of music school training, student teachers will give out information and use techniques (sometimes completely the opposite of what they have been taught) which can be traced directly back to their experiences as high school students, places a great responsibility on every teacher.

You, as music director, character builder, and personal guidance counselor, owe a great deal to these students, to the profession, and to yourself. The chamber ensemble can be a wonderful experience for all concerned, but your leadership must go far beyond the purchase of a table, candles, and some colorful costumes. Great care must be taken in every aspect of your dealings with these students who are at such an impressionable, but equally wonderful age.

5

Choosing Music for Performance

by Harold A. Decker

University of Illinois

Harold A. Decker

is Chairman of the Department of Choral Music in the University of Illinois School of Music, where he conducts many choral groups, including the Oratorio Society, Varsity Men's Glee Club, University Chorus, and Madrigal Singers. His degrees were earned at Morningside College (A.B.-1934), and Oberlin College (Mus.M.-1938). He has completed study leading to a certificate (1953) from Ecole des Beaux Artes in Fountainbleau, France, and has carried on independent research in Europe (1964–65).

Mr. Decker has earned a national reputation as a director, music educator, festival conductor, and lecturer. He has taught as a visiting lecturer at the Oberlin Conservatory of Music, the University of Michigan, the University of Southern California, and George Peabody College. Before moving to the University of Illinois, he was head of the voice and choral departments at the University of Wichita.

He is a member of the Music Educator's National Conference, the American Association of University Professors, and Phi Mu Alpha Sinfonia. He has served the American Choral Director's Association in various positions of leadership, including the presidency.

His duties as choral department head and conductor of numerous performing organizations, and his many appearances as All State Chorus/Choral Clinic Director (Missouri, Illinois, Indiana, Michigan, Wisconsin, Iowa, South Dakota, Kansas, Oklahoma, Texas, Mississippi, Kentucky, Tennessee, Pennsylvania, California, Utah, Colorado, New Mexico) have helped him to develop a very practical approach to the choosing of music for performance. His vast knowledge of choral repertoire is greatly respected by music educators everywhere.

The difficult, but exciting, task of sifting through catalogs, selected lists, clinic notes, books, magazines, pamphlets, advertisements, new music reviews, sample copies, and any other likely source, in search of suitable music for your choral program, actually becomes a year-round, every-waking hour, conscious and sub-conscious sort of occupation.

Every year many new pieces are added to the established catalogs of what may seem like an almost endless list of music publishers (*see* pages 90-97). It is easy to sympathize with the choral director who becomes confused as he wades through stacks of paper trying to choose music for performance which fits his program, his choir, and his own musical personality.

Yet the choices he makes have a direct, and very great, effect on each individual rehearsal, concert, and, ultimately, on the success or failure of the entire choral music program of the school.

Planning the Year's Work

Most choirs can anticipate at least 2 major concerts per year—Christmas and Spring. In Illinois, of course, the Lincoln Day Assembly is a tradition, but each school and each community has its own special observances.

Major concerts should be planned first—dates scheduled, music chosen—then the other events for which the choir is expected to furnish music can be filled in. In this way a reasonable estimate of both the quantity and type of music needed throughout the coming school year can be made.

Know Your Group — and Yourself

The music ordered for your group must be "right." All programs have peak years and lean years; each conductor has strengths and weaknesses in the various styles; every piece does not necessarily "come off" in rehearsal, and some must be abandoned . . . all of these things must be anticipated. A thorough evaluation of the present capability and reasonable potential of the group, as well as some serious self soul-searching, will help you to choose the best music.

The Search Is On

Obviously the first step in choosing music for performance must be to use every possible means to find out just what is available, so that the very best may be selected.

A card index is very useful for keeping a record of the pieces you may want to perform . . . someday. All of us hear fine selections nearly every day, many of which would be appropriate for our own choirs. Unless the name is written down, most of them will be forgotten. By establishing a permanent reference on the file card, you can look up additional information which may be necessary to order the piece when you are ready for it.

Concert programs are a good source, and many directors exchange copies of their programs. Some state and national organizations have attempted program exchanges on a mass scale. I keep a large file of printed programs that have been accumulated through the years and find them to be useful for programming ideas, as well as for selection reference.

Professional magazines have new music review sections, in addition to the many advertisements sprinkled throughout which list the current offerings of many publishers.

Publishers mailing lists should have your name and current address on them. The firms which sell choral music are anxious for their product to be seen, and will send you catalogs and lists, as well as *on approval* and/or *complimentary* copies of their publications . . . if you ask them! When changing positions, a spirit-duplicated letter or post card should be sent to publishers (*see* list of addresses, pages 90-97) containing your name, position, address, former address, the name of the person you are replacing, and your areas of particular interest.

Reference books and pamphlets are often devoted to cataloging choral music. Since publishers tend to concentrate on the new publications in their advertising and promotion, a great deal of material —still in print and still very valuable—may be overlooked unless you check out the more permanent sources as well. The following publications contain many suggestions of really good, though older, choral literature:

> *Handbuch der Chormusik I and II,* edited by Erich Valentin, published by Gustav Bosse, Regenburg, 1958. All cantates are listed, with solo parts, voice distribution, number of accompanying instruments needed, and time of performance.
>
> *Catalogue of Choral Works,* National Federation of Music Societies, 2 Manchester Sq., London, 1953.
>
> *Selected List of Music for Men's Voices,* edited by J. Merrill Knapp, Princeton University Press, 1952.

Selected List of Choruses for Women's Voices, third edition (others 1925, 1946). Compiled by Arthur Ware Locke and Charles K. Fassett. Northhampton: Smith College, 1964.

Conventions can serve your music-hunting needs very well. Programs of performances (with your margin notes) can be filed for future reference; music may be examined at the many publishers' booths; composers, arrangers, editors, and consultants from many areas are available for conversation and advice.

Clinics and workshops, particularly those designed specifically to investigate a great deal of literature, give a director the opportunity to actually hear the pieces performed, and often—in reading sessions—allow him to sing (or sometimes take a turn at conducting) more music in one afternoon than he might encounter normally in a full year of teaching.

Informal conversations with other directors can often add to your knowledge of literature, although it is often the "dessert," the "clinchers" (sometimes, unfortunately, the "potboilers"), which are discussed, rather than the solid and serious, less sensational type of composition. A pocket notebook can help to turn stimulating conversations into a productive part of your constant search for good program material.

THE EXAMINATION

Unfortunately, for the director, the students, the audience, and eventually for both the composer and the publisher, a great deal of choral music has been produced, sold, and performed which is not of very high quality. Therefore it becomes especially important for the school choral director (who also claims to be a music educator) to devise some means of choosing *the best* from the literally *tons* of music which can cross his desk if all available sources have been actively cultivated.

Through many years of careful examination I have learned to discard a great deal of music. I seldom keep more than about 20% of the examination copies received, and gradually pare these down as periodic reexaminations are made.

HOW TO PICK THE BEST

Personal appeal is the first and most important qualification a piece must have. It might be immediately attractive to someone else, but no conductor can ever honestly conduct a composition which does not hold some special appeal *for him*. There are some pieces which I would never program, yet there are others which have such a strong attraction that I feel *compelled* to present them in concert. When looking at music I find that my first consideration is "Would YOU *really* like to perform this music?"

Musical factors must be considered, of course. It is difficult to analyze exactly what makes a piece "sound," but I go through a sort of subconscious mental check list which often includes the following items:

Balance. Is this an artistic composition, or just a harmonized tune? Are the text and the musical setting compatible, meaningful?

Contrast. Drama vs. serenity, full vs. transparent voicings, male vs. female sounds, unison vs. harmony, other harmonic, rhythmic, melodic contrasts.

Accompaniment. Is it playable, and suitable within a choral concept? Does it overshadow the choir? Does it have a musically integrated function within the composition?

Tessitura. A few notes in the extreme ranges can often be effective, but generally pieces which remain within the more comfortable limits of the voices will allow the most pleasant tone quality to come through. (*see* Fig. 5-1)

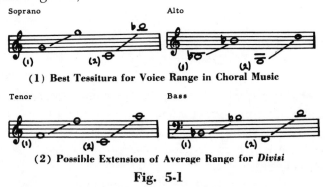

(1) **Best Tessitura for Voice Range in Choral Music**

(2) **Possible Extension of Average Range for *Divisi***

Fig. 5-1

Rhythm. If a difficult rhythmic figure is written for all parts to sing together, it can be taught to the entire group with success, but in pieces with independent rhythms which must be sung *against* other independent rhythms, the problem is much greater.

Potential problems. Advanced harmonies, dissonance, ornaments, wide voice range, difficult intervals, monotonous or poor internal voice leading—all examined in the light of the choir's current capability. An otherwise acceptable piece of music should not be ruled out solely on one of these counts, however, since various rehearsal techniques (even editing and slight revision of parts) can be used to prepare the selection for acceptable performance.

Suitability. The piece should not only fit the occasion for which it is intended, but possibly serve in other contexts as well. Music for performance differs from instructional music in that it should reveal the choir's greatest potential, rather than expose its problems.

Editing and arranging. Edited works should indicate all alterations by the editor in brackets. In early music, dynamic markings other than those of the composer should be minimal. Arrangements must be tasteful and not "overdone." They must reveal the original mood and intent of the music.

Mechanical considerations. The music will receive a better reading, particularly by younger, less experienced singers, if it is neat and uncluttered in appearance. Correct notes, proper alignment of words and music, clarity of *divisi* parts, effective placement of dynamic markings, and other similar items directly related to the skill of the printer (not the musician) will, nonetheless, have a great influence on the musical result, and on the speed with which it can be achieved.

THE PERMANENT REFERENCE FILE

I have found it most useful to file reference copies of the music I would someday like to perform. As music comes across my desk from various sources, one copy of that which is not immediately discarded is put into the appropriate file.

Special. The music I want to perform just as soon as it can be worked into our concert schedules.

Festival. Music which is especially suited to mass chorus, to be used with high school students in my appearances as guest conductor.

Male Chorus. Music for the University of Illinois Men's Gree Club.

Women's Chorus. Although I am not now conducting much of this music, I like to keep a current file of good literature for the use of others in the choral department.

Seasonal. Music useful only during certain periods (Christmas, Easter, Thanksgiving, etc.)

Renaissance. This is subdivided into (1) motets, and (2) madrigals and other secular music.

Baroque, Classic, Romantic. Three separate categories, filed by musical period.

Contemporary. This file always remains the largest, probably because I hate to discard new music until it has had a fair trial; but it is also the file subject to the most frequent reexamination.

Miscellaneous. This includes smaller divisions, such as "Russian," "Contemporary Madrigals," as well as cantatas and large choral works.

Each director will want to adapt his files to his own particular interests, activities, and responsibilities, but if the constant search for good music is to have any permanent and cumulative value, it is essential that *some* form of permanent reference file be started, and expanded regularly.

Since tastes change with age and experience, younger directors may want to file a little extra music now, rather than run the risk of throwing away something today which might be appreciated more fully 10 years from now.

The Core Repertoire

The balanced, educationally sound choral program must present music of all types to the students. A *core repertoire* should be developed containing representative selections from the Renaissance, Baroque, Classic, Romantic, and Contemporary periods, as well as folk songs and spirituals. These basic pieces can then be used to build interesting and varied programs. Seasonal and popular music may be added, as needed. By purchasing music with an eye toward this kind of balance, a permanent library of high quality literature (so necessary for performance, sight reading, and for work with the feeder choirs) can be established.

Ordering the Music

Regardless of how thoroughly you have searched every available source, or how carefully you have chosen the best pieces, your work will be wasted unless you also follow through with an efficient handling of business procedures, so that music can reach the hands of the students in time to rehearse it properly. Here are some practical suggestions, designed to save time and reduce errors in your dealings with the music industry.

Business correspondence should be legible, concise, and well organized. Typewritten letters—carefully proofread for errors (especially in catalog and quantity numbers) on school letterhead, containing consistent signature and position form, with a carbon copy for filing—are the most efficient means of communication. Multipurpose letters waste time, since they must be relayed from one department to another. By limiting yourself to one topic per sheet of paper, and indicating the subject at the top (order, merchandise return), the correspondence may still be mailed in the same envelope.

School business procedures vary. Some may have a central purchasing agency which you must supply with complete and accurate information (in *business*, not musical, terms); others pay "on invoice only," often requiring the countersignature, or at least the "OK" of an administrative officer. Find out the exact procedure used by your school, and then develop a routine for your business affairs which is consistent with the system.

Current catalogs of all publishers should be kept on file. Identify the pieces you order by title, composer-arranger, catalog number, specific arrangement (SATB, SAB), publisher, and price.

"On approval" orders have a time limit, after which the music becomes your property, and is charged to your account. Some companies require that you keep a certain percentage of the material you have requested. Be sure you understand the exact terms of any "on approval" arrangement you may make. When returning unwanted music, affix a separate letter (first class, explaining clearly what you are returning) to the outside of a carefully bound package of music labeled with your school's account number. Send parcel post, insured, marked "Educational materials."

Plan ahead so that the music can be delivered well in advance of the time you will need it. Regardless of the prompt service promises of even the most efficient firms, unexpected delays can develop during a rush season or holiday weekend; pieces can suddenly become "temporarily out of stock—please reorder"; shipping clerks and postal employees can make mistakes in routing . . . and you lose valuable rehearsal time (or go back to "The Green Cathedral").

How to Stretch the Budget

1. Order only those pieces you actually need. While the complete "Messiah" may add prestige to a library, the "Hallelujah Chorus" is available in a separate arrangement.

2. Order only those quantities you need. While it is certainly desir-
    able to have individual copies for each member, sometimes a
    shortage of money makes this impossible. Two, or even three
    people can share the same music, although the speed of learning
    is greatly retarded.
3. Take care of the music you have. Develop an efficient check-out
    system for all music so that when students borrow pieces to take
    home you know where to locate them. Provide adequate shelf
    or file space for your permanent library.
4. Shop around for firms with the most favorable school discount
    policies, the most liberal on approval arrangements, the most fre-
    quent clearance sales, and other fringe benefits (free delivery,
    business advice, etc.).
5. Buy some choral collections, rather than all separate pieces. *Five
    Centuries of Choral Music*, G. Schirmer, Inc., N. Y., 1963 is an
    especially good collection for high schools. There are others.
    Be careful; you may actually *lose* money on a collection, since
    some contain only 2 or 3 really useful pieces.
6. Neighboring schools can set up reciprocal agreements to share
    their libraries. A county or city system can establish a central
    library for the use of all schools. In these situations, music should
    be checked out for the entire school year, then circulated to an-
    other school for the following year's work.
7. There are several libraries throughout the country maintained
    by professional associations and commercial interests, with many
    pieces available for loan or rent. Although useful when certain
    expensive pieces are needed for a special program, the constant
    rental of music is unwise for both financial and musical reasons,
    since it incurs expenses but does nothing to establish a perma-
    nent school library of fine choral music.

Program Building

The choosing of music for performance and the arrangement of
pieces into a program of satisfactory proportions are so interrelated
as to be almost a "chicken-or-the-egg" problem when trying to decide which should come first. Is it better to pick pieces from your
permanent reference file and try to arrange them in some order
which makes sense, or should you plan the type of concert program
which is best for your students and your audience, and then try
to find pieces which will fit into the proper places in the form?

In the final analysis it is really a cooperative process in which educational requirements (the *core repertoire* concept) and principles of proper program structure are integrated, with the aid of adaptations on both sides.

The usual methods of program construction are *chronological* (in order from Renaissance up through Contemporary), *seasonal* (all Christmas, or Spring), and *contrasting groups* (sacred vs. secular, Madrigal group vs. full choir).

The *theme* method offers an opportunity to present good, but possibly unusual music in a unique setting which will appeal to most audiences. As an example, the program in Figure 5-2 investigates music written by four different composers, all inspired by the annual celebrations to the patron saint of music.

Other programs, or groups within programs, can be built on this same idea. A whole program of *Psalms*, for instance, can be very effective, and full of more contrast than might be expected. Composers of many varied styles have written music on psalms—Schütz, Vaughan-Williams, Distler, Kodaly, Hovhannes, Rheinhorst, Gordon Binkard, Zimmerman (jazz idiom, with string bass). A group based on similar texts makes an interesting study of artistic approaches and helps to expose previously unnoticed facets of the text to performers and audience alike. The *Ave Maria* is an obvious possibility. I have also used *O Magnum Mysterium* by Victoria, Gabrielli, and Poulenc.

An effective Christmas program, including a prelude by the instrumental music department, and community singing by the audience can be based entirely on carols. In the program reproduced in Figure 5-3, words for those marked *, included in the original program for the audience's benefit, have been omitted here in order to conserve space.

MAKING FULL USE OF MATERIAL

Just as some composers seem to be able to get the most "mileage" out of each melody, the choral director whose groups perform a great deal must sometimes make the greatest use of the pieces which are ready for performance. For instance, a certain group of selections which has been used to provide a contrast of lightness within a basically "heavy" concert, can be lifted out of that program, intact, and performed for a civic club luncheon. A Renaissance group could be extracted for a church service, a patriotic collection for a D.A.R. meeting, or a folk set for a school assembly.

THE SCHOOL OF MUSIC OF THE UNIVERSITY OF ILLINOIS

presents

THE MADRIGAL SINGERS

in

Music for St. Cecilia's Day

HAROLD A. DECKER, Conductor
JAMES THOMPSON, Assistant Conductor
RICHARD BLOESCH, Harpsichordist

PROGRAM

An Ode for St. Cecilia's Day (1683).....................HENRY PURCELL
   "Welcome to All the Pleasures"   (1659?-1695)

Motet: O beata Cecilia...........................PHILIPPE DE MONTE
                                                                 (1521-1603)

Hymn to St. Cecilia................................BENJAMIN BRITTEN
                                                                 (1913-   )

INTERMISSION

Ode on St. Cecilia's Day (1684)...........................JOHN BLOW
   "Begin the Song"   (1649-1708)

ST. CECILIA'S DAY

For several centuries the custom of celebrating St. Cecilia's Day (November 22) in praise of music by musical performances existed in various countries and according to Grove's *Dictionary of Music and Musicians* "many associations were formed for the purpose." The earliest of such associations known was established in 1570 at Evreux, France, in Normandy on October 12, 1570. In addition to religious rites and a banquet, prizes were awarded for the best motets, part-songs, airs, and sonnets. Among the prominent composers of that age who contributed was Orlando di Lasso.

A century later England first held a series of annual celebrations to the patron saint of music in London in 1683. The practice was to attend divine worship when a choral service and anthem with orchestral accompaniment composed especially for the occasion were performed. They then repaired to another place where an ode in praise of music, again written and composed especially for the occasion, was performed. These odes were written by Dryden, Shadwell, Congreve, and Pope as well as lesser writers. Musicians such as Henry Purcell, John Blow, Dr. Michael Greene, Dr. William Boyce, and others composed the music. These celebrations were observed without interruption in England until 1703, after which they were held only occasionally. Other celebrations are recorded on St. Cecilia's Day in Italy, Germany, and elsewhere. Hymns in her praise have been composed in honor of the martyred saint of music since the early days of Christendom.

Fig. 5-2

Program by University of Illinois Madrigal Singers

CAROL CONCERT PROGRAM

An Instrumental Prelude .... *University of Illinois Wind Ensemble*
    Selections included from the following:

        Suite of Carols for Brass .... LEROY ANDERSON
        Suite of Carols for Woodwinds .... LEROY ANDERSON
        Toccata .... AURELIO BONELLI
        A Lovely Rose Is Blooming .... JOHANNES BRAHMS
        In Dulci Jubilo .... DIETRICH BUXTEHUDE
        Sussex Mummer's Christmas Carol .... ENGLISH CAROL
        Canzon Duodecimi Toni .... GIOVANNI GABRIELI

I

*O Come All Ye Faithful .... LATIN; 18TH CENTURY
The Three Kings .... HEALY WILLAN
        Combined Glee Clubs and Chorus
*O Little Town of Bethlehem .... REDNER

II

Rejoice, Rejoice .... WILLIAM BYRD
Kyrie — Christ Was Born This Day — Eleison .... ALBERT KING
Two Spanish Carols
        December's Ice and Snow .... CATALONIAN CAROL
        See the Shepherds Dancing .... ANONYMOUS (17th Century)
A Carol .... ERNEST BACON
        The Women's Glee Club
*The First Nowell .... ENGLISH CAROL

III

Hacia Belén va un borrico .... TRAD. SPANISH ARR. BY SHAW-PARKER
Angelus ad Pastores .... HASSLER
Allon, Gay Bergeres .... COSTELEY
Go Tell It On the Mountain .... SPIRITUAL ARR. BY JOHN WORK
        The University Chorus
*Hark! the Herald Angels Sing .... MENDELSSOHN
*Deck the Halls .... OLD WELSH

IV

O magnum mysterium (O Mystery Divine) .... JAKOB HANDL
Hodie natus est (Today a Child Is Born) .... DI LASSO
Sweet Was the Song the Virgin Sung ...... ATTEY, ARR. BY HARRINGTON
The Gloucester Wassail .... OLD ENGLISH, ARR. BY ORREY
        The Varsity Men's Glee Club
*Joy to the World .... HANDEL (1742)
*Silent Night .... GRUBER (1818)

V

Fantasia on Christmas Carols .... R. VAUGHAN WILLIAMS
Combined Glee Clubs and Chorus, with Baritone Solo, Organ, and Chimes

* Audience will please join in singing

Fig. 5-3

Many choirs sing a few songs which through the years just seem to *belong* to them. The University of Illinois Men's Glee Club has many such pieces, which the students learn from each other. I spend very little time in rehearsing them, but these songs are always ready for the unexpected encore, the sentimental touch for alumni audiences, and the impromptu song fest.

The Song Is You

The music you choose for performance is a direct reflection on you as a musician, teacher, and person. It is amazing how accurately a choral program reveals the true personality of its director. While it may be safer, and simpler, to depend on the tried and true pieces of your own past successes, the invigorating effect which a constant search for fresh and exciting literature can have on your entire choral music program, as well as on your attitude toward it, is more than worth the extra effort.

Guide to Music Publishers

Since it is essential that choral directors have a thorough knowledge of compositions which are available to them, a list of music publishers is included here. A post card to each one will start an avalanche of mail designed to keep one well informed on the subject. As name and address changes are seen in current periodicals, they should be noted on the list.

The name in SMALL CAPITALS is the code name of the company which is used throughout this book. The address of the company follows. If owned or distributed by another company, the company's code name is put in parenthesis. This list has been compiled with the help of *The Music Educator's Business Handbook* (Music Industry Council), and *Selective Music Lists* (NIMAC), both MENC publications, 1201 Sixteenth Street, N.W., Washington, D.C.; and *The Music Teacher's Guide to the Music Industry* (unpublished), by J. W. Worrel, Supervisor of Music, Cincinnati (Ohio) Public Schools.

Publisher	*Address*
ABC Music Corporation	799 7th Ave., New York City 10000
ABINGDON Music Press	201 8th Ave. S., Nashville, Tennessee 37203
ADVANCED Music Corp.	(MPH)
ALEXANDER, David	Carlsbad, California 92008
ALFRED Music Co., Inc.	145 W. 45th St., New York City 10036

Publisher	*Address*
ALLOWAY	545 Muskingum Place, Pacific Palisades, California 90272
AMPHION	(Leeds)
AMSCO Music Publishing Co.	240 W. 55th St., New York City 10019
ANDRAUD	(SMC)
ANCHOR Books	(Doubleday)
ARNOLD, Edward and Co.	(C. Fischer)
ARROW Press	(Associated)
ART MASTERS Studio	20 W. 26th St., Minneapolis, Minn. 55408
ASSOCIATED Music Publishers, Inc.	1 W. 47th St., New York City (G. Schirmer) 10036
AUGENER, Ltd., London	(Galaxy)
AUGSBURG Publishing House	426 S. 5th St., Minneapolis, Minn. 55415
AVANT Music	2859 Holt Ave., Los Angeles, Calif. 90034
BANDLAND	(Belwin)
BAND SHED	Petal, Mississippi 39465
BARENREITER Verlag	Heinrich Schutz Alee, 29/37, Kassel-Wilhelmshone, Germany
BARGER & Barclay	P.O. Box 663, Great Neck, N.Y. 11020
BARNHOUSE, C. L. Co.	Oskaloosa, Iowa 52577
BARON, M. Co.	Box 149, Oyster Bay, L.I., N.Y. 11771
BEEKMAN	(Presser)
BELWIN, Inc.	250 Maple Ave., Rockville Center, L.I., N.Y. 11570
BENJAMIN	(Associated)
BERKELEY Publishing Company	2244 Dwight Way, Berkeley, Calif. 94700
BIG THREE Music Corporation	1540 Broadway, New York City 10036
BIRCHARD, C. C. and Co.	(Summy)
BLAKE, Whitney, Music Publishers	243 W. 72nd St., New York City 10023
BOOSEY & Hawkes, Inc.	Oceanside, New York 11570
BOOSEY & Co., Ltd., London	(Boosey & Hawkes)
BOSTON Music Company	116 Boylston St., Boston, Mass. 02116
BOURNE Company	136 W. 52nd St., New York City 10019
BREITKOPF & HARTEL	(Associated)
BREGMAN, Vocco & Conn., Inc.	1619 Broadway, New York City 10019
BRIEGEL, George F., Inc.	17 W. 60th St., New York City 10023

Publisher	*Address*
BRITISH AMERICAN Music Company	19 W. Jackson Blvd., Chicago, Ill. (Mills) 60604
BRODT Music Company	Box 1207, Charlotte, N.C. 28201
BROUDE Brothers	56 W. 45th St., New York City 10019
BUXTON Hill	(Chappell)
BYRON Douglas	3812 W. Palmaire Dr., Phoenix, Ariz. 85000
CANYON Press, Inc.	17 Kearney St., East Orange, N.J. 07017
CARLIN Music Co.	4040 W. 173 Place, Torrance, Calif. 90500
CENTURY Music Publishing Co.	39 W. 60th St., New York City 10023
CHAPPELL & Co., Inc.	609 5th Ave., New York City 10017
CHARLES, Frederick, Inc.	434 S. Wabash Ave., Chicago, Ill. 60605
CHART	(Summy)
CHESTER	(G. Schirmer)
CHOIR	Mormon Tabernacle, Salt Lake City, Utah 84100
CHORAL ART	(Fox)
CHORAL PRESS	251 W. 19th St., New York City 10011
CHURCH, John Co.	(Presser)
CLARK & WAY	(Peripole)
COLE, M. M. Publishing Co.	823 S. Wabash, Chicago, Ill. 60605
COLIN, Charles, Music Publishers	315 W. 53rd St., New York City 10019
COLOMBO, Franco	16 W. 61st St., New York City 10023
COMPOSERS Press, Inc.	287 Broadway, New York City 10007
CONCORDIA Publishing House	3558 S. Jefferson Ave., St. Louis Mo. 63118
CONN	(Bregman)
CONSOLIDATED Music Publishers, Inc.	(Amsco)
Consolidated Music Publishing House	(Leeds)
CUNDY-BETTONEY Co., Inc.	96 Bradlee St., Hyde Park, Boston, Mass. 02136
CURWEN, J. & Sons, Ltd., London	(G. Schirmer)
DENISON Music Company	321 5th Ave., South, Minneapolis, Minn. 55415
DE SYLVA, Brown & Henderson	(Chappell)
DITSON, Oliver	(Presser)

Publisher	Address
DOUBLEDAY, and Co., Inc.	Garden City, New York 11530
DURAND & Cie., Paris	(Elkan-Vogel)
EASTMAN	(C. Fischer)
EDITION MUSICUS	333 W. 52nd St., New York City 10019
ELKAN, Henri, Music Publisher	1316 Walnut St., Philadelphia, Pa. 19107
ELKAN-VOGEL Co., Inc.	1716 Sansom St., Philadelphia, Pa. 19103
ELKIN & Co., Ltd., London	(Galaxy)
EPIC	200 Bleecker St., New York City 10000
ERICKSON	415 S. Minnesota, St. Peter, Minn. 56082
FEIST, Leo, Inc.	(Big Three)
FILLMORE	(C. Fischer)
FISCHER, Carl, Inc.	62 Cooper Square, New York City 10003
FISCHER, J. & Bro.	Harrinstown Rd., Glen Rock, N.J. 07450
FITZSIMONS, H.T. Co., Inc.	615 N. LaSalle St., Chicago, Ill. 60610
FLAMMER, Harold, Inc.	251 W. 19th St., New York City 10011
FOLEY, Charles, Inc.	67 W. 44th St., New York City 10018
FOSTER, Mark	Box 4418, Sacramento, Calif. 95821
FORSTER Music Co.	216 S. Wabash, Chicago, Ill. 60604
FOX, Sam, Publishing Co., Inc.	11 W. 60th St., New York City 10023
FRANK Music Corporation	119 W. 57th St., New York City 10019
FRANK'S DRUM SHOP	226 S. Wabash Ave., Chicago, Ill. 60604
FREDERICK, Charles	434 S. Wabash Ave., Chicago, Ill. 60605
FRENCH, Samuel, Inc.	25 W. 45th St., New York City 10036
GALAXY Music Corporation	2121 Broadway, New York City 10023
GALLIARD, Ltd., London	(Galaxy)
GAMBLE Hinged Music Co.	(MPH)
GILLMAN Publications	Box 8671, Crenshaw Station, Los Angeles, Calif. 90008
GINN and Company	Statler Building, Boston, Mass. 02117
GORNSTON, David	117 W. 48th St., New York City 10036
GOWER	(Hansen)
GREGORIAN Institute of America	2132 Jefferson Ave., Toledo, Ohio 43602
GRAY, H.W., Company Inc.	159 E. 48th St., New York City 10017
HANOVER Music Corp.	545 Muskingum Place, Pacific Palisades, Calif. 90272
HANSEN Publications, Inc.	1842 West Ave., Miami Beach, Fla. 33139
HARGAIL Music Press	157 W. 57th St., New York City 10019
HARMS, Inc.	(MPH)
HARMS, T.B.	(Chappell)

Publisher	*Address*
HIGHGATE Press	(Galaxy)
HIGHLAND Music Co.	1311 N. Highland Ave., Hollywood, Calif. 90028
HOFFMAN, Raymond A., Co. (Hoffman Press)	1421 Coolidge St., Wichita, Kansas 67203
HUG	(Peters)
HUNTZINGER, Inc.	(Willis)
INDEPENDENT Music Publishers	65 University Place, New York City 10000
INTERLOCHEN Press	National Music Camp, Interlochen, Michigan 49643
INTERNATIONAL Music Co.	509 5th Ave., New York City 10017
JACOBS, Walter, Inc.	(Big Three)
JENKINS Music Company	1217 Walnut St., Kansas City, Mo. 64142
JOY Music, Inc.	(Mills)
KALI YUGA Music Press	Box 305, Garden City, N.Y. 11530
KALMUS, Edwin F.	P.O. Box 47, Huntington Station, L.I., N.Y. 11746
KALMUS of England	(Associated)
KENDOR Music, Inc.	Delevan, N.Y. 14042
KING, K.L. Music House	Fort Dodge, Iowa 50501
KING, ROBERT, Music Co.	7 Canton St., North Easton, Mass. 02356
KJOS, Neil A., Music Co.	525 Busse Highway, Park Ridge, Ill. 60068
LAWSON-GOULD Music Publishers, Inc.	609 5th Ave., New York City 10017 (G. Schirmer)
LEDUC	(SMC)
LEEDS Music Corp.	322 W. 48th St., New York City 10036
LENGNICK	(Mills)
LEONARD, Hal, Music, Inc.	64 E. 2nd St., Winona, Minn. 55987
LORENZ Publishing Co.	501 E. 3rd St., Dayton, Ohio 45401
LUDLOW Music, Inc.	(Mills)
LUDWIG Music Publishing Co.	557 E. 140th St., Cleveland, Ohio 44110
LUDWIG DRUM CO.	1728 N. Damen Ave., Chicago, Ill. 60647
LUVERNE Publishers	Roselawn Station, Rochester, N.Y. 14618
MAGNAMUSIC Distributors, Inc.	Sharon, Conn. 06069
MALVERNE	(Leeds)
MARKS, Edward B., Music Corp.	136 W. 52nd St., New York City 10019
MC GINNIS & MARX Music Publications	408 2nd Ave., New York City 10010
MC LAUGHLIN & Reilly Co.	252 Huntington Ave., Boston, Mass. 02115

Publisher	Address
MERCURY Music Corp.	(Presser)
MERIDIAN	(Leeds)
MILLER Music Corp.	(Big Three)
MILLS Music, Inc.	1619 Broadway, New York City 10019
MODERN Music Press	(FitzSimons)
MOECK	(Magnamusic)
MORRIS, Edwin H. & Co., Inc.	31 W. 54th St., New York City 10019
MUSIC FOR PERCUSSION	(Plymouth)
MUSIC PRESS, Inc.	(C. Fischer)
Music Publishers Holding Corporation (MPH)	619 W. 54th St., New York City 10019
MUSIC SHOP	512 Nicolet Bldg., Mineapolis, Minn. 55400
NEW SOUNDS in Modern Music	(Colin)
NEW WORLD Music	(MPH)
NOVELLO & Co., Ltd., London	(Gray)
OMEGA Music Edition	19 W. 44th St., New York City 10018
OXFORD University Press, Inc.	417 5th Ave., New York City 10016
PALLMA Music Publisher	Box 145, Beaumont, Calif. 92223
PATERSON's Publications, Ltd., London	(C. Fischer)
PAULL-Pioneer Music Corp.	(Shawnee)
PEER International Corp.	(Southern)
PEPAMAR	(MPH)
PERIPOLE, Inc.	51–17 Rockaway Beach Blvd., Far Rockaway, L.I., N.Y. 11691
PETERS, C. F. Corp.	373 Park Ave. South, New York City 10016
PIEDMONT	(Marks)
PLYMOUTH Music, Inc.	1841 Broadway, New York City 10023
PRENTICE-HALL, Inc.	Englewood Cliffs, New Jersey 07632
PRESSER, Theodore, Co.	Presser Place, Bryn Mawr, Pa. 19010
PRIDE Music Publications, Inc.	230 W. 41st St., New York City 10036
PRO ART Publications, Inc.	469 Union Ave., Westbury, L.I., N.Y. 11591
PRO MUSICA	386 Fulton St., New York City 10000
RECORDER SHOP	(Magnamusic)
REGENT Music Co.	1619 Broadway, New York City 10019
REMICK Music Corporation	(MPH)
RICHMOND Music Press	P.O. Box 465, P.P. Sta., Richmond, Ind. 47374

Publisher	*Address*
RICORDI, G. & Co.	(Colombo)
ROBBINS Music Corp.	(Big Three)
ROCHESTER Music Publications	358 Aldrich Rd., Fairport, N.Y. 14450
RODGERS & Hammerstein	11 E. 44th St., New York City 10000
RONGWEN	(Broude)
ROW	(C. Fischer)
RUBANK, Inc.	5544 W. Armstrong Ave., Chicago, Ill. 60646
SACRED Music Press, The	501 E. 3rd St., Dayton, Ohio 45401
SALABERT Editions, Paris	(Colombo)
SANSONE	(SMC)
SELMER, H&A, Inc.	119 N. Main St., Elkhart, Ind. 46514
SCHIRMER, E.C.	600 Washington St., Boston, Mass. 02111
SCHIRMER, G.	609 5th Avenue, New York City 10017
SCHMIDT, A.P. Co.	(Summy)
SCHMITT, Hall & McCreary Co.	Park Ave. at 6th St., Minneapolis, Minn. 55415
SCHOTT & Co., Ltd, London	(Associated)
SCHROEDER and Gunther	(Associated)
SCHUBERT	(MPH)
SHAPIRO, Bernstein & Co., Inc.	666 5th Ave., New York City 10019
SHAWNEE Press, Inc.	Delaware Water Gap, Pa. 18327
SIKORSKI	(Colombo)
SILVER BURDETT Co.	45 E. 17th St., New York City 10003
SIMROCK, N., Leipzig	(Associated)
SKIDMORE Music Co., Inc.	(Shapiro)
SOUTHERN Music Publishing Co.	1619 Broadway, New York City 10019
Southern Music Company (SMC)	P.O. Box 326, San Antonio, Texas 78206
SPRAGUE-Coleman	(Leeds)
SPRATT, Jack	77 W. Broad St., Stamford, Conn. 06901
STAFF Music Publishing Co.	374 Great Neck Rd., Great Neck, N.Y. 11020
STAINER & Bell, Ltd., London	(Galaxy)
STONE, George B. & Son, Inc.	61 Hanover St., Boston, Mass. 02113
SUMMY-Birchard Co.	1834 Ridge Ave., Evanston, Ill. 60204
TAMS-Witmark Music Library, Inc.	115 W. 45th St., New York City 10036

Publisher	*Address*
TRANSCONTINENTAL Music Publishers, Inc.	1674 Broadway at 52nd St., N.Y.C. 10019
TUSKEGEE Music Press	Tuskegee, Alabama 36088
UNIVERSAL Editions, Vienna	(Associated) (Boosey-Hawkes) (Presser)
UNIVERSITY Music Press	Ann Arbor, Michigan 48103
VILLA-LOBOS Music Corp.	(Big Three)
VOLKWEIN Brothers, Inc.	632 Liberty Ave., Pittsburgh, Pa. 15222
WAHR, George	Ann Arbor, Michigan 48103
WALTON Music Corp.	1841 Broadway, New York City 10023
WALTON'S GALLERIES, Ltd.	2 N. Frederick St., Dublin, Ireland
WEINSTRAUB	(Amsco)
WEELKES, W., England	(Galaxy)
WESTERN Music Company, Ltd., Canada	(Mills)
WILLIAMS, Joseph, England	(Galaxy)
WILLIAMSON	(Chappell)
WILLIS Music Co.	440 Main St., Cincinnati, Ohio 45201
WITMARK, M. & Sons	(MPH)
WOOD, B.F., Music Co., Inc.	250 W. 49th St., N.Y.C. (Mills) 10019
WOODBURY Music Corp.	Woodbury, Conn. 06798
WORLD LIBRARY of Sacred Music	1846 Westwood Ave., Cincinnati, Ohio 45214
WYNN Music Publications	1511 McGee, Berkeley, Calif. 94703

LISTS OF SELECTED MUSIC

The balance of this chapter is devoted to a compilation of lists of music for performance which have been contributed by choral directors in many widely separated sections of the United States. Every state chairman of the American Choral Directors Association was asked to choose 3 outstanding directors in the state (either high school or college), who were then asked for the "*very best* choral compositions you have ever used." Various categories were specified. Those who participated in the project were:

Participating States (with ACDA Chairman)

Arkansas (William R. Trego), California (Lee Kjelson), Colorado (John Held), Connecticut (Gerald R. Mack), Illinois (Kent Newbury), Iowa (Charles D. Matheson), Michigan (Harry Langsford), Minnesota (Harvey R. Waugh),

Missouri (Kent Toalson), New Jersey (Clarence W. Miller), New Mexico (Ronald L. Wynn), New York (Walter Ehret), North Carolina (Paul Fry), Ohio (Ferris E. Ohl), Oregon (Robert E. Robbins), Rhode Island (Ward Abusamra), South Dakota (John L. Rezatto), Texas (Theron Kirk), Utah (A.L. Dittmer), Vermont (Frank W. Lidral), Virginia (Mrs. Viola Painter), Washington (Coyne G. Burnett), Wisconsin (Donald G. Foltz), Wyoming (A. Lester Roberts).

Contributors of Selected Lists

Ward Abusamra	University of Rhode Island (Kingston)
W.H. Beckmeyer	Mt. Vernon (Illinois) High School, Community College
Boyd L. Bohlke	Washington High School (Sioux Falls, S.D.)
C.J. Broadhead	New Rochelle (New York) High School
John Carlson	Rawlings (Wyoming) High School
Joseph Chidley	Clyde (Ohio) High School
Gordon W. DeBroder	University of Denver (Colorado)
H. Harmon Diers	Southern Connecticut State College (New Haven)
Robert H. Ellis	Page High School (Greensboro, N.C.)
P.J. Fitzgerald	Loudoun County Schools (Leesburg, Va.)
John E. Folin	Windom (Minnesota) High School
Murrae N. Freng	Alexandria (Minnesota) Public Schools
Joyce Garver	Camas (Washington) High School
Marvin Gench	St. Joseph (Missouri) Schools
Joseph A. Graves	Bonneville High School (Ogden, Utah)
R. Byron Griest	Massillon (Ohio) High School
George Hansler	Jersey City (New Jersey) State College
Calvin B. Hedegaard	West High School (Davenport, Iowa)
Melvin R. Kornmeyer	Shadle Park High School, (Spokane, Washington)
Fred Leist	Oshkosh (Wisconsin) High School
Arthur Loy	Highland High School (Albuquerque, New Mexico)
Walter J. Michels	El Dorado (Arkansas) High School
Thomas L. Mills	University of Missouri (Columbia)
Robert D. Mix	Duluth (Minnesota) East High School
Weston Noble	Luther College (Decorah, Iowa)
Viola Painter	Byrd High School (Vinton, Virginia)
Mary H. Phillips	Rockingham (North Carolina) High School
A.L. Roberts	University of Wyoming (Laramie)

Contributors of Selected Lists (cont.)

Walter Rodby	The School Musician Magazine (Joliet, Illinois)
Rudolph B. Saltzer	Los Angeles (California) City College
Lynn E. Sjolund	Medford (Oregon) High School
Stephen L. Stone	Beaverton (Oregon) High School
Keith N. Sturdevant	Highland Park (Michigan) High School
Ruth Summers	Edinburg (Texas) High School
Mrs. Paul Trahan	Bellows Free Academy (St. Albans, Vt.)
Angelo Turano	Farmington (New Mexico) High School
Eleanor E. Walden	Granby High School (Norfolk, Virginia)
Edgar L. Wallace	Collingswood (New Jersey) High School
Cloys V. Webb	Perryton (Texas) High School

* indicates one additional director's recommendation

' indicates one additional director's recommendation in another category

Best Concert Selection — Top Quality Music for a Mature Audience

Title	Composer-Arranger	Publisher
Easy		
Adoramus Te ' '	Palestrina	G. Schirmer
Ave Maria	Arcadelt	G. Schirmer
Blessed Is the Man	Corelli-Stone	Boston
Blessing, Glory, and Wisdom '	Bach - Tkach	Kjos
Blessing, Glory, Wisdom, and Thanks	G. Wagner-Ziemer	Lawson-Gould
Bread of Tears	P. Christiansen	Augsburg
Break Forth, O Beauteous Heavenly Light	Bach	Kjos
Cantate Domino ' ' '	Pitoni-Greyson	Bourne
David's Lamentations '	Billings-Siegmeister	C. Fischer
E la Don Don	Greenberg (ed.)	Associated
Fanfare for a Festival	Nelson	Boosey
Gloria Patri	Palestrina	Kjos
Hallelujah, Amen	Handel-Davids	Belwin
Hallelujah (Psalm 150)	Lewandowski-Williams	Plymouth
Hospodi Pomilui	Lvovsky	Kjos
How Sad Flow the Streams	Brahms	Marks

Title	Composer-Arranger	Publisher
Jesu, Word of God Incarnate	Saint-Saëns–Brooks	Spratt
Lord's Prayer, The	Gates	Choir
Malaguena	Lecuona	Marks
My Heart Is Offered Still to You	Lassus	Lawson-Gould
Nightfall in Skye ' '	Roberton	G. Schirmer
O Beloved Shepherds	Hammerschmidt	Concordia
O Bone Jesu	Palestrina	Ditson
O God, Thou Faithful God *	Douglas	Gray
Praise God, Ye Christians	Praetorius	G. Schirmer
Roots and Leaves ' ' ' '	R.V. Williams	Schmidt
Sine Nomine	R.V. Williams	C. Fischer
Song of Galilee *	Chajes	Transcontinental
Tenebrae Factae Sunt ' '	Ingegneri	Kjos

MEDIUM

Title	Composer-Arranger	Publisher
Advent Motet	Schreck-Christiansen	Kjos
Alleluia ' ' ' ' ' '	Thompson	E.C. Schirmer
Alleluia (from "Exsultate Jubilate")	Mozart-Reigger	Flammer
Alleluia, Amen, and Chorale	G. Wagner-Diemer	Lawson-Gould
All Men Now Sing, Rejoice	Bach	Kjos
Almighty God of Our Fathers ' '	James	Wood
Ave Verum '	Mozart	Wood
Beat! Beat! Drums!	Hanson	J. Fischer
Benedictus '	Paladilhe-Christiansen	Kjos
Cantate-Domino ' ' '	Pitoni-Greyson	Bourne
Choose Something Like A Star ' ' ' '	Thompson	E.C. Schirmer
Crucifixus '	Lotti	G. Schirmer
Die Mit Tranen Saen ' '	Schein	Mercury
Fain Would I Change that Note	R.V. Williams	Gray
Gloria	Vivaldi	Ricordi
Hosianna	Gearhart (arr.)	Shawnee
It Is Good to Be Merry	Berger	Kjos
It Lies Not On The Sunlit Hill	Lekberg	Summy-Birchard
Jesu, Dulcis Memoria	Victoria	G. Schirmer

Title	Composer-Arranger	Publisher
Kyrie Eleison (from "Imperial Mass") * ' ' '	Haydn-Hirt	Witmark
Last Words Of David, The ' ' ' ' ' ' ' ' '	Thompson	E.C. Schirmer
Liebeslieder Waltzes	Brahms	Simrock
Lord God, Creator Almighty	Van Hulse	J. Fischer
Matona, Lovely Maiden	di Lasso-Greyson	G. Schirmer
Now Sing We All His Praises	Bright	Marks
O Come, Let Us Sing Unto The Lord	Diemer	C. Fischer
O Magnum Mysterium * ' ' ' '	Victoria-Parker-Shaw	G. Schirmer
O Sing Your Songs	Cain	Flammer
Plorate Filli Israel	Carissimi	Oxford
Roving in The Dew	Chapman (arr.)	Oxford
She Walks in Beauty ' ' '	Foltz	Remick
Silver Swan, The '	Gibbons-Greyson	Bourne
Turtle Dove, The	R.V. Williams	G. Schirmer

DIFFICULT

Adoramus Te	Corsi-Christiansen	Kjos
All Breathing Life	Bach-Williamson	G. Schirmer
Alleluia * ' ' ' ' '	Thompson	E.C. Schirmer
Alleluia (from "Brazilian Psalm") ' ' ' '	Berger	G. Schirmer
Apostrophe To The Heavenly Host, An	Willan	British-American
Ballad Of Brotherhood	Wagner	Elkan-Vogel
Behold! I Build An House	Foss	Mercury
Benedictus '	Paladilhe-Christiansen	Kjos
Cherubic Hymn, The	Hanson	C. Fischer
Choose Something Like A Star ' ' ' '	Thompson	E.C. Schirmer
Die Mit Tranen Saen ' '	Schein	Mercury
Ehre Sei Dir Christe	Schütz-Shaw-Parker	G. Schirmer
Et Incarnatus Est	Bruckner-Heller	Summy-Birchard
For Unto Us A Child Is Born (from "Messiah")	Handel	G. Schirmer
Glorious Everlasting	Cousins	Brodt

Title	Composer- Arranger	Publisher
Hallelujah (from "Mount of Olives")	Beethoven	G. Schirmer
Hallelujah Chorus (from "Messiah")	Handel	Ditson
Hymn To King Stephen	Kodaly	Boosey
Jesu, Meine Freude	Bach	Peters
Jesus And The Traders '	Kodaly	Boosey
Last Words of David, The ' ' ' ' ' ' ' '	Thompson	E.C. Schirmer
Lord, Thou Hast Been Our Refuge	R.V. Williams	G. Schirmer
Make Me, O Lord God, Pure In Heart	Brahms	G. Schirmer
Mass In B Minor	Bach	Novello
Mass In C Major	Beethoven	Peters
Mass In C Minor	Mozart	Complete Works
Mass In G	Schubert	G. Schirmer
Missa Brevis	Kodaly	Boosey
O Magnum Mysterium ' ' ' ' '	Victoria	G. Schirmer
Prayer (from "Cavalleria Rusticana")	Mascagni	Birchard
Tenebrae Factae Sunt ' '	Ingegneri	Kjos
Vineta	Brahms	G. Schirmer

BEST PROGRAM SELECTION — GOOD MUSIC, BUT ALSO IMMEDIATELY APPEALING TO AN AVERAGE AUDIENCE

Title	Composer- Arranger	Publisher
EASY		
Ave Maria	Schubert	Kjos
Charlottetown	Bryan	J. Fischer
Climbin' Up The Mountain	Smith (arr.)	Kjos
Cry Out And Shout ' ' ' '	Nystedt	Summy
Fa Una Canzona (Sing Me A Song) * * ' ' ' ' '	Vecchi	Lawson-Gould
Four Animal Songs '	Koskey	Witmark
Hallelujah, Amen	Handel	Boosey
Hey, Look Me Over	Coleman-Warnick	Morris
Hora	Chajes	Transcontinental
In Heaven Above	Christiansen	Augsburg

Title	Composer-Arranger	Publisher
In Stiller Nacht '	Brahms	Consolidated
Linden Stands, A	German folk-Ahrold	Witmark
Live-a-humble	Hairston	Bourne
Madame Jeanette * * ' '	Murray-Wilhousky	C. Fischer
Master Of Human Destinies '	Hillman	Schmitt
May Night	Brahms-Wetzler	Art Master
O Dear, What Can The Matter Be	Kubik (arr.)	G. Schirmer
O, Lemuel '	Foster-Wagner	Lawson-Gould
O Lord Ruler Of All Nations	Tchaikovsky-Rodby	Plymouth
Onward, Ye Peoples	Sibelius	Galaxy
Paper Reeds By The Brook, The ' '	Thompson	E.C. Schirmer
Pat-a-pan	Davis (arr.)	G. Schirmer
Rock-a-my-soul	deVaux (arr.)	Bourne
Salvation Is Created ' '	Tschesnokoff	J. Fischer
Silver Moon Is Shining, The	Davis (arr.)	E.C. Schirmer
Still, Still, Still	Luboff-Keith	Walton
To The Dawn	Williams	Kjos
Water Is Wide, The	Zaninelli (arr.)	Shawnee

MEDIUM

Title	Composer-Arranger	Publisher
Alleluia ' ' ' ' '	Thompson	E.C. Schirmer
Beautiful Saviour	F.M. Christiansen	Augsburg
Carol Of The Drum '	Davis	Wood
Carol Ye	Wilson	Lorenz
Ching-a-ring-chaw '	Copland	Boosey
Creation, The (w/narrator) ' ' '	Scott	Presser
Crucifixus '	Lotti	G. Schirmer
Cry Out And Shout ' ' ' '	Nystedt	Summy
Early in The Morning	McCormick	Shawnee
Echo Song * ' '	di Lasso	E.C. Schirmer
Elijah Rock '	Hairston	Bourne
Five Nursery Rhymes	Hunter	Lawson-Gould
Go, Lovely Rose ' ' ' ' '	Thiman	Galaxy
Hallelujah Amen ("Judas Maccabaeus") '	Handel	Witmark
He Watching Over Israel	Mendelssohn	ProArt
Hosanna	F.M. Christiansen	Augsburg
I Am An American (w/narrator)	Dragon-Simon	C. Fischer

Title	Composer-Arranger	Publisher
I Have Longed For Thy Saving Health	Byrd-Whitehead	Gray
I Will Lift Mine Eyes	Glarum	Bourne
Interminable Farewell, The	Canby	Associated
I've Been Working On The Railroad	Large (arr.)	Plymouth
Lane County Bachelor	Dickson and O'Hara	Ricordi
Nobody's Business	Jamaican folk-Myrow	Plymouth
O, Holy Child	Pergolesi	Lawson-Gould
O, Lemuel '	Foster-Wagner	Lawson-Gould
Roots And Leaves ' ' ' '	Williams	Schmitt
Sing And Rejoice	James	FitzSimons
Six Folk Songs '	Brahms-Zipper	Marks
There Shall A Star Come Out Of Jacob	Mendelssohn	Schmitt
Three Hungarian Folk Songs ' '	Seiber	G. Schirmer
To Music '	Schubert	Gillman
Turtle Dove, The '	R.V. Williams (arr.)	G. Schirmer
When Israel Went Forth Out Of Egypt	Niklosky	J. Fischer
When The Saints Go Marching In	Jester-Hairston	Bourne
White Evening	Shelley	Mills

DIFFICULT

Title	Composer-Arranger	Publisher
Advent Motet	Schreck-Christiansen	Kjos
Alleluia * ' ' ' ' '	Thompson	E.C. Schirmer
Alleluia (from "Brazilian Psalm") * * ' '	Berger	G. Schirmer
Almighty God Of Our Fathers ' '	James	Wood
Anthem For Spring	Mascagni-Simeone	Shawnee
At The Cry Of The First Bird	Morgan	C. Fischer
Beatitudes, The	Evans	Remick
Benedictus And Hosanna '	Bright	Shawnee
Brazilian Psalm, The * ' ' '	Berger	G. Schirmer
Carmina Burana	Orff	Associated

Title	Composer-Arranger	Publisher
Concert Vocalise	Hayward	Shawnee
Creation, The (w/narrator) * ' '	Scott	Presser
Father William	Fine	Witmark
God Has Gone Up With The Shout	Klein	Shawnee
Halleluia (from "Mount Of Olives") '	Beethoven	Presser
Hodie Christus Natus Est ' '	Sweelinck	Ricordi
Hold On	Hairston	Bourne
Hospodi Pomilui '	Lvovsky	J. Fischer
How Fair The Church	Schumann-Christiansen	Augsburg
I Am The Resurrection And True Life	Schütz	Presser
Jubilant Song, A ' '	Dello Joio	G. Schirmer
Kyrie Eleison (from "Imperial" Mass) ' ' ' '	Haydn-Hirt	Witmark
Last Words Of David, The ' ' ' ' ' ' ' '	Thompson	E.C. Schirmer
Laudamus Te	Mueller	G. Schirmer
Lord Is A Mighty God, The	Davenport	Plymouth
Quest For God	Allen	Shawnee
September Song	Hunter	DeSylva
Six Chansons	Hindemith	Associated
Song of Democracy ' '	Hanson	C. Fischer
Spring '	Grieg-Christiansen	Kjos
Telephone Hour (from "Bye, Bye, Birdie")	Adams & Strouse	Morris
Ye Shall Have A Song ("Peaceable Kingdom") * ' ' '	Thompson	E.C. Schirmer
Yonder! Yonder! '	Russian folk-Gaines	Ditson

BEST CONTEST SELECTION — SHOWS THE GROUP TO ITS BEST POSSIBLE ADVANTAGE

Title	Composer-Arranger	Publisher
EASY		
Alleluia, Glorious Is Thy Name	Olson	Summy
Ave Maria '	Vittoria-Scott	Choral Art

Title	Composer-Arranger	Publisher
Ave Verum '	Mozart	C. Fischer
Birthday Greeting	Kodaly	Boosey
Black Oak Tree, The '	Niles	C. Fischer
Blessing Glory and Wisdom *	Wagner	Gray
Cry Out And Shout * ' ' '	Nystedt	Summy
David's Lamentation '	Billings-Siegmeister	J. Fischer
Down Low In The Valley	Brahms	Lawson-Gould
Fa Una Canzone (Sing Me A Song) ' ' ' ' ' ' '	Vecchi	Lawson-Gould
Four Animal Songs '	Koskey	Witmark
Give Me A Song To Sing	Elliott	Hoffman
Glory Be To God '	Schubert	Marks
Glory To God	Bach-Wilson	Ricordi
Hallelujah Amen ("Judas Maccabaeus") '	Handel	G. Schirmer
He Shall Come Down Like Rain	Berger	Shawnee
Lamb Of God	Christiansen (arr.)	Augsburg
Long Day Closes, The	Sullivan-Perry	Belwin
Non Nobis Domine	Quilter	Boosey
Now April Has Come '	Shaw-Parker (arr.)	G. Schirmer
Praise Ye The Lord Of Hosts	Saint-Saëns	G. Schirmer
Psallite	Praetorius	Bourne
Scarborough Fair	Henderson (arr.)	Kjos
Thou Must Leave Thy Lowly Dwelling	Berlioz	Gray
Three Hungarian Folk Songs ' '	Seiber	G. Schirmer
To Music '	Schubert-Wilson	Schmitt

MEDIUM

Alleluia ' ' ' ' '	Thompson	E.C. Schirmer
Be Thou My Judge, O Lord	Morgan	J. Fischer
Cherubim Song	Musitcheskoo	J. Fischer
Choose Something Like A Star ' ' ' '	Thompson	E.C. Schirmer
Come Softly Now	Young	Young
Creation, The	Richter	Flammer
Drum	Fetler	Associated

Title	Composer-Arranger	Publisher
Eyes Of All Wait Upon Thee, The '	Berger	Augsburg
Go, Lovely Rose * ' ' ' ' '	Thiman	Galaxy
God Is Gone Up	Hutchings	Novello
God Is Our Refuge	Bender	Augsburg
Glory To God	Nelson	Boosey
Hosanna In The Highest	Soderman	Walton
In Stiller Nacht '	Brahms	Presser
Let All The Nations Praise The Lord	Leising-Hoggard	Shawnee
Let The Words Of My Mouth	Hyde	FitzSimons
Let Thy Holy Presence '	Tschesnokoff-Cain	Birchard
Lord Is My Shepherd, The	Matthews	FitzSimons
Mighty Fortress, A	Luther-Mueller	G. Schirmer
Nightingale, The	Tchaikovsky-Schindler	Ditson
O Clap Your Hands	R.V. Williams	Galaxy
On The Marrow	English folk-Gaines	Galaxy
Out Of The Depths	Vierra	Boosey
Plorate Fillii Israel '	Carissimi-Christiansen	Kjos
Prayer To Jesus	Oldroyd	Oxford
Psalm 150	Newbury	G. Schirmer
Psalm 150	Peterson	Willis
Regina Coeli (from "Cayalleria Rusticana")	Mascagni	G. Schirmer
Rise Up, My Love, My Faire One	Willan	Oxford
Spring '	Grieg-Christiansen	Kjos
Suddenly There Came A Sound	Aichinger	Frank
Sure On This Shining Night	Barber	G. Schirmer
Tenebrae Factae Sunt	Palestrina	Choral Press
Time And Space '	P. Christiansen	Augsburg
Turtle Dove, The '	R.V. Williams	G. Schirmer
Ye Sons And Daughters	Leisring	E.C. Schirmer

DIFFICULT

All Breathing Life	Bach	G. Schirmer
Angelic Choir	Goldbeck	Witmark

Title	Composer- Arranger	Publisher
Brazilian Psalm ' ' ' '	Berger	G. Schirmer
Choose Something Like A Star ' ' ' '	Thompson	E.C. Schirmer
Christmas Eve	Pooler	Summy
Eili, Eili (Invocation)	Yiddish folk- Schindler	G. Schirmer
Falcon, The	Wilkinson	Novello
Hodie Christus Natus Est * '	Sweelinck	Wood
Honor And Glory ' '	Bach	Plymouth
How Great Are Thy Wonders	Christiansen	Augsburg
How They So Softly Rest '	Willan	Gray
Ideo Gloria In Excelsis Deo	Kraehenbuhl	Associated
If By His Spirit ' '	Bach-Carlton	Boosey
Il Est Bel Et Bon	Passerau	Bourne
Jesus And The Traders '	Kodaly	Boosey
Jubilant Song ' '	Dello Joio	G. Schirmer
Kyrie Eleison (from "Imperial" Mass) ' ' ' '	Haydn-Hirt	Witmark
Last Words Of David, The ' ' ' ' ' ' ' '	Thompson	E.C. Schirmer
Let Their Celestial Concerts	Handel	Wood
Make A Joyful Noise Unto The Lord	Lekburg	Galaxy
Master Of Human Destinies '	Hillman	Schmitt
Misericordias Domini	Durante	G. Schirmer
Now Thank We All Our God	Mueller	G. Schirmer
O Brother Man	Ringwald	Shawnee
O Gladsome Light	Gretchaninoff	J. Fischer
O Magnum Mysterium * ' ' ' '	Victoria-Parker- Shaw	G. Schirmer
Omnipotence, The	Schubert	G. Schirmer
Prayers of Steel	P. Christiansen	Augsburg
Revelation Motet	Franck	Broude
Sing A New Song	Kreutz	Summy
Time	Effinger	C. Fischer
Virga Jesse Floriut	Bruckner	Peters

Wake, Awake, For Night
  Is Flying
	Christiansen
	  (arr.)
		Augsburg

Wall of Heaven O Saviour Rend, The	Brahms	E.C. Schirmer

OTHER SACRED SELECTIONS

Title	Composer-Arranger	Publisher
EASY		
Adoramus Te * '	Palestrina	E.C. Schirmer
Agnus Dei	Hassler	Bourne
Cantate Domino * ' '	Pitoni-Greyson	Bourne
Canticle Of Peace, A	Clokey	Summy
Come Thou, Holy Spirit	Tschesnokoff-Tkach	Kjos
Cry Out And Shout ' ' ' '	Nystedt	Summy
Gloria In Excelsis	Mozart	G. Schirmer
Glory Be To God '	Schubert	Marks
He Shall Come Down Like Rain	McCormick	Shawnee
Heavenly Light	Kopylow	C. Fischer
Heavens Resound, The	Beethoven	Birchard
Hosanna To The Son Of David	Moe	C. Fischer
I Sing Of A Maiden	M. Shaw	Oxford
If By His Spirit ' '	Bach-Carlton	Boosey
Let There Be Peace On Earth	Miller & Jackson	Hansen
Let Thy Holy Presence '	Tschesnokoff-Cain	Summy
Mary Magdalene *	Brahms	Gray
O Man Thy Grief And Sin Bemoan '	Williams	Schmitt
O Spirit, Who From Jesus Came	Havey	G. Schirmer
Out Of The Depths I Cry To Thee	James	Willis
Plorate Filii Israel '	Carissimi-Christiansen	Kjos
Poor Man Lazrus	Hairston	Bourne
Praise We Sing To Thee	Haydn-Luvaas	Kjos
Prayer To Jesus * *	Oldroyd	Oxford
Prophecy	Purvis	Flammer
Psalm 150	Lewandowski	C. Fischer
Sing Praises	Glarum	Schmitt
There Is A Balm In Gilead	Smith (arr.)	Plymouth
MEDIUM		
Agnus Dei	Pergolesi	Mercury
Ave Maria ' *	Vittoria	C. Fischer
Benedictus And Hosanna '	Bright	Shawnee
Blessing, Glory, Wisdom, And Thanks '	Bach-Tkach	Kjos

Title	Composer-Arranger	Publisher
Cherubic Hymn	Gretchaninoff	Kjos
Eyes Of All Wait Upon Thee, The '	Berger	Augsburg
Commit Thy Way Unto The Lord	Liebhold	Concordia
Hodie Christus Natus Est	Palestrina	Kjos
Honor And Glory * '	Bach-Ehret	Plymouth
I Will Life Mine Eyes	Glarum	Bourne
Kyrie Eleison	Dieterich	Boosey
Last Words Of David, The * ' ' ' ' ' ' '	Thompson	E.C. Schirmer
Lovely Things	Klemma	Fox
Lullaby For Christmas, A	Lockwood	Kjos
Make A Joyful Noise Unto The Lord	Seay	Flammer
Morning Hymn	Henschel	Choral Press
Now Let Us All Praise God And Sing	Young	Young
O Be Joyful	Glarum	Presser
O Filii Et Filias	Leisring	Bourne
O Lord God	Tschesnokoff	Boston
O Rejoice Ye Christians	Bach	E.C. Schirmer
O Sacred Head	Christiansen	Augsburg
O Sacred Head Now Wounded *	Bach-Hassler	E.C. Schirmer
Of The Father's Love Begotten	Chenoweth	Lawson-Gould
Paper Reeds By The Brook ' '	Thompson	E.C. Schirmer
Psalm 100	R.V. Williams	Oxford
Psalm 100	Weaver	Boosey
Salvation Is Created ' '	Tschesnokoff	Bourne
Silent Devotion And Response	Bloch	Summy
Sing Unto God	Fetler	Augsburg
Tenebrae Factae Sunt ' '	Ingegneri	Boston
Thine Is The Greatness (Kol Slaven)	Bortniansky	C. Fischer
Three Kings, The	Willan	Oxford
Time And Space '	P. Christiansen	Augsburg
Venite, Exsultemus Domino	Sweelinck	Summy
With A Voice Of Singing	M. Shaw	G. Schirmer

DIFFICULT

All Things That Rise Will Fall	Berger	Associated
Almighty God Of Our Fathers ' '	James	Wood
Ascendit Deus	Gallus	Associated
Ave Maria	Bruckner	Peters

Title	Composer- Arranger	Publisher
Born Today	Sweelinck	Gray
Coronation Anthem	Houghton	Wood
Deo Gracias	Britten	Boosey
De Profundis (Out of Great Depths)	Bright	Shawnee
Die Mit Traenen Saen ' '	Schein	Bourne
Earth Is The Lord's, The	Nikolsky	J. Fischer
Exultate Deo	Scarlatti	Mercury
Gloria	Bruckner	Marks
Glorious Everlasting	Cousins	Brodt
Glory Be To God	Berger	Kjos
Glory To God In The Highest	Thompson	E.C. Schirmer
Great And Mighty Wonder, A	Sateren	G. Schirmer
Have Ye Not Known (from "Peaceable Kingdom") *	Thompson	E.C. Schirmer
Hosanna	Lockwood	G. Schirmer
If By His Spirit ' '	Bach-Carlton	Boosey
Last Words Of David, The * ' ' ' ' ' ' '	Thompson	E.C. Schirmer
Let All The Nations	James	Wood
Lord, Make Me An Instrument Of Thy Peace	Wilson	Robbins
O Day Full Of Grace	F.M. Christiansen	Augsburg
O Magnum Mysterium ' ' ' ' '	Victoria	G. Schirmer
O Man Thy Grief And Sin Bemoan '	Williams	Schmitt
Psalm 98	Distler	Barenreiter
Send Out Thy Spirit	Schuetky	Wood
Shepherds Had An Angel, The	Besly	G. Schirmer
Spirit Also Helpeth Us, The	Bach	Novello
Vesperae Solennes	Mozart	Universal
Vinea Mea Electa	Poulenc	Salabert
Ye Shall Have A Song ("Peaceable Kingdom") * ' ' '	Thompson	E.C. Schirmer

OTHER SECULAR SELECTIONS

Title	Composer- Arranger	Publisher
EASY		
Come, Close The Curtain	Hokanson	Summy
Dancing & Springing	Hassler-Greyson	Bourne
Down By The Sparkling Fountain	Lekring	Summy

Title	Composer-Arranger	Publisher
Fa Una Canzone (Sing Me A Song) * ’ ’ ’ ’ ’ ’	Vecchi	Lawson-Gould
Fare Thee Well My Honey	Forsblad	Shawnee
Five Nursery Rhymes	Hunter	Lawson-Gould
Frere Jacques	Gardner (arr.)	Staff
Gloucester Wassail	Scott (arr.)	Shawnee
I Beheld Her Beautiful As A Dove	Willan	Oxford
Kismet (selections)	Rappaport (arr.)	Frank
Longing For Home	Hansen	Kjos
Lullaby (from "Bavarian Highlands")	Elgar	Mills
Madame Jeanette * ’ ’ ’	Murray	C. Fischer
May Day Carol	Taylor	J. Fischer
Monotone	Lockwood	Kjos
Mountain High, Valley Low	Scott-Ades	Shawnee
Nightfall In Skye * ’	Roberton	G. Schirmer
O Brother Man	Ringwald	Shawnee
O Lovely Heart	Roberton	G. Schirmer
Poor Wayfaring Stranger ’	Siegmeister (arr.)	C. Fischer
Song Of My Land, The	Wilson	Marks
Sweet Day	R.V. Williams	Mills
Three Hungarian Songs	Bartok	Boosey
Valse (Speaking Chorus)	Toch	Mills
When Rooks Fly Homeward	Baynon	Boosey

MEDIUM

Title	Composer-Arranger	Publisher
Annie Laurie	Kubik (arr.)	Southern
Black Oak Tree, The ’	Niles	C. Fischer
Carol Of The Drum ’	Davis	Wood
Charm Me Asleep	Leslie-Krone	Witmark
Ching-a-ring-chaw	Copland	Boosey
Creation, The (w/narrator) ’ ’ ’	Scott	Presser
Der Abend	Brahms	G. Schirmer
Echo Song ’ ’ ’	diLasso-Widman	G. Schirmer
Elijah Rock ’	Hairston	Schuman
Fa Una Canzone (Sing Me A Song) * ’ ’ ’ ’ ’ ’	Vecchi	G. Schirmer
Fanfare For A Festival ’	Nelson	Boosey
Glory ’	Rimsky-Korsakoff	Witmark
Go, Lovely Rose ’ ’ ’ ’ ’	Thiman	Galaxy
Holiday Song	Schuman	G. Schirmer

Title	Composer-Arranger	Publisher
I Hear A Voice A-Prayin' ' '	Bright	Shawnee
I Hear America Singing	Lockwood	Shawnee
Melodies Of The Middle Ages	Langstroth (arr.)	Ditson
Now April Has Come '	Shaw (arr.)	G. Schirmer
Nursery Rhyme Suite	Simeone	Shawnee
Old Mother Hubbard	Diack (arr.)	C. Fischer
Rain Song	Bright	Associated
Rocka Ma Soul	Cain (arr.)	Flammer
Roots And Leaves * * ' '	Williams	Schmitt
She Walks In Beauty * ' '	Foltz	Witmark
Six Folksongs '	Brahms	Marks
Song Of Gallilee	Chajes (arr.)	Transcontinental
Sure On This Shining Night	Barber	G. Schirmer
Three Hungarian Folk Songs ' '	Seiber	G. Schirmer
Weep, O Mine Eyes *	Bennet	Bourne
Westside Story (selections)	Bernstein	G. Schirmer
Yankee Doodle	Hunter (arr.)	Lawson-Gould

DIFFICULT

Title	Composer-Arranger	Publisher
August Noon	Bright	Shawnee
Cool Prayers	Foss	G. Schirmer
Chorus Of Homage	Gericke	G. Schirmer
Ezekiel Saw De Wheel	Dawson (arr.)	Music Press
Fable, The	Dello Joio	C. Fischer
Four Slovak Folk Songs	Bartok	Boosey
Geographical Fugue (Speaking Chorus)	Toch	Mills
Glory	Rimsky-Korsakoff	Witmark
How They So Softly Rest '	Willan	Gray
Hymn To Saint Cecilia	Dello Joio	C. Fischer
I Love My Love	Holst	G. Schirmer
Jubilant Song, A ' '	Dello Joio	G. Schirmer
Lilium Regis	Creston	Ricordi
Little Bird	Kubik	Southern
Neighbor's Chorus	Offenbach-Meyerowitz	Broude
Now Let Us All Sing	Kirk	Shawnee
Now Sleeps The Crimson Petal	Quilter-Cain	Boosey
Partita Piccola	VanDelden	Peters
Poor Wayfaring Stranger	Seigmeister (arr.)	C. Fischer
Revecy Venir du Printans	LeJeune	Flammer

Title	Composer-Arranger	Publisher
Six Chansons	Hindemith	Schott
Song Of Democracy ' '	Hanson	C. Fischer
Stomp Your Foot	Copland	Boosey
Three Quatrains	Bright	Associated
Three Whitman Excerpts	Strang	Associated
Tribute	LoPresti	C. Fischer
Wheel, On Wheel	Sowanda	Ricordi
'Yoer Vous Nestes qu'un Villain	Debussy	Salabert
Yonder. Yonder '	Russian folk-Gaines	Ditson

6

A Practical Guide to Style

by Hugh Thomas

Birmingham-Southern College

Hugh Thomas

is Choral Director and Chairman of the Department of Music at Birmingham-Southern College. He holds the Bachelor of Music and Master of Music degrees from the Birmingham Conservatory of Music (piano major), and has spent two terms in advanced study at the Berkshire Music Center (conducting under Robert Shaw and advanced analysis under Julius Herford). He has appeared as piano soloist with Andre Kostelanetz and the Curtin String Quartet, and made his professional debut as a conductor (The Hugh Thomas Chorus) *in Town Hall, New York, 1951. This concert received favorable reviews in leading New York newspapers, as well as in* Musical America *and other publications.*

Mr. Thomas, a native of Birmingham, became Dean of the Conservatory in 1947 and its Director in 1955. In 1964 he was named Chairman of the Department of Music. He is music critic for the Birmingham Post-Herald, *Minister of Music at Canterbury Methodist Church, is active in the southeast as a choral adjudicator and work shop conductor, and has directed first performances of more than 30 major choral works in Alabama.*

As a composer, his versatility ranges from art songs, through a concerto for Two Pianos and Orchestra, to original music for a college show, "Caught Dead."

Hugh Thomas' practical, knowledgable, good-humored-but-sincere approach to the communication of style (as displayed in this chapter) has served his students, who go on to professional and/or teaching careers, extremely well.

116

All of us hear performances by school choirs in which the right notes are sung at the proper time, the diction is clear, the intonation is accurate, the blend is pleasant—in short, the music is being sung *properly,* and yet it just doesn't "come off"!

The *style* is not right. This is simply not Mozart (or Brahms, or whomever). Why? It is extremely difficult to pin down; there are so many factors which go into the creation of a style, and the printed page—a series of complicated symbols from which an aural experience is supposed to be evoked—is only the very beginning of this process.

The purpose of this chapter is to supply the choral director with a *basic guide* to style, not the final answer to every artistic consideration. That, thank goodness, is impossible for one person to dictate to another.

You Must Believe

Singing is the most personal experience in all music, because the "instrument" is one's own flesh and blood. But there is a great difference between honest subjectivity, true personal involvement, and the externally imposed "effect" introduced by a tasteless conductor lacking artistic restraint, who thinks, "We can go all out here, and there won't be a dry eye in the house." On the other hand, some conductors seem to be almost afraid to allow themselves to become involved, lost in the music, and as a result present a *correct*, but dull and sterile performance.

Unless you are really *in love* with a piece of music, unless you believe in it completely, unless it actually begins to glow in your mind's ear, how can you ever expect a group of students to understand, believe, and eventually love it?

The Conductor's Responsibility

One of the marks of great creative talent is that somehow, through both natural gifts and acquired technical skills, relatively few people have been able to transform raw materials (which are available to every mind) into great works of art. By probing more deeply within themselves than most of us are able to do, these geniuses reveal the great potential capability of the human mind and spirit.

It is the conductor's obligation to search for the true meaning of that vague sketch on the printed page just as deeply as the composer searched within himself when he created it.

Thus, every choral director has inherited a trust which carries with it a tremendous amount of responsibility.

Do Your Homework

Assuming the school choral conductor has earned at least a Bachelor's degree in music, including certain required music history and literature courses, he is now only ready to *begin* learning. Four years of diligent study in a good music school merely allow one to "hit the high spots."

Even a very short piece with few technical problems—a 2 page composition by di Lasso, for instance—may require hours of serious study before a conductor is able to grasp the deeper meanings from which he will be able to help the printed page to come alive.

Functional Phrases

I have found one statement to be especially helpful when attempting to understand the composer's intentions: *The phrase is the functional basis of all good music.*

A good literary writer depends on nouns and verbs for the basis of his sentence structure, but also uses adjectives and adverbs to modify meanings, and prepositions and conjunctions to connect the important words. Music "sentences" (phrases) also contain important "words", as well as modifying and connecting ones.

When dealing with real music, you may be sure that at any one isolated instant you have either

1. reached an important point
2. are moving toward it, or
3. are leaving it.

Every phrase is functional; rarely is a good composer guilty of merely "killing time."

Personal Musical Taste and Analysis

There is a man in this country who has served music with genuine deep-seated ideals. He has an amazing ear for sound and a natural instinct for musical taste. He has a friend who is the best musical analyst I have ever had the pleasure of working with anywhere. This combination of impeccable taste and exhaustive analysis leads to a stylistic performance which is close to perfection. You can rely on Robert Shaw, who has worked regularly with analyst Julius

Herford, to present a model of correctness surrounded by warmth and perception.

So, obviously, the recordings of Mr. Shaw (and other outstanding choral conductors) may be a valuable source of study materials. A list of some recommended recordings is supplied below, but the wise school choral director will refer to these only as an aid to discovering the truth. He will choose according to the dictates of *his own* developed taste and careful analysis, since all questions concerning musical interpretation and style are, within certain obvious limitations, of the open-end variety. Fortunately, no one person is the final authority. In fact, I would far rather listen to a well-prepared, thoughtful young conductor make what might be called "mistakes" in style, rather than present a "carbon-copy" of a Shaw recording, no matter how beautiful the latter may be.

Musical interpretation can never be finalized, and yet when conducting you must feel that the way you are doing it is the way *it must be*—at this time, for you . . . provided there is a background of study and honest personal conviction.

Recommended Choral Collection Recordings [1]

Boulanger, Nadia	
French Renaissance	Decca 9629, Decca 3201
Dartmouth Glee Club	United Artists 3037
Fleetwood Singers	
Italian Music	Lyrichord 75 (775)
Greenberg, NY Pro Musica Antiqua	
Evening of Elizabethan Verse and	
Its Music	Columbia ML - 5051
Elizabethan & Jacobean Ayres,	
Madrigals, and Dance	Decca 9406(79406)
Play of Daniel	Decca 9402(79402), 3200
Harvard Glee Club, Forbes	Carillion 118
16th & 17th Century Motets	Carillion 124
Songs of the World	Carillion 122
Harvard-Radcliffe Music Clubs	
Sacred Polyphony	Cambridge 405
Hindemith, Yale Collegium Musicum	
Bach, Gesualdo, Weelkes, Monteverdi	Overtone 4
Dufay, Palestrina, di Lasso, etc.	Overtone 5
Princeton University Glee Club, Nollner	
Bach to Old Nassau	Carillion 125
Randolph Singers	

Recommended Choral Collection Recordings [1]

Catch Clubs	Elektra 162(7162)
Modern American Madrigals	Composer's Recordings, Inc. 102
St. John's College Choir	London Argo 340 (5340)
San Jose College, Choir, Copeland	Music Library 7007
R.V. Williams, Willan, Ginastera, etc.	Music Library 7065
Shaw, Robert, Chorale	
Easter	Victor LM-1201
America, The Beautiful	Victor LM-2662(LSC-2662)
Chorus of Love	Victor LM-2402(LSC-2402)
Deep River	Victor LM-2247(LSC-2247)
Great Sacred Choruses	Victor LM-1117
I'm Goin' to Sing	Victor LM-2580(LSC-2580)
Mighty Fortress	Victor LM-2199(LSC-2199)
On Stage	Victor LM-2231(LSC-2231)
On Tour	Victor LM-2676(LSC-2676)
Operatic Choruses	Victor LM-2416(LSC-2416)
Sea Shanties	Victor LM-2551(LSC-2551)
23 Glee Club Favorites	Victor LM-2598(LSC-2598)
What Wondrous Love	Victor LM-2403(LSC-2403)
With Love from a Chorus	Victor LM-1815
Yours Is My Heart	Victor VCM-7023 (VCS-7023)
Shaw, Robert, Cleveland Orchestra and Chorus	
Hallelujah	Victor LM-2591(LSC-2591)
Smith, Gregg, Singers	Verve 2137 (6151)
Trapp Family Singers	
Evenings of Folk Songs	Decca 9793
Best	Decca DX-162
Farewell Concert	Decca 9838
Sad Am I Without Thee	Decca 9759
Tuskegee Institute Choir	
Spirituals	Westminster 18080
Vienna Choir Boys	
Children's Songs	Epic LC-3588
Madrigals	Phillips 500011(900011)
Wagner, Roger, Chorale	
Echoes from 16th Century Cathedral	Capitol P-8460(SP-8460)
Holy, Holy, Holy	Capitol P-8498(SP-8498)
House of the Lord	Capitol P-8365(SP-8365)
Negro Spirituals	Capitol P-8600(SP-8600)

Recommended Choral Collection Recordings [1]

Virtuoso	Capitol P-8431(SP-8431)
Vive la France	Capitol P-8554(SP-8554)
Voices of South	Capitol P-8519(SP-8519)
Washington Cathedral Men and Boys Choir, Callaway	
4th Century Liturgical Music	Vanguard 1036
Welch Chorale	
15th and 16th Century Motets	Lyrichord 52
Westminster Abbey Choir	London 5800(25800)

---

[1] Record numbers in parenthesis are stereo versions.

How To Study

Although the *degree* to which one's own abilities can be developed may have been predetermined, this inborn capability must be cultivated in order to grow.

Musical taste, the seemingly intuitive perception of what constitutes the best, can be nurtured by constant exposure, but since it is the sum total of years of experience, progress is often slow and can be quite intangible.

Musical analysis, however, can be a much more exacting procedure. The following outline of musical elements can be used as an aid to analysis.

A Guide to Analysis

Melody

What basic type?
    major, minor, modal, pentatonic, tone-row, etc. (or alterations)
Can it be placed in some special category?
    folksong, recitative, arioso, etc.
How is the melody organized?
    long arch, shorter phrases—contrasts, repeats, sequences
What type of interval motion?
    conjunct (by step), disjunct (by leap), combination
What harmonies are outlined by the intervals?
Is the range basically wide or narrow?
Is the contour mainly smooth or angular?
Where is the climax? How achieved?

What is the basic plan of declamation?
    syllabic (one note-one syllable), melismatic (several notes-one
    syllable), reciting (one note-several syllables).
Do the word accents match those in the music? Exceptions?

Rhythm

Reexamine the melody with rhythm as the primary concern. Are
the regular metrical accents, expected at the beginning of each
measure, actually the proper emphasis points?
How does the true rhythmic accent affect the phrasing?
How is the rhythm organized?
    where are beginnings and endings of phrases (pickup notes, strong
    and weak cadence beats)? how are phrases grouped into periods
    and larger structures? will a form diagram aid in the analysis of
    this piece?
What special rhythmic effects are used?
At which tempo is the piece most effective (if the composer was
not specific)?

Harmony and Counterpoint

What is the basic texture?
    contrapuntal (melody vs. melody), harmonic (melody with
    chords)
Is emphasis on the voice leading of individual parts (counterpoint),
or on the chord progression (harmony)?
Can the piece be placed in some special category?
    imitation, canon, fugue, etc.
What are the chordal aspects of a contrapuntal type piece?
How are the voices led in a harmonic work?
How do individual parts affect the over-all ensemble traits?
What type modulation is used? How is it done?
How complex is the harmony?
    non-harmonic tones, secondary dominants (V of V), special chro-
    matic chords (+6, Neopolitan, non-grammatical chords — those
    which cannot be analyzed by conventional methods).
What is the effect of the "harmonic rhythm" (the rhythm pattern
created by the full series of chord changes throughout a piece)?
Have the usual resources been extended by various devices?
    polytonality, 12 tone, "chords" for sonority or percussive effect
    only.
How are cadences used?

Are cadences of a particular type?
"textbook," "doctored," or "borrowed" from another period of music history.

ESTABLISHING THE IDENTITY

Each composer in each musical period has his own particular "trademarks." In the following brief period-by-period discussion it is my intention to point out those aspects which are most important to the establishment of a musical identity.

PRE-BACH

The best music for school choral groups (from the standpoint of beauty of vocal sonority) is to be found within the pre-Bach era, in the compositions of Byrd, Tallis, di Lasso, Vittoria, Palestrina, Sweelinck, Schütz, Weelkes, and many others, some of whom are little known. For the choral man, this was a magical period. The sonority, the phrasing, and the interesting rhythms which grow out of the text—written right into the parts—will appear, almost automatically, when the music is sung cleanly, accurately, and honestly. No special "tricks" are needed, just a neat, uncomplicated performance . . . at which you have arrived through a careful process of study and rehearsal!

The Text. Begin as the composers did, with the words. Each fragment of a sentence with a new thought or a new idea of any kind, is usually introduced by a new musical fragment, which, at times, will need some slight emphasis for projection.

Rhythm. Accents cannot be anticipated according to any regular plan, but grow strictly out of the words. When imitation occurs in another voice, it may come on what would be (in traditional terms) an "odd" beat, thus creating a sort of "rhythmical counterpoint." Your rhythmic concept, therefore, must come from investigation of *word emphasis*, rather than searching for a regular duple, triple, or mixed meter based on the repetitive accents found in music of later periods.

Tone. The quality should be clean, unaffected, free-flowing, somewhat ethereal. The music of this period can help students to learn what is almost certainly a new concept in tone quality for most of them, since they are constantly exposed to the throaty, husky, popular-type commercial singing, and the "foggy *sotto voce*" affected by so many in present-day social circles.

Phrasing. The phrasing grows completely out of the text. One

RECOMMENDED CHORAL COMPOSITIONS – RENAISSANCE

Mixed Voices – SATB

TITLE	GRADE	COMPOSER	NUMBER	PUBLISHER
Adoramus Te	M	Aichinger	6000	Walton
Adoramus Te, Christe (Latin)	E	Palestrina	769	Belwin
Agnus Dei	D	Morley	1771	E.C. Schirmer
Agnus Dei	D	Palestrina	312-40616	Presser
Allon, Gay Bergeres (French)	E	Costeley-Shaw	10178	G. Schirmer
Almighty and Everlasting God	M	Gibbons	5349	Summy
Angelus Ad Pastores Ait	M	Hasler	8600	G. Schirmer
Ave Maria (Latin)	M	Victoria	2W2712	Witmark
Ave Maris Stella (Latin-English)	M	Anerio	ES 55	Bourne
Cantate Domino (Latin)	E	Hassler	ES 18	Bourne
Cantate Domino (Latin)	E	Pitoni	ES 5	Bourne
Crucifixus	M	Lotti	1192	E.C. Shirmer
Ecco quomode Moritur (Latin-English)	M	Haendl	1226	E.C. Schirmer
Echo Song	E	di Lasso	5802	G. Schirmer
Fa Una Canzone (Italian)	E	Vecchi	LG 556	G. Schirmer
Glory Be to God on High	E	Victoria	1416	Schmitt
Hodie, Christus Natus Est (Latin) (SSATB)	D	Sweelinck	R 133	Choral Art
How Long, O Lord	M	di Lasso	1409	Schmitt
If Ye Love Me	M	Tallis	2269	E.C. Shirmer
Little White Hen, A	M	Scandello	ES 29	Bourne
Look Down, O Lord	M	Byrd	ES 58	Bourne
O Jesu Christe	M	de Melle	E 560	Bourne
O Magnum Mysterium	M	Victoria	10193	G. Schirmer

Title		Composer	Number	Publisher
O Rex Gloriae	M	Marenzio	381	Mills
O Sing Joyfully	M	Batten	A 190	Oxford
Revecy Venir Du Printans	D	Le Jeune	RB 5	Flammer
Remember Our Saviour	M	Eberlein	1422	Schmitt
Sancta Trinitas (Latin-English)	M	DeFeuin-Riedel	1410	Schmitt
Suddenly There Came a Sound from Heaven	M	Aichinger	F 441	Frank
Tenebrae Factae Sunt (Latin)	M	Ingegneri	W 3028	Witmark
This Is the Record of John	D	Gibbons	TCM 42	Oxford
Venite, Exsultemus Domino (Latin-English)	D	Sweelinck	5517	Summy

WOMEN'S VOICES

Title		Composer	Number	Publisher
Assumpta Est Maria (Latin)	D	Aichinger	2 W 2899	Witmark
Benedictus (Latin)	M	Palestrina	MC 352	Mercury
Hodie Christus Natus Est (Latin)	M	Nanino	89158	Flammer
Il est bel, et bon	D	Passereau	ES 54	Bourne
Regina Coeli (Latin)	M	Aichinger	2 W 2900	Witmark

MEN'S VOICES

Title		Composer	Number	Publisher
Adoramus Te	E	Palestrina-Gibb	2098	G. Schirmer
Ave Maria	M	Arcadelt	526	E.C. Schirmer
Coenam Cum Discipulis	E	Gumpelzhaimer	9961	G. Schirmer
Inimici Autem	E	di Lasso	954	E.C. Schirmer
Mater Patris et Filia	M	Brumel	11011	G. Schirmer
O Bone Jesu	E	Palestrina	527	E.C. Schirmer
O Magnum Mysterium	M	Handl	7539	J. Fischer
O Sacrum Convivium	M	Viadana	47	J&W Chester
Regina Coeli (TTB)	D	Aichinger	NY 1848	Ricordi
That Virgin Child	E	Tallis-Precht	98-1366	Concordia
Vere languores nostros	M	Lotti	70	E.C. Schirmer

needs only to understand the text in order to follow the "directional urge" of each phrase.

Tempo. This must be adjusted, within reasonable limitations, to the size and strength of the group, and to the acoustical properties of the performance site. Since the choral music of this period was generally written to be sung in large cathedrals with great reverberation span, ample time was allowed for the notes to sound.

Extra-musical knowledge. It is very valuable for the serious choral conductor to broaden both his knowledge and sensitivity in relation to many of the other fine arts. My visits to Westminster in London, St. Mark's in Venice, and St. Peter's in Rome have helped me to understand why these men wrote as they did, how their composition was influenced not only by the clean, angelic refinement of the prevalent architectural style (the aesthetic side), but also by the acoustical properties of the actual structures which resulted (the practical side).

Many times one intangible can best be defined through reference to another intangible. In comparing the style of Palestrina and di Lasso, for example, the parallel relationships of polished glassware and old gold from this historical period can be infinitely more meaningful than words like "clean" vs. "warm."

THE BAROQUE PERIOD

The present-day performance of music from the 17th and early 18th centuries (through 1750) is often hampered by the musician's overly literal adaptation of the term *Baroque.* Besides, this word has regained its reputation during our 20th Century.

This music must come alive! Up off the printed page with the wonderful sense of internal rhythmic flow which is always there, but too often obscured by conductors who allow the texture to thicken.

Rhythm. The conductor's ability to produce correct rhythmic figures over a steady pulse is very necessary, but assumed. The really important aspect is the spirit, the "inner personality" of the rhythm. Much of this music actually *dances* across the page.

The Phrase. If the conductor has conveyed to the choir the function of the phrase, there should be no serious problem for either singers or audience to follow the contrapuntal writing so common in this music. The subject need not be "yelled out" above the counterpoint; it will sound — the composer took care of that. It is somewhat like a number of beautiful silk threads, each a different shade, running across a wall. If each one functions in a pleasing color relationship with the others, we say that the colors "blend." But even though there may be a strong interdependence of all threads in the resulting pattern, each strand also maintains its independence, since it can be traced (because of its own particular color) from beginning to end.

Some of the so-called "thickness" of the contrapuntal music of this period, particularly in Bach, is often a result of the dissonance which occurs when independent lines cross — become slightly tangled, if you will. This can be disturbing to the vertically oriented ear which must be trained to realize that the horizontal movement — the place the phrase is "going" — is far more important than any one isolated spot at which it may be compared to other phrases in earlier or later stages of their own independent development.

The Sound. Conductors are tempted to superimpose the very full, richly orchestrated, "stereo" resonance, which we all hear daily in symphonic music written during the 19th Century, on choral music from the Baroque period. It is the movement of individual lines *across* the page which not only determines the sense of the phrase in the music of Bach, Handel, and their contemporaries, but also dictates a basically *horizontal* concept of sonority — one far removed from the vertical texture produced by overtone-filled chords voiced from the lowest double bass notes to the extremes of the piccolo range.

The Text. In *Jesu Meine Freude* (Jesus, Dearest Master) by Bach —25 minutes of choral music that is as great as any ever written— there is a strong temptation to "swim through" the very florid, ornate texture with a great amount of physical effort. But the words, "Ye are not of the flesh, but of the spirit," suggest a basically light, lyrical, almost lilting quality. Other texts are equally revealing and helpful when they are studied thoroughly.

THE CLASSICAL PERIOD

Elegance, purity, balance, clarity, and emotional reservation, with the emphasis on a clear and concise form are characteristics of classical art, be it architecture, literature, the dance, sculpture, painting, or music. However, many surprises await those who will search even just a short distance below this formal surface. In the clever, enticing, intriguing, ear-tickling, happy music of Haydn there are serious harmonic shocks, and in Mozart's seemingly child-like simplicity there is great power along with consummate grace.

Beethoven is, of course, another matter. I am sure that many high school choirs perform music that is beyond their years, and this giant composer is often one of their victims. For young voices to perform any section of the *Missa Solemnis* (or even most portions of the *Mass in C*) is to deny the music its basic sonority and at the same time strain youthful voices beyond their normal capacity. This mighty music that is such a masterful combinaton of personal and universal utterance seems to be woven through the very sinews of one of music's unique personalities, and is not for high school voices! [2]

We are zealous for the progress of our choirs and, as a result we sometimes give them music (much of it from the classical period) which acts as a deterrent rather than an aid. No chorister enjoys trying to sing beyond his range or his dynamic limits, no matter what his age.

The music of the Classical period calls for careful control of every detail — the ultimate in tasteful restraint and intellectual poise.

THE ROMANTIC PERIOD

The composers of this time, in league with writers who reacted against what many felt to be an arid formalism of the classical period, participated in an emotional overflow of personal expression.

Whenever a style becomes so personal, so subjective (almost autobiographical), it causes a near dearth of choral composition. While many composers of this period were able to create highly successful instrumental music, most could not solve the problem of setting words of universal concept. The Psalms, a Jubilate Deo, or a Mass (which had been ground out through the cumulative experience of many generations) do not adapt themselves to a musical style which is primarily personal or subjective.

Franz Schubert and Johannes Brahms were two notable exceptions, however. But then neither Schubert nor Brahms were "Romantic" in quite the same way that we usually think of the term.

Everything Schubert wrote for the voice is a song, a *lied*. Even *Credo* from the *Mass in G*, for instance, with its many syllables repeated on the same chord, is still in the spirit of a song. When approached with this concept in mind, the music of Schubert can be a very lovely experience for students. There is a great deal of usable literature for mixed chorus, many part songs, and enough male chorus music to last for a long time without repetition.

---

[2] While we are on this subject I might point out that I have never heard a satisfying performance (in adjudicating or in public concert) of one of the high school favorites "How Lovely Is Thy Dwelling Place" from *A German Requiem*, by Brahms. Temperamentally and mechanically it too is beyond the capacity of high school voices.

A Comparative Style Guide – Baroque – Bach and Handel

	Bach	*Handel*
Background of the musical style	Uniquely personal and cosmic at the same time, absorbing the achievements of Italy and France, plus his own North German Lutheran heritage. Strong subjectivity to text.	Completely international–German seriousness, Italian suavity, French grandeur, expressed through the English choral tradition.
Qualities of the style	Tight construction, but satisfying equilibrium of harmony and counterpoint. Technical perfection of details. Intensity of expression controlled by a ruling architectural idea. Continuing vitality. Lavish choral color with unsurpassed sense of fluent, lyrical phrasing. Wide range of temperament in choral music from robust (even frenzied at times) to complete tranquility.	The dramatist, the master of grandiose effects. Choral parts extremely well written. Sonority often less complex than that of Bach. Pictorial musical symbolism, word painting. Great power to incarnate in music the essence of a mood, with overwhelming poetic depth and suggestiveness.
Personal traits affecting the style	Virtuoso organist. Simple, steady man. Practical composer who wrote for whatever combination of voices and/or instruments he had available, and for specific occasions as well as routine output from week to week. Innovator in keyboard performance.	Artist, producer and business man, deliberately appealing to middle class audiences. Lived in the glare of public life. Wrote oratorios for the concert hall (therefore this is *theatre*, not *church* music).

RECOMMENDED CHORAL COMPOSITIONS – BAROQUE

Mixed Voices – SATB

TITLE	GRADE	COMPOSER	NUMBER	PUBLISHER
All Breathing Life, Sing and Praise Ye the Lord	D	Bach	7470	G. Schirmer
Alleluia (Cantata 142)	E	Bach	42-227	Peters
Beside Thy Cradle	E	Bach	1601	E.C. Schirmer
Break Forth, O Beauteous Heavenly Light	E	Bach	302	E.C. Schirmer
Ehre Sei Dir Christe	E	Schutz-Shaw	10123	G. Schirmer
Exultate Deo	D	A. Scarlatti	312-40166	Presser
Four Psalms	E	Schutz	MC 6	Mercury
Gloria (excerpts-Latin)	M	Vivaldi		Walton
Hallelujah	D	Bach	2453	McLaughlin
Hallelujah, Amen	E	Handel	304	E.C. Schirmer
Hallelujah Chorus (Messiah)	D	Handel	2020	G. Schirmer
Is God for Us	D	Schutz		Chantry
Jesu, I Will Ponder Now	M	Schutz	1004	Concordia
Jesu, Joy of Man's Desiring	E	Bach	332-14703	Presser
Lasciatemi Morire (Italian)	D	Monteverdi	NY 841	Ricordi
Lord, Have Mercy on Us	M	Buxtehude	CM 6	Fox
Now Christ Our Lord Is Ris'n Again	M	Bodenschatz	CM 5	Fox
Now God Be Praised in Heav'n Above	M	Vulpeus	1693	E.C. Schirmer
Now Let Heaven and Earth Adore Thee	E	Bach	287	Wood
Our Father (English-German)	D	Schutz		Broude
Sicut Locutus Est (Magnificat) (SSATB)	M	Bach		G. Schirmer

Women's Voices

Title		Composer	Number	Publisher
As from the Earth a Flower Grows	E	Monteverdi	45	Marks
Morning Star, The	E	Praetorius	8953	Galaxy
Suscepit Israel (Magnificat) (Latin-English)	M	Bach	1307	Pro Art
We Hurry with Tired, Unfaltering Footsteps	D	Bach	904	Galaxy

Men's Voices

Title		Composer	Number	Publisher
All Glory, Laud and Honor	M	Bach	2135	E.C. Schirmer
Cantate Domino	M	Pitoni-Greyson	ES 56	Bourne
Come Now, Sweet Death	M	Bach	8956	G. Schirmer
Lord Jesus, Thy Dear Angel Send	M	Bach-Barrow	2143	E.C. Schirmer
O Bone Jesu O Mighty God, Our Lord (TB)	E	Schütz	ES 527	E.C. Schirmer
"Wake, O Wake," The Watch Is Crying	M	Bach-Treharne	8349	G. Schirmer

A COMPARATIVE STYLE GUIDE – CLASSICAL – HAYDN AND MOZART

	Haydn	*Mozart*
Background of the musical style	Developed mostly from his own inner communion, but also: 1. Viennese and Italian symphonists. 2. "Storm and Stress" movement. 3. KPE Bach style 4. Mozart (lyricism and chromaticism)	Developed from his instinctive amalgamation of these influences: 1. German roccoco style (father) 2. Italian singing style (JC Bach) 3. Mannheim school 4. Padre Martini (counterpoint) 5. German Singspiel 6. Rediscovery of the music of Bach and Handel 7. Haydn (form experiments, unity through economy of material, polyphony)
Qualities of the style	1. peasant 2. folk music themes 3. constantly experimenting with new forms 4. "pie-throwing" type humor 5. full use of melodic material 6. primarily diatonic tonality 7. primarily instrumental in concept	1. aristocratic 2. sophisticated themes 3. symmetrical, regular, preconceived forms 4. subtle, restrained humor with intellectual appeal. 5. seemingly endless supply of pure melody 6. feeling for chromaticism 7. a rare balance of choral vs. instrumental appropriate for the media.
Personal traits affecting the style	1. competent performer 2. very late musical maturity 3. composing a laborious task 4. composed at keyboard	1. outstanding, world-renowned virtuoso 2. musical maturity at an early age 3. learning process rapid 4. composed in mind, copied down later

Recommended Choral Compositions – Classical

Mixed Voices – SATB

TITLE	GRADE	COMPOSER	NUMBER	PUBLISHER
Agnus Dei	E	Pergolesi	MC 147	Mercury
Ave Verum Corpus	E	Mozart	6813	G. Schirmer
David's Lamentations	E	Billings	CM 6572	C. Fischer
Gloria in Excelsis (12th Mass)	M	Mozart	3515	G. Schirmer
Glory to God in the Highest	M	Pergolesi	CM 551	C. Fischer
Kyrie Eleison (Lord Nelson Mass)	M	Haydn-Hirt	5W 3543	Witmark
Laudate Dominum (Latin-English)	M	Mozart	2280	E.C. Schirmer
Sanctus (Imperial Mass)–Latin-English	M	Haydn	SC 12	Plymouth
When Jesus Wept	E	Billings	Mp 102	Mercury

Women's Voices

TITLE	GRADE	COMPOSER	NUMBER	PUBLISHER
Like As A Father (SSA)	E	Cherubini	5297	Summy
Stabat Mater–9 selections–(SA)	M	Pergolesi		Oxford

Men's Voices

TITLE	GRADE	COMPOSER	NUMBER	PUBLISHER
Viva Tutti (TTB)	E	Ed. Hunter	778	Lawson-Gould
Requiem in D minor	M	Cherubini		Associated

A COMPARATIVE STYLE GUIDE – ROMANTIC – SCHUBERT AND BRAHMS

	Schubert	Brahms
Background of the style	1. Haydn, Mozart, early Beethoven 2. Little formal instruction in compositional techniques; no contrapuntal study.	1. Opposition to the new theories of Liszt, Wagner, etc., with a desire to revitalize the classical approach and remain true to Beethoven. Admirer of Bach. Close friend of the Robert Schumanns. 2. Great compositional technique.
Qualities of the style	1. Melody of rare beauty, sometimes undisciplined, over-exuberant. Contour expressive of the text. Choral music written in the nature of a *lied*–almost as much so as his solo songs.	1. Melody well-constructed for development possibilities. Free, flowing, lyrical, but with characteristic wide spacing, downward sweeps, and folk flavor.
	2. Classical balance of form and content—Romantic ideas in material.	2. Mixture of warmth and restraint, intellect and emotion. Instinct for logical form sometimes concealed by overlapping of phrases.
	3. Rythm often repetitious, even monotonous.	3. Rhythm complicated, dotted, syncopated, cross-accented. Phrases shifted from the normal metrical accent.
	4. Harmony both diatonic and chromatic with color chords, enharmonic relationships, interchange of major and minor modes, casual modulations–often to distant keys.	4. Harmony sometimes vague, inconclusive, suggesting atonality; otherwise used much of the Romantic vocabulary (as Schubert), but with sombre keys, and emphasis on the flat side of an established tonality.

5. Inner parts often dull and uninteresting.

5. Inner parts full, often rhythmically independent. Sonority and color in different registers used to advantage, penetrating low range of upper with the high range of the lower voices.

Personal traits affecting the style

1. Tragic, untimely death (age 31) means all music is from his "early period."

2. Unassuming, modest, poetic. Poverty-stricken life, supported by friends, all in Vienna.

1. Compositions include a mature period (lived to age 64).

2. Strong, masculine, firm character and purpose. Experienced choral conductor, especially women's. Champion of own convictions in arguments with other composers; very good self-critic; great attention to small detail, edited other's works for his own choral concerts.

The music of Brahms has a texture which is so difficult to describe ("lovely warm grays", perhaps) but so easily identifiable. Structure and sound are so perfectly interrelated as to be inseparable in this carefully constructed music. However, it is difficult to keep it from becoming too thick. Brahm's truly outstanding trait, the one which lifts him to the highest level of achievement, is his marvelous sense of *phrase strength*. This is the man with the long line! Of course, the strength can be achieved only through the length . . . and this is the difficulty for most school performing groups.

Singing a Brahms phrase is much like the sensation of resistance you feel when pulling your arm through water—as in swimming— except that you never seem to get to the end of the stroke. This forward progress against partially self-imposed resistance must be accomplished in relation to time, but to be really successful, it must overcome time, go beyond it, seemingly disregard it . . . a difficult thing to do.

Contemporary Music

It is a great deal easier for most students to grasp a contemporary style, with its frictional harmony and striving for "newness" than it is for some directors. Students, *without* years of training in tonal music, have less to forget!

Two characteristics of contemporary music seem to offer the greatest difficulty:

1. The tendency of this music is frequently to suggest, rather than fully explain what is intended. Somewhat like Morse code, these brief symbols — the understated phrases of many compositions — represent a great deal more to those who can transcribe the full text of the message, than to those who just hear dots and dashes flying by.
2. Harmony is based more on progression from tension to tension, rather than the constant complete resolution of dissonance. We have become all too accustomed to the latter.

The conductor of today, conducting the music of today, does have an advantage in that the influences of his own environment correspond basically to those of the composer whose music he is attempting to interpret.

Since any contemporary movement is either based on a direct reaction against the period immediately preceding it, reflects a desire for nostalgic return to the practices of some earlier time, or is the result of an attempt to update the best of all previous periods, it seems obvious, but nonetheless absolutely essential, for anyone attempting to understand the music of the 20th century to be well-schooled in the music of the past.

RECOMMENDED CHORAL COMPOSITIONS – ROMANTIC

Mixed Voices – SATB

TITLE	GRADE	COMPOSER	NUMBER	PUBLISHER
Christus factus est	D	Bruckner	5249	Summy
Create in Me Oh God	M	Brahms-Williamson	7504	G. Schirmer
Der Abend	M	Brahms	10134	G. Schirmer
Easter Anthem	M	Billings	9949	G. Schirmer
Forth From Jesus Sprang a Rose	M	Bruckner	5405	Boosey
Four Folk Songs (German)	M	Brahms	AJ 23	Marks
He, Watching Over Israel	M	Mendelssohn	2498	G. Schirmer
How Lovely Is Thy Dwelling Place	D	Brahms	5124	G. Schirmer
Let Nothing Ever Grieve Thee (German-English)	D	Brahms	6093	Peters
Liebeslieder Waltzes, Op. 52 (German)	D	Brahms	ES 929a	Associated
Locus Iste A Deo Factus Est	M	Bruckner	6314	Peters
Mary Magdalene	M	Brahms	2230	E.C. Schirmer
Nunc Dimittis	M	Gretchaninoff	7039	Kjos
Sanctus	E	Schubert		Plymouth
Six Folk Songs	M	Brahms	AJ 9	Marks
Summer Day	M	Dvorak	A 404	Associated
To Music	E	Schubert	5575	Summy
Virgin Child, The	D	Fauré	1005	Galleon
Wash Me Thoroughly	M	Wesley	321	E.C. Schirmer
White Dove, The	M	Brahms	370	Wood

TITLE	GRADE	COMPOSER	NUMBER	PUBLISHER
Women's Voices				
Ave Maria (SSAA)	E	Brahms	4	G. Schirmer
Far and Wide (SSA)	M	Brahms	2 W 2985	Witmark
Gardener, The (The 4 Trios) (Horns)	E	Brahms	530	Gray
Greetings (Horns, Piano)	M	Brahms	2503	E.C. Schirmer
Laudi Alla Virgine Maria (SSAA)	D	Verdi	4256 C	Peters
Marienlieder (German-English)	M	Brahms		E.C. Schirmer
Magdalena			885	
The Hunter			886	
Angelic Greeting			887	
Mary's Journey to Church			894	
Call to Mary			895	
Praise of Mary			896	
Mary's Pilgrimage			897	
May Night (SSAA)	M	Brahms	4182	Summy
Miller's Daughter, The (SSAA)	D	Brahms	1071	E.C. Schirmer
Minnelied, Op. 44, No. 1	E	Brahms		Kalmus
So Clear Thine Eyes	E	Brahms	2079	Schmitt
Thought Like Music, A	E	Brahms	332-15186	Ditson
Three Sacred Choruses (SSAA)	D	Brahms		Broude
O Bone Jesu				
Adoramus Te				
Regina Coeli				
Whene'er the Sounding Harp Is Heard	E	Brahms	Trios 180	Novello

Men's Voices

Title		Composer	Number	Publisher
Brother James' Air (TB)	E	Arr. Jacob	166	Oxford
Chorus of Camel Drivers	M	Franck	63	E.C. Schirmer
Dedication	E	Franz-Wyatt	308	Gray
Festgesang an die Kunstler	D	Mendelssohn	615	King
Gram	M	Dvorak	9813	G. Schirmer
Hermitage, The	E-M	Schubert	12333	Universal
Inveni David	D	Bruckner	6318	Peters
Laura Lee (tenor solo)	E-M	Foster-Parker-Shaw	874	Lawson-Gould
Lieder Und Romanzen (German-English)	D	Brahms	10711	G. Schirmer
Maegdlein Im Walde	M	Dvorak	9812	G. Schirmer
My Horn Shall Weight A Willow Bough	M	Brahms	1464	G. Schirmer
Pastorella, La	D	Schubert	LG 512	G. Schirmer
Serenade	D	Schubert	68	Marks
Song of the Spirits over the Waters (double chos.)	D	Schubert	41	Marks
Spirit of Love	D	Schubert	LG 774	G. Schirmer
Three Folk Songs	E	Brahms	4247	Marks
To Music	M	Schubert	8378	J. Fischer
To Spring	M	Schubert	10100	G. Schirmer
Widerspruch (Contradiction)	M	Schubert-Parker	513	Lawson-Gould

RECOMMENDED CHORAL COMPOSITIONS — CONTEMPORARY

Mixed Voices — SATB

TITLE	GRADE	COMPOSER	NUMBER	PUBLISHER
Adoramus Te, Christe	M	Goodman	392	Associated
Alleluia	D	Thompson	1786	E.C. Schirmer
Alleluia (Brazilian Psalm) (8 pt.)	D	Berger	9992	G. Schirmer
All Glorious God	M	Rorem	6389	Peters
And in a Dream, Our Lady	M	Bauernfeind	A 401	Associated
Anthony O Daly	D	Barber	8909	G. Schirmer
As the Hart Panteth	D	Hawkins	A 195	Oxford
Boatman's Dance, The	M	Copland-Fine	1904	Boosey
Carol of the New Prince	D	Sitten	2203	Galaxy
Ceremony of Carols	M	Britten		Boosey
Ching-A-Ring-Chaw	M	Copland	5024	Boosey
Christ The Lord Is Ris'n Today	D	Rorem	6390	Peters
Communion	D	Kodaly	5574	Boosey
Concord	M	Britten	5014	Boosey
Cradle, The	D	Kelly	X115	Oxford
Ding Dong! Merrily on High	M	Paget	2669	Galaxy
Drei Volksliedersatze (German-English)	D	Schoenberg		Marks
Two Comely Maidens			AJ 17	
Now May Has Come with Gladness			AJ 18	
To Her I Shall Be Faithful			AJ 19	
Easter Chorale	M	Barber	11265	G. Schirmer
E'en So, Lord Jesus, Quickly Come	M	Manz	98-1054	Concordia
Fantasia on Christmas Carols	D	R.V. Williams		Galaxy

Title		Composer	Number	Publisher
Father William	M	Fine	5 W 3182	Witmark
Felices Ter (thrice Happy They)	M	Thompson	2416	E.C. Schirmer
Five Nursery Rhymes	M	Hunter	525	Lawson-Gould
Five Songs on Old Texts	D	Hindemith		Associated
True Love				
Ladies Lament				
Of Household Rule				
Troopers Drinking Song				
The Devil a Monk Would Be				
Give Thanks Unto The Lord	D	Storer	2196	Galaxy
Glory to God (SSATB)	E	Nelson	5321	Boosey
Glory to God	M	Vincent	406	Mills
Heart Not So Heavy As Mine	D	Carter		C. Fischer
Here Repose, O Broken Body	D	Pinkham	HP 10	Highgate
Hodie Christus Natus Est (*divisi*)	D	Poulenc	RL 12528	Salabert
Hodie Christus Natus Est	D	Vun Kannon	403	Gray
Hosanna to the Son of David	D	Hannahs	2631	Associated
How Excellent Thy Name	M	Hanson	CM 6808	C. Fischer
Hymn for Christmas Day, A	D	Parry	X 32	Oxford
Hymn of St. Columba, A	D	Britten	5569	Boosey
Hymn to the Virgin (Latin-English)	M	Britten	1856	Boosey
Jubilate Deo	D	Britten	5551	Oxford
Jubilate Deo	M	Owens	8012	Schmitt
Last Words of David	D	Thompson	2294	E.C. Schirmer
Laudate Dominum	D	Goodman	A 298	Associated
Lord Shall Give Thee Rest, The	D	Storer	416	Leeds
Lord Star, The	D	Bacon	MP 125	Associated

TITLE	GRADE	COMPOSER	NUMBER	PUBLISHER
Lo, The Messiah	D	Castelnuevo-Tedesco	1404	Galaxy
Make A Joyful Noise To The Lord	D	Newbury	51069	Lawson-Gould
Mary Hynes	D	Barber	8908	G. Schirmer
Musicians Wrestle Everywhere	D	Carter	Mp 119	C. Fischer
New Song, Three Psalms for Chorus, A		Kay		Peters
Sing Unto The Lord (Psalm 149)	D		6136 A	
Like As a Father (Psalm 103)	M		6222 A	
O Praise The Lord (Psalm 117)	D		6229 A	
Nicolette (#1, Trois Chansons-French-English)	D	Ravel		Durand
O Clap Your Hands (SSATTBB)	D	R.V. Williams	CCL 222	Galaxy
O How Amiable	E	R.V. Williams	A 94	Oxford
O Magnum Mysterium (Latin-English)	D	Poulenc	RL 12525	Salabert
O Praise The Lord	D	Kay	6229	Peters
O Queeem Gloriosum (English)	M	Powell	6230	Schmitt
Oves, Omnis	D	Casals		Broude
Pater Noster	E	Stravinsky	1833	Boosey
Praise	M	Bergsma	2165	Galaxy
Prelude Aud Hodie	D	Moe	312-40489	Presser
Promise of Living, The	D	Copland	5020	Boosey
Psalm 98	D	Distler	AE 111	Arista
Psalm 114	D	Kodaly	5328	Boosey
Psalm 121	D	Kodaly	5330	Boosey
Salve Regina	D	Poulenc		Salabert
Sanctus Benedictus	M	Titcomb	434	C. Fischer
Sea Charm (11 short choruses)	D	Piket	A 141	Associated
Sing Hollyloo	M	Vincent	404	Mills

Title		Difficulty	Composer	Number	Publisher
Sing Praise To God		E	Dressler	107	Abingdon
Sing Unto The Lord		D	Kay	6136	Peters
Six Chansons (French-English)		M-D	Hindemith	10454-59	Schott
The Doe	Springtime				
The Swan	In Winter				
Since All Is Passing	The Orchard				
Star of the Mystic East		D	Rubbra	269	Mills
Sure on This Shining Night		M	Barber	10864	G. Schirmer
Sweet Sunny		M	Dello Joio	6718	C. Fischer
Te Deum		D	Fox	885	Schmitt
Tenebrae Factae Sunt (Latin-English)		D	Poulenc		Salabert
This Is Truly The House of God		D	Rubbra		Mills
Three Hungarian Folk Songs		E	Bartok	5326	Boosey
Three Epitaphs		M	Halffter		Peer
For the Tomb of Don Quixote				Mi 74	
For the Tomb of Dulcinea				Mi 75	
For the Tomb of Sancho Panza				Mi 76	
Veni, Veni Emmanuel		M	Kodaly	5564	Boosey
With a Voice of Singing		E	M. Shaw	8103	G. Schirmer

Women's Voices

Title	Difficulty	Composer	Number	Publisher
All in Green Went My Love Riding	D	Diamond	WO 501	Southern
American Psalm, An	D	Sanders	MP 107	C. Fischer
Ave Maria	M	Kodaly	1711	Boosey
Blessed Land of Heaven Above	E	Powell	2570	Schmitt
Bread Baking (SA)	E	Bartok	1669	Boosey

TITLE	GRADE	COMPOSER	NUMBER	PUBLISHER
Ceremony of Carols	M	Britten	H 15576	Boosey
Woleum Yole				
This Little Babe				
There Is No Rose				
In Freezing Winter Night				
The Yonge Child				
Spring Carol				
Balulalow				
Deo Gracias				
As Dew in Aprille				
Ching-A-Ring-Chaw (SSAA)	M	Copland-Fine	5025	Boosey
Come In (Frostiana)	M	Thompson	2539	E.C. Schirmer
Early in the Spring (4 Seasons)	M	R.V. Williams	54-222	Oxford
Father William (SSA)	M	Fine	2 W 3204	Witmark
Girl's Garden, A (Frostiana)	D	Thompson	2540	E.C. Schirmer
Hist Whist (SSA)	D	Persichetti	CM 6651	C. Fischer
I Sing of a Maiden (SSAA or TTBB)	M	Kraehenbuehl	A-213	Associated
Lamb, The	D	Toch	AMI 2306	Mills
Lines from Milton	M	Branden	3722	Witmark
Little Bird, Little Bird (SSAA divisi)	D	Kubik	WO 503	Southern
Lullaby (Hodie)	M	R.V. Williams	46-502	Oxford
Lullaby of the Duchess (SSA)	M	Fine	2 W 3206	Witmark
Missa Brevis in D	D	Britten		Boosey
O Can Ye Sew Cushions	E	Britten	5213	Boosey
Petites Voix (French-English)	M-D	Poulenc	16124	Salabert
Sam Was a Man (SA)	M	Persichetti	9791	G. Schirmer
Three Carols (SSAA)	D	Warlock	554	Oxford
Velvet Shoes (SA)	E	Thompson	2526	E.C. Schirmer
Virgin Martyrs, The (SSAA)	M	Barber	8386	G. Schirmer
Young Joseph	D	Diamond		C. Fischer

Men's Voices

Title		Composer	No.	Publisher
Alleluia (Brazilian Psalm)	D	Berger-Heath	11020	G. Schirmer
Arriero, Canta!	M	Ginastera	2968	Boston
Boatmen's Dance, The (baritone solo)	M	Copland-Fine	1908	Boosey
Chorale Fanfare for Christmas	M	Nelson	5337	Boosey
Concento di Voci	D	Orff		Associated
December	D	Ives	812-2	Peer
Dirge for Two Veterans	D	Holst	8323	Curwen
Dodger, The (campaign song) (baritone solo)	E	Copland-Fine	1909	Boosey
Drinking Song	D	R.V. Williams		Oxford
Eine lichte Mitternacht	D	Hindemith		Associated
Emblems	D	Carter	MP 120	C. Fischer
Fanfare for Christmas Day	M	Shaw	10467	G. Schirmer
Farmer's Boy, The	M	R.V. Williams	78	Galaxy
Frostiana (TBB)	M-D	Thompson	2181-82	E.C. Schirmer
(2) Pasture				
(6) Stopping by the Woods on a Snowy Evening				
Gate of Heaven, The	D	Thompson	2175	E.C. Schirmer
Glory Be To God	D	Rachmaninoff	1781	Gray
Last Words of David, The	M	Thompson	2154	E.C. Schirmer
Linden Lea	E	R.V. Williams	1991	Boosey
Love Nay, Nay!	D	Piket	A 177-82	Associated
Here's to the Maiden				
Where Be You Going				
Dear Jane				
Who Tames The Lion Now				
Lullaby				
Her Triumph				

TITLE	GRADE	COMPOSER	NUMBER	PUBLISHER
Maria	M	Bernstein	10704	G. Schirmer
Nun Takes the Veil, A	M	Barber	10859	G. Schirmer
Sunt Lacrimae rerum	D	Orff		Schott
Peacocks, The	D	Kodaly	1819	Boosey
Pirate Song	M	Bernstein	9915	G. Schirmer
Plank Round	M	Bernstein	9918	G. Schirmer
Shepherds Rejoice	D	Frackenpohl	612	King
Sleep Little One	M	Nelson	5337	Boosey
Vagabond, The	M	R.V. Williams	1661	Boosey
Vale of Tuoni	M	Sibelius	310	Row

FOLK, CHRISTMAS, AND HYMNS — ARRANGED

Mixed Voices — SATB

TITLE	GRADE	COMPOSER	NUMBER	PUBLISHER
Above A Star	E	Graham	1153	Elkan-Vogel
Ah, Jesus Lord, Thy Love To Me	E	Johnson	513	Augsburg
Ain-a That Good News	M	Dawson	103	Tuskegee
As It Fell Upon A Night	M	Davis	1291	Galaxy
Babe Lies in the Cradle, A	M	Droste	A 462	Associated
Brother James' Air	M	Jacob	763	Oxford
Carol of the Birds	M	Shaw-Parker	10173	G. Schirmer
Carol of the Drum	M	Davis	568	Wood
Cert'n'y Lord	M	Johnson	6641	C. Fischer
Christmas Carol, A	D	Dello Joio	4237	Marks
Christmas Day	M	Holst	983	Novello
Christmas Eve	M	Donato	1950	Boosey
Christ Was Born on Christmas Day	E	Shaw-Parker	731	G. Schirmer

Title		Composer/Arranger	Number	Publisher
Come All You Fair and Tender Ladies	M	Sheppard	724	Row
Death, 'Tis A Melancholy Day	E	V. Thomson	CCS 9	Gray
De Camptown Races	M	Shaw-Parker	865	Lawson-Gould
Deep River	M	Shaw-Parker	813	Lawson-Gould
De Ol Arks A-Moverin'	M	Sowande	6121	Chappell
Dodgin'	E	Simeone	A 722	Shawnee
Didn't My Lord Deliver Daniel	M	Genuchi	O 17	Ludwig
Ding Dong Merrily On High	M	Candlyn	CM 6565	C. Fischer
Ezekiel Saw De Wheel	D	Dawson	110	Tuskegee
For All the Saints	M	R.V. Williams	9908	G. Schirmer
Four Slovak Folk Songs (German, Hungarian, English)	D	Bartok	7437	Boosey
Glory to God	M	Henderson	663	C. Fischer
He Is Born	M	Wagner	10169	Lawson-Gould
How Unto Bethlehem	M	Shaw-Parker	1680	G. Schirmer
Hunter, The	M	Brahms	81208	E.C. Schirmer
I Know Where I'm Goin'	M	Engel	346	Flammer
Is There A Fair In Bethlehem	M	Graves	697	Mills
I Was Born Almost 10,000 Years Ago	M	Hunter	905	Lawson-Gould
I Will Arise	E	Shaw-Parker	986	G. Schirmer
Jump Tune	M	Campbell	10819	Lawson-Gould
Lay Down Your Staffs	M	Shaw-Parker	5389	G. Schirmer
Linden Lea	E	R.V. Williams	NY 1924	Boosey
Lolly Too-Dum	D	Kubik	513	Ricordi
Lone, Wild Bird, The	E	Johnson	MI 8	Augsburg
Listen to the Mocking Bird	D	Kubik	OCS 750	Southern
Make Me Joy Now In This Fest	D	Walton		Oxford

TITLE	GRADE	COMPOSER	NUMBER	PUBLISHER
My Dancing Day	M	Shaw-Parker	731	G. Schirmer
My Ways Cloudy	M	Sowande	6119	Chappell
O Dear! What Can The Matter Be?	M	Kubik	9853	Lawson-Gould
On the Gallows Tree	M	Engel	81203	Flammer
Pat-A-Pan	M	Davis	1616	E.C. Schirmer
Pensive Dove	M	Shaw-Parker	916	Lawson-Gould
Rejoice and Be Merry	E	Hinton	40-918	Oxford
Rejoice In Bethlehem	M	Pfautsch	621	Lawson-Gould
Rocking	M	Ossewarde	2843	Gray
Saw You Never In the Twilight	E	Graham	1180	Elkan-Vogel
Sing We Now of Christmas	M	Terri	51013	Lawson-Gould
Soon One Mornin' Death Comes Creepin'	D	Kubik	9855	G. Schirmer
Spotless Rose, A	M	Howells		Oxford
Star in the South	M	Sargent	X 50	Oxford
Sweet Baby, Sleep	M	R.V. Williams	51134	Lawson-Gould
To Our Little Town	E	Malin	A 206	Mills
Touro-louro-louro	D	Shaw-Parker	10167	G. Schirmer
Turtle Dove, The	M	R.V. Williams	8105	G. Schirmer
Two Chorales from "Hodie"	D	R.V. Williams	43-929	Oxford
The Blessed Son of God				
No Sad Thought				
Two Mexican Carols	M	Sargent	84-111	Oxford
Jesus Sleeps				
Earth's Joy				
Venite Adoremus	M	Wright	5110	Canyon
When Christ Was Born of Mary Free	M	Friedell	1705	Gray

When Jesus Left His Father's Throne	E	Johnson		Augsburg
While Shepherds Watched Their Sheep	E	Jungst	515	Gray
Why Thus Cradled Here?	E	Lynn	103	Abingdon
Zither Carol	M	Sargent	138	Oxford
			X 50	

Women's Voices

Christmas Dance of the Shepherds	M	Kodaly	5172	Boosey
First Mercy, The	M	Warlock	3262	Boosey
Hodie Christus Natus Est	M	Monteverdi	MC 24	Mercury
Little Drummer Boy, The (SSA)	M	Davis	670	Mills
Love Is Come Again (Easter)	M	Sommerville	542	Boosey
Mayday Carol	E	Taylor	4872	J. Fischer
St. Hellen's Tune	E	Merrill	94-204	Oxford
Star of the East	E	Frankeepohl	512	Elkan-Vogel

Men's Voices

Across the Western Ocean	M	Dougherty	10413	G. Schirmer
Adios, Cathedral de Burgos (contralto solo)	M	Parker-Shaw	658	Lawson-Gould
All 'round de Glory Manger	M	de Paur	709	Lawson-Gould
All This Night Shrill Chanticleer	M	Stevens	ME 1015	Peer
Al Olivo (Spanish)	D	Shaw-Parker	LG 670	G. Schirmer
Ariang (Korean)	E	Forbes	10995	G. Schirmer
A-Roving	M	Luboff	1004	Walton
Aura Lee (TTBB)	E	Hunter-Parker-Shaw	527	Lawson-Gould
Battle of Jericho (TB)	E	Bartholemew	9776	G. Schirmer
Blow Ye Winds	M	Dougherty	10412	G. Schirmer
Boars Head Carol (TTBB)	E	Shaw-Parker	10179	G. Schirmer

TITLE	GRADE	COMPOSER	NUMBER	PUBLISHER
Bonnie Eloise	M	Hunter-Shaw	528	Lawson-Gould
Bound for the Rio Grande	M	Shaw	51056	Lawson-Gould
Cheerful Arm, The	M	Gibb	9357	J. Fischer
Coffee Grows on White Oak Trees	M	Fergusen	51016	Lawson-Gould
Companions All Sing Loudly	E	Sheppard	3062	Boston
Didn't My Lord Deliver Daniel	M	Genuchi	008	Ludwig
Do-Don't Touch-a My Garment	M	Shaw	9954	G. Schirmer
Down by the Sally Gardens	M	Shaw-Parker	51019	Lawson-Gould
Down in the Valley	E	Mead	1716	Galaxy
Erie Canal, The	M-D	Forbes	10732	G. Schirmer
Good Night Ladies	M	Hunter-Shaw	531	Lawson-Gould
Holly and the Ivy, The	M	Barrow	2117	E.C. Schirmer
Hullabaloo Balay	M-D	Rowley	1822	Boosey
Hundred Pipers, The	E	Whiting	7003	G. Schirmer
If I Got My Ticket, Can I Ride? (TBB)	M	Shaw	9852	G. Schirmer
In dulci jubilo	M	Davison	25	E.C. Schirmer
I Wonder As I Wander	M	Niles	9202	G. Schirmer
La Tarara	D	Shaw-Parker	51046	Lawson-Gould
La Virgen lava pavales (TTBB)	M	Shaw-Parker	10198	G. Schirmer
Little Innocent Lamb	M	Bartholemew	9907	G. Schirmer
Lo, How a Rose E'er Blooming	E	de Paur	555	Lawson-Gould
March of the Kings (French)	M	Shaw-Parker	10190	G. Schirmer
Mary Had a Baby	E-M	Shaw-Parker	10191	G. Schirmer
One More River	M	Warlock	1854	Boosey
O Tannenbaum	M	Shaw-Parker	10195	G. Schirmer
Ox Driving Song, The	M	Reed	1121	Mills

Title		Arranger	Number	Publisher
Pat-A-Pan	M	Davis	2100	E.C. Schirmer
Poor Man Lazrus	M	Hairston	1022	Bourne
Remember, O Thou Man	E	Sheppard	11132	G. Schirmer
Rowing	M	Rowley	1900	Boosey
Set Down Servant	M	Shaw	C 26	Shawnee
Shenandoah	M	Bartholemew	7211	G. Schirmer
Still, Still, Still	M	Luboff	1009	Walton
Streets of Laredo	M	Hunter	777	Lawson-Gould
Swansea Town	M	Holst	8096	G. Schirmer
They Call The Wind Maria	M	Loewe-Stickles	1222	Chappell
Wait for the Wagon	M	Hunter-Shaw	541	Lawson-Gould
What Shall We Do with a Drunken Sailor	D	Shaw-Parker	51053	G. Schirmer
What Sweeter Music	M	Stevens	ME 1016	Peer

SOME ILLS AND MISCONCEPTIONS

While I feel a positive approach to the solution of problems is generally most desirable, there are certain ills and misconceptions which have crept into the performance of choral music that disturb me very much.

1. *Historical dryness.* We seem to have "discovered" the history of music, which has produced, in some people, an attitude that almost seems to negate performance. They become so overly concerned with explanations, like "this is the first time we find the use of the Neopolitan 6th," that they never do get around to actually enlivening any of the music.

2. *The gimmick performance.* Some conductors use isolated sounds, colors, vowels, or consonants, with no regard either for the phrase line or for the period of composition. With this theatrical concept of twisting rhythms and sounds, they sprinkle very obvious tricks throughout music and thus create an effect that would do justice to a variety show or a Hollywood epic, but leave Mozart or di Lasso in a most ludicrous position.

3. *Physical interference from conductors.* It is difficult, especially if you have a young group, to wait for them to fit a rhythmic pattern into your conducting diagram. It is so much easier (at least in the beginning) to "peck it out for them as it goes by." Soon a conductor absolutely kills the composition by picking it to pieces with his baton. I remember one gentleman who used to go through a very strenuous ballet exercise every time he reached "tis of thee" in a performance of "America." He felt that he simply must "beat" that eighth note! A chorus is, first and foremost, a musical instrument . . . one which is uniquely equipped to create a beautifully smooth phrase line. The conductor must not interfere with this wonderful quality.

4. *The day of the long line.* There is nothing more moving than to hear a phrase line—a musical sentence—spun out to its conclusion in a way that is both compatible with the music and complete within itself. Among those who are genuinely serious about music, this is the day of the "long line." In festival performances I have often heard young conductors pass over rests and stagger the breathing so much that the line becomes endless . . . less . . . less . . . ly long. This doesn't always fulfill the requirements of the piece at hand. In the field of literature, at the very same time

that William Faulkner was experimenting with the stream of consciousness, Hemingway was using simple sentences, writing in a very short, almost choppy style. It is the same with composers. All music is not necessarily long-lined, and our awareness of phrase-length has led to considerable musical affectation.

5. *Prevalent Misconceptions.*
   a. The rrr . . . ich, rrr . . . esonant rrr . . . ing is a fine choral sound, therefore it should be used for *all* music. (But this sound was not any part of the Baroque aural experience).
   b. Haydn was a clever composer of happy, rather folksy music. (But what about his prophetic harmonic originality?)
   c. Mozart was a dainty and gay composer of drawing room music. (But what about the other ⅞ of his work?)
   d. Sacred means sombre, and secular means carefree. (But how about examining each piece on its own merits?)
   e. Church music and dance music are entirely separate. (But what about "For Unto Us a Child Is Born," from Handel's *Messiah?*)
   f. Madrigals are happy, light and gay. (But what about many deeply subjective pieces, like Monteverdi's "The Tears of a Lover at the Tomb of His Beloved" — *Legrime d'Amante al Sepolero del Amata?*)

COMMUNICATING STYLE

A choral conductor's concept of style, based on years of listening, study, analysis, and comparison, must be communicated to his choir members if the knowledge is to serve any practical purpose.

Every effective communicator of ideas (and you, the choral director, are no exception) must be salesman, actor, cajoler, preacher — all of these things, sometimes during a single rehearsal — in order to kindle a desire in the singers which is already glowing within you. At times the greatest conceivable restraint is called for, and other times the most exaggerated histrionics may be necessary. Often you must risk making a complete fool of yourself in front of other human beings in order to achieve your goal.

A newspaper reporter who had attended one of my rehearsals once wrote an article containing numerous direct quotes from my comments during that session. I was quite surprised to see in print those things which I really couldn't quite recall having said. They apparently had simply erupted as I was working to convey to the

chorus my intense love for the "Ode to Joy" movement of the Beethoven 9th Symphony which we happened to be working on at the
time.

Students come to you happily, willingly, without any strong feelings regarding interpretation. They have no "musical will" as such
and it is up to you to create this in them. While it is a very difficult
task at times, it is really one of the most rewarding experiences in
all of music. Those of us who have been granted this rare opportunity must not abuse it, but, through the most thorough preparation,
provide these students with an honest and thoughtful concept of
the various stylistic traits of choral music from every period in our
extremely rich heritage.

STYLE — THE INNER CHARACTERISTICS

Remember that the words *style* and *form* are far from synony-
mous.

Form is concerned with the larger use of musical structure; the
Sonata-Allegro form has been used by Mozart, Beethoven, Brahms,
and Bartok, even though each has his own "sound."

Style is a more flexible, a more intimate thing: the composer's own
peculiar vocabulary is in evidence. The curve, arch, lift and fall
of a phrase, the voicing of the parts, the key relationhip, the method
of setting words, harmonic and rhythmic traits ... these are the
things that point to a particular composer. They are also the things
which lead us beyond the profile and the silhouette to a look at the
inner characteristics of a composer.

When we seek these deeper features we are more nearly identifying ourselves with the creative musician we hope to represent, both
to our singers and to our listeners.

It is worth the effort.

7

Contests and Festivals

by Dallas Draper

Louisiana State University

Dallas Draper

*is Professor of Music and Director of
Choral Activities at Louisiana State
University. He holds academic degrees
from Northeast Missouri State College
and Louisiana State University, and
has also done graduate work at the
Eastman School of Music and New
York University. He moved to LSU in
1946 from St. Louis, where for over 3
years he had served as Assistant Conductor of the St. Louis A Capella Choir
and the St. Louis Bach Festivals. He is
the founder and conductor of the LSU
A Capella Choir.*

*Professor Draper's personal singing engagements have taken him to
most of the 50 states and Canada. He has been soloist with the St. Louis
and New Orleans Symphony Orchestras, and has presented a recital in
Carnegie Hall. He is an active member of the Music Teachers National
Association, the National Association of Teachers of Singing, and the
American Choral Directors Association, all of whom he has served in
various positions of responsibility. The University of Minnesota, Washington State University, University of Missouri, University of Texas, and
Northeast Missouri State College have enjoyed his services as visiting
professor.*

*Mr. Draper has been selected as contest judge and festival conductor
for many events throughout the country, including appearances in
Nebraska, Iowa, Missouri, Alabama, Texas, Arkansas, Georgia, Tennessee,
Louisiana, Mississippi, Oklahoma, Kentucky, Florida, West Virginia,
Minnesota, New Mexico, Washington, and Alaska.*

156

Contests and festivals serve as a major incentive for both students and directors. When conducted properly they can help to raise the musical standards of school performing organizations.

Students who have been well-trained and properly conditioned look forward to the annual trip to the state contest where they have the opportunity to hear the work being done by students from other schools. Choral directors may compare their own finished product with the fruits of their colleague's efforts during the same school year.

Participants in choral festivals receive the benefits of skillful direction by an outstanding conductor, as they experience the thrill of massive sound. Through careful observation of the work habits and techniques of a first rate festival conductor, a local director can pick up many procedures and mannerisms, thus benefiting from the experience as much or more than his students.

When contests and festivals are carried on over a period of time, and organizers and managers are careful to secure well-qualified judges and conductors who insist on very high musical standards, the achievements of choral programs throughout the entire state are seen to improve at a steady rate.

WHEN TO ENTER CONTEST

Directors should be prepared for the administrators and townspeople who may point with pride to their winning basketball team and call for a "winning chorus" right now as well. The only person who really knows when the group is ready to compete is you... the regular conductor. It is best to survey the other performing organizations in your area, and determine when you will be able to make a decent showing. Since a notably unsuccessful contest appearance has such a demoralizing effect, an entire year's efforts towards the establishment of a fundamentally sound music program may be destroyed in just 20 minutes on stage... if the group is not ready.

STEPS IN CONTEST PREPARATION

Since the choir should always be prepared to perform to the best of its ability—on every occasion, whether for an afternoon meeting of the Brownie Scouts or a contest appearance in front of a judge with a "tough" reputation—no drastic change in the manner of preparation for contest is necessary.

Still, many directors select music specifically for contest during the summer preceding the school year in which it will be used, announce the three selections to the students early in September, and rehearse meticulously for months . . . only to discover that the piece is not sounding at all like it looked in the music store — it seems not to be especially suited either to the ability or particular personality of the choir — in short, it is just not "jelling."

The Spring Concert, rather than the contest/festival, should be the peak of performance preparation. Contest material can then be selected from the very best of the concert music (even though long ago you may have picked 3 pieces you would *like* to take to contest, if everything works out).

CHOOSING MUSIC FOR CONTEST

The music must fit the ability of the choir and its conductor. It is extremely dangerous to choose a piece simply because it is a wonderful composition, you have always wanted to conduct it, and your group last year could have sung it well. Too many times conductors, in an attempt to impress the judge and/or their colleagues, will choose something so ambitious as to lead to certain disaster.

The first step, therefore, is to evaluate, objectively and without prejudice, your own ability and the specific strengths and weaknesses of the students in your choir. Next, make some attempt to predict accurately the amount of technical progress and musical maturation you might normally expect from both yourself and your students by the time concert/contest time arrives. Only then are you ready to begin a search through the thousands of good pieces available in order to find material for an exciting and educational year of work.

FESTIVAL LIST OF REQUIRED MUSIC

Many state organizations have certain required numbers; some insist that all compositions be chosen from an official list. I favor a *suggested* list of outstanding choral works, to be used as a guide. In this way directors become familiar with the best literature, but are not restricted to the performance of a limited repertoire.

The Southern California Vocal Association publishes an excellent list of acceptable compositions for both Junior and Senior High School Festivals.

Southern California Vocal Association
Festival List of Required Music [1]

SENIOR HIGH SCHOOL

MIXED CHOIR
SATB unless otherwise indicated

TITLE	GRADE	COMPOSER	NUMBER	PUBLISHER
Adoramus Te, Christe (Latin)	E	Palestrina	769	Belwin
Agnus Dei (Latin)	M	Hassler	ES 1	Bourne
Agnus Dei	M	Morley-Dart	603	Galaxy
Agnus Dei (Latin)	E	Pergolessi	MC 147	Presser
All Breathing Life	D	Bach	7470	G. Schirmer
Alleluia (Brasilian Psalm)	D	Berger 8 part	9992	G. Schirmer
Alleluia	D	R. Thompson	1786	E.C. Schirmer
Alleluia, Glorious Is Thy Name	M	Olson	B 1575	Summy
Alleluia, Sing Praise (Cantata #142)	E	Bach-Hirt	CM 7140	C. Fischer
Alleluja (Motet VI)	E	Bach SATB-Continuo	6106A	Peters
All My Hearts Desiring	M	Brahms SSATBB	5406	Summy
Allon, Gay Bergeres (French)	E	Costeley-Shaw	10178	G. Schirmer
Alma Redemptoris Mater (Latin)	M	Palestrina	921	McLaughlin
Ave Maria (Latin)	D	Bruckner 8 part	AJ-47	Marks
Ave Maria (Latin)	M	Vittoria	W 2712	MPH
Ave Maria (Latin)	E	Villa-Lobos		V-Lobos
Ave Regina Coelorum	M	di Lasso-Richter	A-406	Associated
Ave Verum	M	Byrd	Lib 520	Galaxy
Ave Verum Corpus (Latin)	E	Mozart	6813	G. Schirmer
Benedictus	D	Paladilhe-Christiansen	15	Kjos
Birthday Greeting	M	Kodaly	312-40579	Presser
Caligaverunt Oculi Mei (Latin)	D	Victoria-Deis	8409	G. Schirmer
	D	Victoria-Wilhousky	CM 6579	C. Fischer
Cantate Domino	M	Croce-Martens	2095	Walton
Cantate Domino (Latin)	E	Hassler	ES 18	Bourne
Cantate Domino (Latin)	E	Pitoni	ES 5	Bourne
Cantate Domino (Latin)	D	Schutz	ES 33	Bourne
Ceremony of Carols ONE	M	Britten		Boosey
Cherubim Song	E	Tschaikowsky	491	Boston
Chester	E	Billings	LG 501	G. Schirmer
Christe Eleison (Greek)	M	Francesco Durante	NY 2003	Colombo
Christo Paremus Conticum	D	Albert L. Carr SSATTBB	51037	G. Schirmer
Christus Factus Est (Latin)	D	Bruckner	748 LG	G. Schirmer
Come Again, Sweet Love	M	Dowland	81274	Flammer
Come Soon	M	Brahms	3112	Boosey
Create in Me, Oh God	M	Brahms-Williamson	7504	G. Schirmer
Cry Out and Shout	E	Nystedt SSATTB	1574	Summy
Dancing and Springing	M	Hassler	ES 8	Bourne
Dark Eyes	M	Vasquez	F 520	Frank
David's Lamentations	E	Billings	CM 6572	C. Fischer
Dear Love, Be Not Unkind	E	Dering	F 484	Frank
Drei Volksliedersatze (German-English) ONE	D	Schoenberg		
#1 Two Comely Maidens (German-English)			AJ #17	Marks
#2 Now May Has Come With Gladness			AJ #18	Marks
#3 To Her I Shall Be Faithful			AJ #19	Marks
Early One Morning	M	Arr. Ahrold	W 3557	MPH
Ecce Vidimus (Latin)	E	Palestrina	1883	Choral Press
Echo Song	E	di Lasso	5802	G. Schirmer
			1184	E.C. Schirmer
Ehre Sei Dir Christe (German)	E	Schutz-Shaw	10123	G. Schirmer
Elegy (Strings (GS))	M	Beethoven	AJ 42	Marks
Eloquence (German)	M	Haydn-Geiringer	CM 6341	C. Fischer
			51066	G. Schirmer
Fair Maiden, Thy Charm and Loveliness	E	Hassler	ES 43	Bourne
Farewell, My Love	E	Anonymous-Hirt	CM 7041	C. Fischer
Fa Una Canzone (Italian)	E	Vecchi	LG 556	G. Schirmer
Felices Ter (Thrice Happy They)	M	R. Thompson	2416	E.C. Schirmer
Five Flower Songs (Published sep.)	D	Britten	1871-1875	Boosey
Five Centuries of Choral Music	E-D	A Collection		G. Schirmer
(Excellent Material)				

[1] *Editor's note*: This list, published annually (including current prices of music) has been made available through the cooperation of Anthony J. Palmer, Alhambra (California) High School, President of the Association.

TITLE	GRADE	COMPOSER	NUMBER	PUBLISHER
Five Songs Op. 104 (German) ONE	D	Brahms	NY 356	Colombo
For All the Saints	M	R. V. Williams-Shaw	9908	G. Schirmer
Four Folk Songs (German) ONE	M	Brahms	AJ 23	Marks
Four Gypsy Songs (German) TWO	D	Brahms		Boosey
Four Psalms TWO	E	Schutz	MC 6	Presser
Four Slovak Folk Songs TWO (Ger.-Hungarian-Eng.)	D	Bartok		Boosey
Girl With the Buckles On Her Shoes	E	Arr. Nelson Accomp.	10968	G. Schirmer
Gloria (Heiligemesse) (Latin-English)	E	Haydn-Woolman	2301	Walton
Gloria (Mass in E Minor) (Latin)	D	Bruckner	4050	Marks
Gloria Excerpts (Latin)	M	Vivaldi		Walton
Gloria in Excelsis Deo (E Flat Magnificat) (Latin)	M	Bach SSATB	505	Kjos
Gloria in Excelsis (Twelfth Mass) (Latin)	M	Mozart	3515	G. Schirmer
Glory Be To God	D	Berger six part	5206-A	Kjos
Glory to God	E	Ron Nelson SSATB	5321	Boosey
Glory to God in the Highest	M	Pergolesi	CM 551	C. Fischer
Glory to God in the Highest	D	R. Thompson	2470	E.C. Schirmer
Go, Lovely Rose	M	Eric Thiman	1537	Galaxy
Great is the Lord, Our Maker	M	Michael Haydn	10529	G. Schirmer
Gute Nacht (German & English)	M	Schumann	AJ 39	Marks
Hallelujah, Amen (Judas Maccabeus)	M	Handel-Deis	9835	G. Schirmer
Hallelujah Chorus (Messiah)	D	Handel	2020	G. Schirmer
Hear the Murmuring Waters	D	Monteverdi SSATB	NY 837	Colombo
He, Watching Over Israel	M	Mendelssohn Acc.	2498	
Here Is Thy Footstool	M	Creston	11146	G. Schirmer
Hodie, Christus Natus Est (Latin)	D	Poulenc Divisi		Colombo
Hodie, Christus Natus Est (Latin)	D	Sweelinck SSATB	R 133	Fox
Hodie, Christus Natus Est (Latin)	D	Healy Willan Divisi	CM 469	C. Fischer
Holy Radiant Light	D	Gretchaninoff 8 part	8081	G. Schirmer
How Excellent Thy Name	M	Hanson Acc.	CM 6808	C. Fischer
How Lovely Is Thy Dwelling Place	D	Brahms Acc.	5124	G. Schirmer
Hunter's Song (German & English)	M	Schumann	AJ 39	Marks
Hymn to the Virgin (Latin and English)	M	Britten Double Choir	1856	Boosey
I Cannot Conceal It	E	Certon	ES 42	Bourne
If I Should Die	M	Arr. Ahrold SSATTBB	W 3556	MPH
I Have Longed For Thy Saving Health	E	Byrd-Whitehead	1679	Gray
I Know a Young Maiden (German)	E	Lassus-Hirt	CM 7039	C. Fischer
In Thee, O Lord (In Te Domine Speravi)	M	Halsey Stevens Organ	P 6520	Peters
Invocation and Chorale	M	Christiansen	1178	Augsburg
It Was A Lover and His Lass	M	Kirk	A 426	Shawnee
I Will Not Let Thee Go	D	CPE Bach 8 pts.	8427	G. Schirmer
Jesu Dulcis Memoria (Latin)	M	Victoria	5573	G. Schirmer
Jubilate Deo Omnis Terra (Latin)	D	Peeters	2096	McLaughlin
Jubilant Song	D	Dello Joio Acc.	9680	G. Schirmer
Kyrie Eleison (Lord Nelson Mass)	M	Haydn-Hirt	W 3543	MPH
Lasciatemi Morire (Italian)	D	Monteverdi	NY 841	Colombo
Last Words of David	D	R. Thompson Acc.	2294	E.C. Schirmer
Let All Mortal Flesh Keep Silence	E	Holst	#5	Galaxy
(Accomp.-Baritone Solo)				
Let All the Nations Praise the Lord	M	Leisring-Hoggard Dbl. Choir		Shawnee
Let Nothing Ever Grieve Thee (German & Eng.)	D	Brahms Acc.	6093	Peters
Let Thy Holy Presence	M	Tschesnokoff 8 part	B 12	Summy
Liebeslieder Waltzes Op. 52 (TWO) (German)	D	Brahms Acc.	ES 929a	Associated
Lieder und Romanzen Op. 93a (TWO) (German)	D	Brahms	10856	G. Schirmer
Like as a Culver on the Bared Bough	D	Halsey Stevens SSATB	A 218	Associated
Linden Lea	E	Vaughn Williams	5389	Boosey
Lord is a Mighty God, The	E	Mendelssohn 2 pt. Acc.	9	Kjos
Many A Song	M	Dvorak-Mason	7008	Walton
Miserere Mei (Latin)	M	Lotti	1938	Boosey
Modern Music	E	Billings	MC 88	Presser
Music, Spread Thy Voice Around (Solomon)	M	Handel SSATB Acc.	4132	Marks
My Heart Is Offered Still To Thee (French)	E	Lassus	LG 563	G. Schirmer
Never Weather-beaten Sail (Campion)	M	Morgan Acc.	2295	E.C. Schirmer
Nicolette (#1 Trois Chansons) (Fr. & Eng.)	D	Ravel Tenor Divisi		Elkan-Vogel
Now Sing We All This Day	M	Hassler SAATB	333	Mills
O Admirabile Commercium	M	Palestrina-Sargent	354	Oxford
O Be Joyful, All Ye Lands	M	Gretchaninoff SATB-Divisi	#5	Kjos
O Clap Your Hands	D	R. V. Williams SSATTBB	CCL 222	Galaxy
O Eyes of My Beloved	E	di Lasso	1146	E.C. Schirmer
O God, Thou Faithful God	M	Brahms-Douglas	1647	Gray
O Lovely May	M	Brahms SATBB	5576	Summy

TITLE	GRADE	COMPOSER	NUMBER	PUBLISHER
O Lord God	D	Tschesnokoff	1500	Boston
O Magnum Mysterium (Latin-English)	D	Poulenc		Colombo
O Magnum Mysterium (Latin-English)	D	Victoria	ES 20	Bourne
			7626	G. Schirmer
O Mistress Mine	M	R. V. Williams	243	Mills
O Rejoice Ye Christians Loudly	M	Bach	367	E.C. Schirmer
O Stay Sweet Love	M	Farmer	312-40091	Presser
Oh, My Love Is Like A Red, Red Rose	E	Arr. Henderson SATB-Acc.	1099	Kjos
Oh No, John	EM	Arr. Henderson	1044	Kjos
Oh No, John	M	Eric Thiman	MT 1052	Gray
150th Psalm	D	Berger SATB-Divisi	8512	J. Fischer
Pater Noster (Latin)	E	Stravinsky	1833	Boosey
Pilon L'Orge (French)	M	Poulenc	Rouart	Colombo
Praise Ye the Lord	D	Hovhaness	A 208	Associated
Prayer of St. Francis	M	Lekberg SATB-Divisi	5208	Kjos
Psalm XLVII	D	Bourgeois SATB-Divisi	CM 6858	C. Fischer
Psalm 96 (French-English)	M	Sweelinck	MC 4	Presser
Psalm 150	D	Newberry SATB-Divisi	638	G. Schirmer
Reincarnations (Published Sep.)	D	Barber	8908-09-10	G. Schirmer
Road Not Taken, The (Frostiana)	E	R. Thompson	2485	E.C. Schirmer
Safe In Thy Hand	E	Bach-Ohl	5567	Summy
Salvation is Created	M	Tschesnokoff 8 part	4129	J. Fischer
Sanctus (Imperial Mass) (Latin-English)	M	Haydn	SC 12	Plymouth
Scarborough Fair	M	Arr. Henderson	1051	Kjos
Serve the Lord with Gladness	M	Handel	LG 794	G. Schirmer
She Walks in Beauty	D	Foltz	R3171	MPH
Sicut Locutus Est (Magnificat) (Latin)	M	Bach SSATB		G. Schirmer
Silent Devotion and Response (Heb.-Eng.)	M	Bloch		Broude
Six Chansons (French-English) TWO				
(The Doe; The Swan; Since All is Passing;	M-D	Hindemith	10454-59	Associated
Springtime; In Winter; The Orchard)				
Six Folk Songs—ONE	M	Brahms	AJ 9	Marks
Six Love Songs (from Op. 52 & 65) ONE	D	Brahms	388	E.C. Schirmer
Song of the Open Road	D	Dello Joio SATB-Acc.	O 3826	C. Fischer
Stars Are With the Voyager	M	Bright	A 513	Shawnee
Stomp Your Foot	D	Copland SATB-Acc.	5019	Boosey
Surely He Hath Borne Our Griefs	D	Carl H. Graun	LGC 661	C. Schirmer
Sure on This Shining Night	M	Barber	10864	G. Schirmer
Super Flumina Babylonis (Latin)	D	Palestrina	7259	J. Fischer
Surrexit Pastor Bonus (Latin)	D	di Lasso SSATB	7685	G. Schirmer
Sweet Day	E	V. Williams	241	Mills
Swell the Full Chorus (Solomon)	M	Handel	2144	Galaxy
Tenebrae Factae Sunt (Latin)	M	Ingegneri	W 3028	MPH
Tenebrae Factae Sunt (Latin) (English)	D	Poulenc		Colombo
This Day We Do Honor	M	Mozart	B 64	Summy
Three Hungarian Folk Songs	E	Bartok	5326	Boosey
Three Hungarian Folk Songs	M	Seiber	10715	G. Schirmer
Three Shakespeare Songs ONE	E	V. Williams		Oxford
Thrift	E	W. Schuman	342-40001	Presser
Though You Are Young (Campion)	D	Rubbra		Galaxy
Tune Thy Music To Thy Heart (Campion)	M	Rowley	8443	G. Schirmer
Turtle Dove, The	E	V. Williams SSATB	8105	G. Schirmer
Two Madrigals (Italian) ONE	M	Palestrina	MC 58	Presser
Vinea Mea Electa	D	Poulenc	Sal. m II	Colombo
Weep O Mine Eyes	E	Bennet	ES 30	Bourne
Weep O Mine Eyes	D	Halsey Stevens SSATB		Row
When Jesus Wept	E	Billings	Mp 102	Presser
Willow Song, The	M	V. Williams	242	Mills
Wondrous Cool, Thou Woodland Quiet	M	Brahms	40631	G. Schirmer
Your Dancing, My Dearest	MD	Costeley-Mason	7017	Walton

WOMEN'S VOICES
SSA unless otherwise indicated

Adieu, Mignonne, When you are gone	M	Dello Joio	CM 6784	C. Fischer
Adoramus Te, Christe (Latin)	E	Corsi	R 117	Fox
Adoramus Te, Christe (Latin)	M	di Lasso	1508	E.C. Schirmer
Adoramus Te, Christe (Latin)	M	Gasparini	8154	G. Schirmer
Adoramus Te, Christe (Latin)	M	Tenero SSAA	2327	Choral Press
Agnus Dei (Latin only) (3 pt. canon)	M	Thomson SSS	MC 153	Presser

TITLE	GRADE	COMPOSER	NUMBER	PUBLISHER
Ah, My Dear Son	D	Warlock	1431	C. Fischer
Alleluia (Cantata #142)	E	Bach-Lefebre Acc.	1056	Galaxy
Alleluia	E	Mozart Acc.	CM 536	C. Fischer
All in Green Went My Love Riding	D	David Diamond		Southern
All the Pretty Little Horses (9th)	M	Arr. Owen	312-40518	Presser
All Ye Saints Be Joyful	E	K. K. Davis SSAA	R 3330	MPH
As Costureiras (Portuguese & English)	D	Villa-Lobos SSAA Div.	9395	G. Schirmer
(The Sewing Girls)				
As From the Earth a Flower Grows	E	Monteverdi	45	Marks
Assumpta Est Maria (Latin)	D	Aichinger Acc.	2W2899	MPH
At the Gate of Heaven	E	Marjory Allen	B 1570	Summy
Ave Maria (Latin)	E	Arcadelt	ES 3	Bourne
Ave Maria (Latin)	E	Brahms SSAA Acc.	4	G. Schirmer
Ave Maria (Latin)	E	Michael Head Acc.	5124	Boosey
Ave Maria (Latin)	M	Kodaly	U. 0756	Presser
Ave Maria (Latin)	D	Trappistine Nun		World Library
Ave Maria (Latin)	D	Hovhaness SSAA Acc.	A 277	Associated
Ave Verum Corpus (Latin)	E	des Pres	R 101	Fox
Ave Verum Corpus (Latin)	E	Mozart Acc.	WE 1	Bourne
Benedictus (Latin)	M	Palestrina	MC 352	Presser
Benedictus (Latin)	E	Vittoria	NY 2040	Colombo
Bread Baking	E	Bartok SA	1669	Boosey
Breakers Off Barranquilla	M	Clokey Acc.	1409	Summy
Cantiones Duarum Vocem (Latin) TWO	D	di Lasso SA	11	Presser
Ce Moys de May (French)	M	Janequin-Finch	1987	E.C. Schirmer
Ceremony of Carols ONE	M	Britten Acc.	H 15576	Boosey
(Welcome Yole: There Is No Rose: The Yonge Child: Balulalow: As Dew in Aprille:				
This Little Babe: In Freezing Winter Night: Spring Carol; Deo Gracias)				
Ching a Ring Chaw	M	Copland-Fine SSAA Acc.	5025	Boosey
Come All You Christian Gentlemen	M	Pitfield	2548	Galaxy
Come In (Frostiana)	M	R. Thompson	2539	F.C. Schirmer
Come Shepherd Swains	M	Wilbye-Greenberg	N 2	AMP
Country Girls (Ninth Grade)	E	Britten SA	5016	Boosey
Dancing Song	D	Kodaly SSAA Div.	544	Oxford
Danza, Danza, Fanciulle Gentile (Italian)	M	Durante Acc.	LG 940	G. Schirmer
Divertissement (Seven—Sing any TWO)	D	Pitfield SSAA	266	Peters
Early in the Spring (Four Seasons)	M	Vaughan Williams		Oxford
Echo Song	E	di Lasso	83098	Flammer
Enchanting Song	M	Bartok	1954	Boosey
Evening Rondeau	E	Purcell-Jacques	OM 6	Oxford
Fain Would I Change That Note	M	Vaughn Williams	636	Gray
Five Prayers for the Young TWO	D	Ned Rorem	312-40307	Presser
Follow Me Down to Carlow (Ninth Grade)	E	Bell Acc.	B 66	Shawnee
Four Love Songs ONE	M	Brahms-C.L. SSAA Acc.	810	E.C. Schirmer
Four Russian Peasant Songs TWO	D	Stravinsky SSAA Acc.	27	Marks
Four Sacred Songs of the Night TWO	M	Houston Bright	B 190	Shawnee
Fragments from the Mass TWO	D	Emma Lou Diemer SSAA	AJ 96	Marks
Gardener, The (The Four Trios) (Horns)	E	Brahms Acc.	530	Gray
Girl's Garden, A (Frostiana)	D	R. Thompson Acc.	2540	E.C. Schirmer
Go Lovely Rose	D	Eric Thiman SSAA	1537	Galaxy
Greensleeves	E	Holst	584	Oxford
Greetings (Horns, Piano)	M	Brahms Acc.	2503	E.C. Schirmer
Griddle Cakes	M	Koshetz Acc.	W 2917	MPH
Gute Nacht (German-English)	E	Brahms Acc.	819	E.C. Schirmer
Gypsy Lament	M	Kodaly	536	Oxford
Hodie Christus Natus Est (Latin)	M	Nanino	89158	Flammer
House on the Hill, The	M	Copland SSAA	445	E.C. Schirmer
How Merrily We Live	M	Este	5359	G. Schirmer
I Gave My Love a Pretty Little Ring (Ninth Grade)	E	K. K. Davis	B 140	Summy
In Silent Night	M	Brahms Acc. Violin	83089	Flammer
Joyful Song, A	M	Duro	CM 6742	C. Fischer
Jubilate Deo	E	Mozart Acc.	1193	Belwin
Lamb, The	D	Toch	AMI 2306	Mills
Lambs To The Lamb	M	Creston	CM 6649	C. Fischer
Lark in the Morn (Four Seasons)	M	Vaughn Williams		Oxford
Lass with the Delicate Air	E	Arne	515	Gray
Laudi Alla Virgine Maria	D	Verdi SSAA	4256C	Peters
Laud We Thy Name	E	Bach-Davis Acc.	2054	Galaxy
Lift Thine Eyes	E	Mendelssohn	332-00820	Presser
Linden Lea	MD	Vaughn Williams	219	Boosey

TITLE	GRADE	COMPOSER	NUMBER	PUBLISHER
Litanies—a la Vierge Noire (French only)	D	Poulenc		Elkan-Vogel
Little Bird, Little Bird	D	Kubik SSAA Div.		Southern
Loafer, The	E	Bartok	1671	Boosey
Long Time Ago	M	Copland-Straker	5423	Boosey
Lord's Prayer, The	E	Peeters SA	6202	Peters
Love at My Heart Came Knocking	E	Deale SSAA		Oxford
Love Has Now Become a Stranger	E	Gabrieli	43	Marks
Love is a Sickness	D	Leo Smit SSAA Acc.		Broude
Love Lives Over the Hills	M	Rowley	8320	G. Schirmer
Lovely Appearing (Pur Dicesto—Italian)	M	Lotti	LG 942	G. Schirmer
Lovely Star (Sop. Solo)	D	Sorozabal SSAA	W3637	MPH
Lover and His Lass, A	E	Forsblad	6080	Kjos
Lullaby (Sop. Solo)	M	V. Williams SA		Oxford
Lullaby, My Sweet Little Baby	E	Byrd	ES 10	Bourne
Magnificat in the Eighth Mode	D	Dufay-Boepple	MC 29	Presser
Marienlieder (German & English) ONE	M	Brahms SSAA		
Magdalena (German & English)			885	E.C. Schirmer
The Hunter			886	E.C. Schirmer
Angelic Greeting			887	E.C. Schirmer
Mary's Journey to Church			894	E.C. Schirmer
Call to Mary			895	E.C. Schirmer
Praise of Mary			896	E.C. Schirmer
Mary's Pilgrimage (German & English)			897	E.C. Schirmer
Mayday Carol	E	Taylor Acc.	4872	J. Fischer
May Night	M	Brahms SSAA	4182	Summy
Miller's Daughter	D	Brahms SSAA	1071	E.C. Schirmer
Minnelied Op. 44 #1	E	Brahms	248	Kalmus
Minnie and Winnie	E	Berger	9169	J. Fischer
Mocking of Youth	M	Bartok	1955	Boosey
Morning Star, The	E	M. Praetorius	8953	G. Schirmer
Mother, I Will have a Husband	M	Vautor	ES 11	Bourne
My True Love Has My Heart	E	Theron Kirk Acc.	5021	Summy
My Spirit Be Joyful (Cantata 146)	E	Bach Acc.	2507	E.C. Schirmer
Nightingale	M	Weelkes	671	Gray
Now I Lay Me Down To Sleep	E	R. Thompson	1985	E.C. Schirmer
Now Is the Month of Maying	E	Morley	332-14329	Presser
Now Sleeps the Crimson Petal	E	Quilter	1678	Boosey
Nun Takes a Veil	D	Barber SSAA	10860	G. Schirmer
O Can Ye Sew Cushions	E	Britten	5213	Boosey
Oh, Had I Jubal's Lyre	M	Handel	3001	Gillman
O Filii et Filiae (Latin)	E	Gevaert	868	E.C. Schirmer
O Magali, my most beloved	E	Arr. Glaser	2512	E.C. Schirmer
O Sleep Fond Fancy	MD	Morley	4216	Marks
Only Tell Me	E	Bartok	1670	Boosey
Old Rhymes for Treble Voices		Halsey Stevens		AMP
When Good King Arthur Ruled This Land	M	SAA	A 259	
Anna Elise	D		A 260	
When I Was a Little Boy	E	SA	A 261	
Infirtaris	M		A 262	
O Vos Omnes (Latin)	E	Croce	89096	Flammer
O Waly, Waly	M	Arr. Fleming	5343	Boosey
Pater Noster (Latin)	E	Gevaert	2502	E.C. Schirmer
Petites Xoix (French) (English)	M-D	Poulenc	16124	Colombo
Penniless Sweetheart, The	M	Martinu	1948	Boosey
Piping Down the Valleys Wild (Latin)	M	Howells SA	5357	Boosey
Praise Ye the Lord	M	Mendelssohn	AJ 81	Marks
Pueri Hebraeorum (Latin)	M	R. Thompson SSAA-SSAA	492	E.C. Schirmer
Recordata	M	Palestrina	NY 2033	Colombo
Regina Coeli (Latin)	M	Aichinger	W 2900	MPH
Regina Coeli, Laetare (Latin)	D	Healey Willan SSAA		Gray
Rejoice, Rejoice	M	Byrd-G.W.W. SSAA	2200	Galaxy
Riddle, The	E	Arr. Owen	312-40884	Presser
Rosemary (Four choruses) (Nonsense Song)	MD	R. Thompson SSAA	1023	E.C. Schirmer
Sacerdotes Domini (Latin)	E	Byrd-G.W.W. SSAA	815	E.C. Schirmer
Sacrae Cantiumculae (Latin) (#12 and #16) ONE	D	Monteverdi	MC 24	Presser
1—Angelus ad Pastorem Ait				
2—Hodie Christus Natus Est				
St. Gregory's Day	D	Kodaly SSAA	W 39	Oxford
Sam was a Man	M	Persichetti SA	9791	G. Schirmer
Serenade	D	Schubert SSAA Acc. Alto	MC 15	Presser

TITLE	GRADE	COMPOSER	NUMBER	PUBLISHER
Seven Choruses from the Medea of Euripedes ONE	D	Virgil Thomson SSAA	MC 128	Presser
Sheep Shearing (Four Seasons)	E	Vaughan Williams SA		Oxford
Shepherd, Shepherd, Leave Decoying	E	Purcell	285	Wood
Silent Strings	E	Bantock	1467	Boosey
Simple Gifts	E	Copland SA Acc.	1903	Boosey
Sing Aloud to God	E	M. Haydn	10871	G. Schirmer
Sing, O Ye Saints	M	Schuetz SA	98-1414	Concordia
Sing Ye to the Lord	M	Byrd	2201	Galaxy
Sister Awake	M	Gardner Read	8845	J. Fischer
So Clear Thine Eyes	E	Brahms	2079	Schmitt
So Delicious	D	Picket	A 254	Associated
Softly the Echo Ringing (French)	E	Bornschein	2037	Schmitt
Song of Galilee	E	Arr. Chajes	TCL 332	Transcontinental
Song of Music, A	D	Hindemith SSA-Acc.		Associated
Sound the Trumpet	E	Purcell SA Acc.	LG 787	G. Schirmer
Spell	D	Picket	A 253	Associated
Spring	M	Bartok	1953	Boosey
Spring	D	Pfautsch SSAA	W 3515	MPH
Spring at Summer's End	M	Cowell	WO-509	Peer
Spring Greeting	E	Biresak	332-40007	Presser
Stabat Mater (Nine selections) ONE	M	Pergolesi SA		Oxford
Summer is a Coming and Cuckoo (Four Seasons)	M	V. Williams U-SSAA		Oxford
Suscepit Israel (Magnificat) (Latin & Eng.)	M	Bach Acc.	1307	Pro Art
Swallow's Wooing	M	Kodaly	542	Oxford
Sweet Lovers Love the Spring	D	Powell Acc.	CM 7042	C. Fischer
Tell Me What Master Hand	M	Palestrina	595	Gray
Though Philomena Lost Her Love	M	Morley	4217	Marks
Thought Like Music, A	E	Brahms Acc.	332-15186	Presser
Three Carols (#I or #II and III)	D	Warlock SSAA Acc.	554	Oxford
Three Folk Songs ONE	E	Brahms	4017	Marks
Three Love Songs Op. 52 #4 ONE	E	Brahms SA	1055	E.C. Schirmer
Three Sacred Choruses ONE	D	Brahms SSAA		Broude
(O Bone Jesu; Adoramus Te; Regina Coeli)				
Three Songs from Sweden	E	Arr. Hallstrom (1 & 3)	B 215	Shawnee
To the Sunshine (Ninth Grade)	E	Schumann	5200	Summy
Tutu Maramba (Ninth Grade)	E	Erb	LG 637	G. Schirmer
Two Purcell Songs	M	Jacques	OM 18	Oxford
(Ah How Pleasant Tis to Love; Fairest Tale)				
Velvet Shoes (Ninth Grade)	E	R. Thompson SA Acc.	2526	E.C. Schirmer
Veni Sponsa Christ (Latin and English)	D	Monteverdi	NY 2032	Colombo
Verdant Meadows	M	Handel	9096	J. Fischer
Vere Languores Nostros (Latin)	M	Lotti	ES 22	Bourne
Village Where They Ring No Bells	M	Hendl	CM 6653	C. Fischer
Visitor, The	M	Thiman	2356	Galaxy
Way to Paradise	M	Martinu (Violin)	1943	Boosey
Welcome Sweet Pleasure	E	Weelkes	738	Wood
Welcome to Spring, A	M	Gordon	SK 3006	Shapiro
We Hasten with Eager Yet Faltering Footsteps	M	Bach SA Acc.	2506	E.C. Schirmer
Whene'er the Sounding Harp is Heard	E	Brahms Acc.	Trios 180	Gray
When Love is Kind	E	Cain	2094	Schmitt
Which is the Properest Day to Sing	M	Arne	8444	G. Schirmer
Wtih a Voice of Singing (Ninth Grade)	E	Martin Shaw SA Acc.	10227	G. Schirmer
Wooing of a Girl	M	Bartok	1956	Boosey
Your Voices Raise	M	Handel Acc.	W 3565	MPH

MEN'S VOICES

TITLE	GRADE	COMPOSER	NUMBER	PUBLISHER
Acre of Land, An	M	Williams, R. V.	636	Oxford
Adios, Catedral de Burgos (Contralto Solo)	M	Spanish-Parker, Shaw	658	G. Schirmer
Adoramus Te, Christe (Latin)	D	Palestrina	950	E.C. Schirmer
Agnus Dei (Latin)	M	Morales TTB	MC 359	Presser
Album for Male Voices Op. 30 (Baritone Solos)	M-D	Grieg-Grainger	2492a	Peters
Alleluia "Let Thy Hand Be Strengthened"	M-D	Handel-Darne TTBB	8834	G. Schirmer
Amo, Amas, I Love a Lass	M	Bartholomew TBB	MC 149	Presser
A-Roving	M	Arr. Luboff	1004	Walton
All Through the Night	E	TB	9999	G. Schirmer
All Ye Saints Be Joyful	M	K. K. Davis	R 3329	MPH
Al Olivo (Spanish)	D	Shaw-Parker	LG 670	G. Schirmer
Ave Maria (Latin)	D	Arcadelt	526	E.C. Schirmer
Bachelor, The	D	Kodaly TBB	1893	Boosey

TITLE	GRADE	COMPOSER	NUMBER	PUBLISHER
Battle of Jericho	E	Bartholomew TB	9776	G. Schirmer
Beautiful Savior	M	Arr. Fry	322-35462	Presser
Before Sleep	D	Holst, G.	5359	Boosey
Bells in the Steeple	M	Bartholomew	MC 172	Presser
Benedictus (Latin)	M	Palestrina TTB	MC 352	Presser
Benedictus (Latin)	E	Victoria TTB	NY 2040	Colombo
Blue of Heaven Is In Her Eyes (Basque)	M-D	Sorozabal-Davis	W3633	MPH
Boatmen's Dance, The (Baritone Solo)	M	Copland-Fine	1908	Boosey
Bonnie Eloise	M	Thomas-Shaw	LG 529	G. Schirmer
Bound for the Rio Grande	M	American Shanty-Shaw	51056	G. Schirmer
Broken Melody	M	Sibelius	5781	G. Schirmer
Brothers, Sing On!	M	Grieg-McKinney	6928	J. Fischer
Cantate Domino (Latin)	D	Hassler-Davidson	ES 56	Bourne
Carol, Brothers, Carol	M	Ringwald	C 152	Shawnee
Chant des Bretons, Le	E-M	Berlioz-Kunzel	5401	Boosey
Christ of the Snow	M	Gaul-Morgan	9-W 3486	MPH
Colorado Trail	M	Arr. Luboff	1005	Walton
Come Let Us Start a Joyful Song	M	Hassler-Greyson TBB	ES 31	Bourne
Come Sing This Round With Me	M	Martini-Greyson TBB	ES 32	Bourne
Der Hern Segne Euch (German-English)	M	Bach TB	6079	Peters
(May God Smile On You)				
Dirge For Two Veterans	D	Holst, G.	8323	G. Schirmer
Do-Don't Touch-a My Garment	M	Arr. Shaw	9954	G. Schirmer
Dodger, The (Campaign Song) (Baritone Solo)	E	Copland-Fine	1909	Boosey
Down by the Sally Gardens	M	Arr. Mishkin	2153	E.C. Schirmer
Drink to Me Only With Thine Eyes	M	Arr. Hunter	LG 538	G. Schirmer
Du, Du Liebst Mir Im Herzen (German-English)	E	Shaw-Parker TTBB	51043	G. Schirmer
Faire, If You Expect Admiring	M		684	G. Schirmer
Turne Back, You Wanton Flyer	M		684	G. Schirmer
Farmer's Boy, The	M	Williams, R. V.	78	Galaxy
Five Slovak Songs	M	Arr. Bartok, B.		Boosey
Four Carols ONE	D	Halsey Stevens TBB	1015-1018	Peer
#1 All This Night Shrill Chanticleer				
#2 What Sweeter Music				
#3 As I Rode Out This Enderes Night				
#4 A Virgin Most Pure				
Four Old Hungarian Folk Songs	M-D	Arr. Bartok, B.	UE 8891	Presser
Fratres in Unim	D	Fitzgerald	NY 1479	Colombo
Frostiana 2) Pasture	M-D	Thompson, R.	2181-82	E.C. Schirmer
6) Stopping by Woods on Snowy Evening				
Gaudeamus Igitur — Humoreske	M	Liszt	5408	Boosey
Geographical Fugue (Speaking Chorus)	D	Toch, E.	347	Mills
Glory Be To God On High	E	Kirk TTB	2073	Fox
Glory To God	D	Gretchaninoff TTBB	53	Marks
Go, Lovely Rose	M	Thiman, E.	1537b	Galaxy
Gondolier, The	D	Schubert-Erb	LG 747	G. Schirmer
Good-Bye, Fare Ye Well	M	Parker-Shaw	51050	G. Schirmer
Good Fellows, Be Merry (Peasant Cantata)	D	Bach-Duey	2944	Boston
Goodnight, Ladies (Baritone Solo)	M	Trad.-Hunter, Shaw	531	G. Schirmer
Grandfather's Clock (Baritone Solo)	M	Work-Hunter, Shaw	532	G. Schirmer
Gratias Agimus Tibi (Latin-English)	M-D	Hassler TTBB	782	G. Schirmer
Grave and the Moon, The	M-D	Schubert-Plott	DC 1	Brodt
Gute Nacht (German)	M	Schumann-G. W. W.	901	E.C. Schirmer
Hangtown Gals	E	Harley, Aschbrenner	CM 6218	C. Fischer
Happy Wanderer, The	M	Moller-Ehret		Fox
Heart Worships, The	D	Holst	2952	Galaxy
Hello, Girls	E	American-Pfautsch	B-1630	Summy
Henry (Humorous)	M	Lewis, J. L.	82180	Flammer
Here is Thy Footstool	D	Creston	9793	G. Schirmer
Hermitage, The	E-M	Schubert	UE 12333	Presser
He Who Comes Here?	M	Morley-Fellowes	71	Galaxy
Hills of the North, Rejoice	M-D	Cassler TTBB	10599	G. Schirmer
Hope for Tomorrow	D	Berger, J.	10727	G. Schirmer
How Merrily We Live	M	Bartholomew	MC 173	Presser
Hul-a-ba-lu-be-lay	E	Arr. Churchill, S.	1643	Belwin
Hunters Farewell	D	Mendelssohn	4992	G. Schirmer
Hunting the Hare	M	Arr. Jones	82192	Flammer
Hush to Peace	M	Arne-Hunter TBB	LG 775	G. Schirmer
I Am a Good Musician (Novelty) (Solo Leader)	E	German Folk-Schilling	996	G. Schirmer
I Bought Me a Cat	M-D	Adapted-Copland-Fine	1910	Boosey

TITLE	GRADE	COMPOSER	NUMBER	PUBLISHER
I Hear a Voice A'Prayin'	M	Bright	C 155	Shawnee
If I Got My Ticket, Can I Ride?	M	Shaw	9852	G. Schirmer
I'll Sail Upon the Dog-Star	M	Purcell-Tkach	82189	Flammer
In Silent Night	E-M	Brahms-Gibb	1664	Boston
In That New Jerusalem	M	De-Cormier TTBB	51091	G. Schirmer
Infant Holy	E	Ferucci (Polish)	S 007	Boston
Intercession	M-D	Holst, G.	5360	Boosey
In the Doorways I Will Linger	M-D	Schubert-Rider	875	G. Schirmer
I Travel Far But Take No Rest (Basque) (Tenor Solo)	D	Sorozabel-Davis	W 3634	MPH
I Wish I Was Single Again	E-M	Scott	C-94	Shawnee
I Wonder As I Wander	M	Niles	9202	G. Schirmer
Jack Was Every Inch A Sailor	E	Hunter TB	LG 778	G. Schirmer
Jesu, Joy of Man's Desiring	M	Bach-Treharne	8389	G. Schirmer
Johnny Stiles (Bass Solo)	M-D	Kubik		Southern
Keep A-Inchin' Along	E	Johnson	10485	G. Schirmer
Komm, Susser Tod (German)	M-D	Bach	7565	J. Fischer
L'Amour de Moy (Tenor Solo)	M	Parker, Shaw	51044	G. Schirmer
Land Sighting	M	Grieg	1013	G. Schirmer
Laudes de Saint Antoine de Paduoe (Set of 4. one)	D	Poulenc TTBB	Ed Salabert	Colombo
Laura Lee (Tenor Solo)	E-M	Foster-Parker, Shaw	874	G. Schirmer
Let All the World in Every Corner Sing	E	Lang TB	E 86	Oxford
Let Me Go Warm	M	Gordon, P.	SK 1002	Shapiro
Let Me Wander Not Unseen	M-D	Handel	41602	Hoff
Let Not Your Song End	M	Cain	82172	Flammer
Let There Be Music	E	Williams	82145	Flammer
Lieder Und Romanzen (German & English)	D	Brahms	10711	G. Schirmer
Linden Lea	E	R. V. Williams	1991	Boosey
Little Drummer Boy	M-D	Simeone (Davis)	C 160	Shawnee
Loch Lomand	M-D	Ringwald		Shawnee
Lo, How A Rose E'er Blooming	E-M	Praetorius	LG 555	G. Schirmer
Love In Her Eyes Sits Playing	M-D	Handel-Horrocks	2594	Galaxy
Maiden Fair, O Deign To Tell (Humorous Serenade)	M	Haydn	527	Gray
Make A Joyful Sound	M	Ramsfield TTBB-Acc.	C 174	Shawnee
Marianina	E	Parker, Shaw	974	G. Schirmer
Marry a Woman Uglier Than You (Solo)	M	de Paur	543	G. Schirmer
Mary Had A Baby	E-M	Shaw-Parker	10191	G. Schirmer
Melodies of the Middle Ages	M	Langstroth	332-40109	Presser
Must I Then (German-English)	M	Arr. Lynn TTBB	901	G. Schirmer
My Heart Commends Itself to Thee	M	diLasso-Daltry	368	Wood
My Horn Shall Weight A Willow Bough	M	Brahms	1464	G. Schirmer
My Lord, What a Mornin'	E	Stewart-Reynolds TBB and/or SSA	K17	Hansen
Na Bahia Tem	M	Villa-Lobos, H.	ME 2312	Associated
Nachtliches Standehen (Night Song)	E-M	Schubert	U 12332	Presser
Navy Hymn, The	E-M	Dykes-Scott	137	Witmark
Night	M-D	Schubert-Erb	LG 786	G. Schirmer
Noel, Noel	E	Gevaert	5513	Kjos
Non Nobis Domino	E	Quilter TB	348	Boosey
Now Let Every Tongue Adore Thee	M	Bach	30	E.C. Schirmer
Now Thank We All Our God	M	Cruger-Barrow	2115	E.C. Schirmer
O Bone Jesu (Latin)	M-D	Palestrina	ES 45	Bourne
O Bone Jesu, O Mighty God, Our Lord	E	Schutz TB	ES 527	E.C. Schirmer
Oh Rejoice, Ye Christians Loudly	D	Bach-Saar	545	E.C. Schirmer
Old Dusty Trail, The	E	Miller	3109	Choral Press
Old King Cole	E-M	Okun, M.	51089	G. Schirmer
One More River	M	Anon-Warlock	1854	Boosey
O Nightingale	E	Gordon, P.	SK 1001	Shapiro
O Peaceful Night	M	German	497	Gray
Passing By	M	Purcell-Shaw	LG 795	G. Schirmer
Pastorella, La	D	Schubert	LG 512	G. Schirmer
Pasture, The	D	Thompson TBB	2181	E. C. Schirmer
Peacocks, The	D	Kodaly	1891	Boosey
Poor Lonesome Cowboy	E	Luboff	1007	Walton
Prayer	M	Malin	3123	Summy
Punch	M	Bartholomew	MC-150	Presser
Red Iron Ore	M	Forbes	10733	G. Schirmer
Red, Red, Rose, A	M	Schumann	LG 781	G. Schirmer
Regina Coeli (Latin)	D	Aichinger TTB	NY 1848	Colombo
Ruins, The	D	Kodaly TBB	U 10877	Presser
Rustics and Fisherman "Gloriana"	M	Britten	5017	Boosey

TITLE	GRADE	COMPOSER	NUMBER	PUBLISHER
Serenade	M-D	Thiman, E.	1132	Mills
Serenaders, The (Canto di Caccia)	E	A.T.D.	929	E. C. Schirmer
Silver Moon Is Shining, The (Tu mi vuoi tanto bene)	M	A.T.D.	929	E. C. Schirmer
Simple Gifts	E	Copland-Fine TB Acc.	1903	Boosey
She Is My Slender Small Love	D	Thiman	10671	G. Schirmer
Shepherds, Awake	E	K. K. Davis	G 1580	MPH
Sing, Maiden, Sing	D	Palmgren	7553	J. Fischer
Sing of the Noble Selim's Glory	E-M	Mozart-H. G. M.	2144	E. C. Schirmer
Song of the Guerillas	M	Copland TTB	1729	Boosey
Songs Mein Grossmama Sang	D	Pfautsch Acc.	51021	G. Schirmer
Soon One Mornin'	E	Gilliam	10770	G. Schirmer
Spanish Ladies (Baritone Solo)	E-M	Shaw	51051	G. Schirmer
Spirit of Love	D	Schubert	LG 774	G. Schirmer
Stars of the Summer Night	M	Woodbury-Shaw	LG 539	G. Schirmer
Stopping by Woods on a Snowy Evening	D	Thompson TBB	2182	E. C. Schirmer
Streets of Laredo	M	Hunter	LG 777	G. Schirmer
Studentenschmauss	M	Schein-G. W. W.	10571	G. Schirmer
Swansea Town	M	Holst, G.	8096	G. Schirmer
Swansea Town	M	Parker, Shaw	51052	G. Schirmer
Sweet Love Doth Now Invite	M	Dowland	ES 7	Bourne
Tell Me, Fair One (Dimmi, O Bella) (Tenor Solo)	M	A.T.D.	929	E. C. Schirmer
Ten Glees (Madrigals & Airs)	M	Sel. & Ed. Bartholomew	MC 121	Presser
Thanks Be to Thee	E	Handel Acc.	1222	Galaxy
This Is My Country (Festival Edition)	M	Jacobs-Ringwald TTBB-Acc.	C 170	Shawnee
Three Folk Songs TWO	E	Brahms	4247	Marks
Three German Folk Songs	E-M	Arr. Linn		G. Schirmer
1. The Hunter from Kurpfalz			900	
2. Must I Then			901	
3. Holla Hiaho			902	
Timber	E	House-Hoffman	PS 65	Fox
To Spring	M	Schubert	10100	G. Schirmer
Tranquility	M	Gibbs	M 6	Oxford
Treue Liebe (German)	M	Shaw	LG 669	G. Schirmer
Turne Backe, You Wanton Flyer	M		684	G. Schirmer
Tutti Venite Armati	M	Gastoldi	964	E. C. Schirmer
Vagabond, The	M	Vaughan Williams	5454	Boosey
Veni Sponsa Christi (Latin)	M	Monteverdi TTB	NY 2032	Colombo
Virgen Lava Panales, La (Contralto Solo)	M	Shaw, Parker	10198	G. Schirmer
Viva L'Amour	M	Shaw-Parker	51026	G. Schirmer
Viva Tutti	E	Hunter TTB	LG 778	G. Schirmer
Verdant Meadows	M	Handel TTB	9145	J. Fischer
Waltzing Matilda	E-M	Cowan	CM 7091	C. Fischer
Warning	M	Mozart	2146	E. C. Schirmer
We Be Soldiers Three	M	Bartholomew TBB	MC 151	Presser
We Be Soldiers Three & We Three Poor Mariners	M	Ravenscroft TBB	ES 13	Bourne
We Hasten to Ask Thine Aid	D	Bach TB Acc.	7552	J. Fischer
We Pray to Thee	M	Palestrina	5540	Kjos
What Do We Plant?	M	Copland TB Acc. and/or SA	1639	Boosey
When Johnny Comes Marching Home	E	Heath	10873	G. Schirmer
Widerspruch (Contradiction)	M	Schubert-Parker	513	G. Schirmer
With Voices Rejoicing	E	Mozart	2183	E. C. Schirmer
Women	M	Gordon, P.	129	Elkan-Vogel
World It Went Well With Me Then, The	M	Williams	637	Oxford
World's Good Morrow, The	E-M	A. Woodgate, L.	5238	Boosey
Zion Hears the Watchman Singing	D	Buxtehude TB	538	E. C. Schirmer

MADRIGAL LIST
SATB unless otherwise indicated

TITLE	GRADE	COMPOSER	NUMBER	PUBLISHER
A Cappella Singer	E-D	Clough-Leighter SATB-SSATB	1682	E. C. Schirmer
Ah, May the Sun	M	Palestrina	ES 61	Bourne
Ah, Wilt Thou Leave Me?	D	Stanton	838	G. Schirmer
All Creatures Now Are Merry Minded	M	Bennett SSATB	665	Gray
All Happiness Love Gives to Me	E	Hassler	ES 62	Bourne
Allon, Gay Bergeres (French)	E	Costeley	10178	G. Schirmer
All Ye Who Music Love	M	D. Donato SSATB	ES 63	Bourne
Amarilli, Mia Bella (Italian & English)	D	Caccini-Vree	LG 927	G. Schirmer

TITLE	GRADE	COMPOSER	NUMBER	PUBLISHER
April is in My Mistress Face	E	Morley-Churchill	748	Bourne
Ballett	E	Stephanie SSATB	2144	Pro Art
Big Fat Goose (German-English)	M	di Lasso-Mason	7002	Walton
Cold Winter, Villain That Thou Art	D	Debussy		Elkan-Vogel
(#3 Trois Chansons - French & English)				
Come Again, Sweet Love	M	Dowland	81274	Flammer
Come Away Death	M	Vaughan Williams SSATB	13	Galaxy
Come, Let Your Hearts Be Singing	E	Gastoldi	ES 26	Bourne
Come Now, Let Us Be Joyful (Italian & English)	M	Vecchi	ES 64	Bourne
Cor Mio Mentre vi Miro (Italian & English)	M	Monteverdi SSATB	10432	Associated
Dancing and Springing	M	Hassler SSATB	CM 4645	C. Fischer
Echo Song	E	DiLasso	5802	G. Schirmer
Fair Maid, Thy Charm, Thy Loveliness	E	Hassler	ES 43	Bourne
Fa, la, la, I Cannot Conceal It	E	Certon	ES 42	Bourne
Fain Would I Change That Note	E	Vaughan Williams	587	Gray
Fair Phyllis I Saw	M	Farmer	1664-15	Galaxy
Farewell My Love	E	Anonymous-Hirt	CM 701	C. Fischer
Fa Una Canzone (Italian)	E	Vecchi	LG 56	G. Schirmer
Fire, Fire My Heart	D	Morley SSATB	ES 65	Bourne
Go Lovely Rose	D	Halsey Stevens		Row
Good Day, My Dear (French-English)	E	di Lasso	ES 49	Bourne
Hard By A Fountain	E	Waelrant	543	Gray
I Know a Young Maiden (German)	E	Lassus-Hirt	CM 7039	C. Fischer
Il Est Bel Et Bon (He is Good) (French)	M	Passereau	ES 9	Bourne
Innsbruck, I Now Must Leave Thee	M	Isaac	CM 4704	C. Fischer
In the Merry Spring	M	Ravenscroft	W 2631	MPH
It Was a Lover and His Lass	E	Morley	275	Galaxy
Like As A Culver	D	Stevens SSATB	A 218	Associated
Little White Hen, A (German)	M	Scandello	ES 29	Bourne
Lord, Lovely Hast Thou Made My Dear	D	Debussy		Elkan-Vogel
(#1 Trois Chansons - French & English)				
Love Is A Sickness	E	Vaughan Williams	97	Galaxy
My Bonny Lass	E	Morley-Harris	81277	Flammer
My Heart is Offered Still to Thee (French)	E	Lassus	LG 563	G. Schirmer
My Heart With Love Is Springing	E	Hassler	ES	Bourne
Nicolette (#1 Trois Chansons) (French & English)	D	Ravel		Elkan-Vogel
O Eyes of My Beloved (Italian & English)	E	Di Lasso	1146	E. C. Schirmer
O Lovely Splendor	E	Palestrina-Mason	7013	Walton
O Mistress Mine	M	Vaughan Williams	243	Mills
O Stay, Sweet Love	M	Farmer	312-40091	Presser
Revecy Venir du Printemps (French)	D	LeJeune (Divisi)	RB-5	Flammer
Roundelay (#3 Trois Chansons) (French & English)	D	Ravel		Elkan-Vogel
She, Now Seeing the Time	M	Janequin	312-40448	Presser
Silver Swan, The	D	Gibbons	ES 18	Bourne
Since First I Saw Your Face	E	Thomas Ford	W 2967	MPH
Since My Tears and Lamenting	E	Morley-Hirt	CM 7040	C. Fischer
Sing We and Chant It	E	Morley SSATB	81276	Flammer
Six Chansons (French and English)	D	Hindemith	10454-59	Associated
(The Doe, The Swan, Since All Is Passing.				
Springtime, In Winter, The Orchard)				
Sweet Honey Sucking Bees	D	Wilbye SSATB	GS 8781	G. Schirmer
Sweet Suffolk Owl	M	Vautor SSATB	10297	G. Schirmer
Three Lovely Birds From Paradise	D	Ravel Sop. Solo		Elkan-Vogel
(#2 Trois Chansons - French & English)				
Tomorrow the Fox Will Come to Town	M	Ravenscroft	41	Oxford
To Take the Air a Bonny Lass Went Walking	M	Farmer	MT 488	Gray
Two-Faced Love	M	Costeley	869	G. Schirmer
Two Madrigals (Italian-English)	E	Palestrina	MC 58	Presser
Weep O Mine Eyes	E	Bennet	ES 30	Bourne
Weep O Mine Eyes	D	Halsey Stevens SSATB		Row
Whene'er the Tambourine I Hear	D	Debussy		Elkan-Vogel
(#2 Trois Chansons - French & English)				
Willow Song, The	M	Vaughan Williams	242	Mills
Renaissance to Baroque	M-D	Lehman Engel		Flammer

1. French
2. Italian
3. English
4. German
5. Spanish

JUNIOR HIGH SCHOOL

Note:

Consideration was given by the committee to the special problems of the intermediate school (grades 7 and 8 only). It is hoped that sufficient materials are contained herein to encourage such groups to participate in festivals.

UNISON

TITLE	GRADE	COMPOSER AND/OR ARR.	NUMBER	PUBLISHER
Brother James' Air (Unison w/descant)	EM	Arr. Jacob	OCS166	Oxford
Canticle of Peace, A	M	Clokey	B340	Summy
Come, Together Let us Sing (any unison arr.)	E	J. S. Bach	1001	E.C. Schirmer
Et Exultavit Spiritus Meus	M	Bach-Whittaker	OCS 1440	Oxford
Friday Afternoons (select any two of the twelve)	EM	B. Britten		Boosey
If With All Your Hearts	M	Mendelssohn	GS 5896	G. Schirmer
Jewish Year in Song, The (select one)	MD	A. W. Binder	Ed 1330	G. Schirmer
For All These Our Sins				
O Give Thanks				
Come To Me My Little One				
Let All Things Now Living	EM	Arr. K. K. Davis	1819	E.C. Schirmer
(unison with descant) Festival, Spring, Graduation				
Like As a Father (3 equal voices)	E	Cherubini	5297	Summy
She's Like the Swallow	E	Arr. R. V. Williams	U47	Oxford
Spacious Firmament (with descant)	M	Haydn-K. K. Davis	1829	E.C. Schirmer
Through All The Year (unison with descant)	EM	Arr. Pitcher	30	Birchard
Velvet Shoes	E	Thompson	2526	E.C. Schirmer
Wondrous Love (with descant)	E	Arr. Thiman	MF 593	Berkeley

UNISON (OR *BOYS' VOICES)

TITLE	GRADE	COMPOSER AND/OR ARRANGER	NUMBER	PUBLISHER
*Gentle Jesus Ever Blest (Pie Jesu)	EM	Faure-Kjelson		Belwin
(English or Latin)				
Grant Us Light (Unison w/descant)	E	Thiman	10280	G. Schirmer
Hush Baby; No More Weeping (recorder part opt.)	E	arr. Copely	U97	Oxford
My Heart Ever Faithful	D	J. S. Bach	ECS 1009	E. C. Schirmer
Sheep May Safely Graze	M	J. S. Bach		
(any unison arrangement)				
The Singers from THREE CHILDREN'S SONGS	E	R. Vaughn Williams	OCS 1032	Oxford
*Verdant Meadows	E	Handel		
(any unison arrangement)				

WOMEN'S VOICES

SA unless otherwise indicated

TITLE	GRADE	COMPOSER	NUMBER	PUBLISHER
Alleluia from Motet "Exsultate Jubilate"	M	Mozart-Riegger		Flammer
All Praises to the Lord	M	Bach-Baird	9491	G. Schirmer
Barbara Allen	M	Arr. Ager	1878	Boosey
Break Forth, O Beauteous Heavenly Light	E	Bach		
(Any standard 2 pt. arrangement				
also found in collections)				
Bonnie Wood of Craigielea	E	Arr. Nightingale	2008	Walton's Galleries
Christmas Dance of The Shepherds (opt. piccolo)	E	Kodaly	5172	Presser
Come All Ye Fair and Tender Ladies	E		51120	Lawson-Gould
(with instrumental accompaniments)				
Come, Ye Children and Hearken to Me	E	Steffani-Weinhorst	98-1593	Concordia
Deaf Old Woman, The (also SB and TB for	E	Arr. K. K. Davis	1645	Galaxy
Boys Voices instruments opt.)				
Down in Trinidad	EM	Arr. Schillio	312-40498	Presser
Give Ear Unto Me	M	Marcello	1522	Gray
How Lovely are Messengers	E	Mendelssohn-Moss	4397	J. Fischer
In Dulci Jubilo	MD	Praetorius-Greer	CM 411	C. Fischer
Ipse Te Cogat Pietas (Latin)	M	di Lasso	1995	E.C. Schirmer
Kyrie Eleison & Agnus Dei	MD	Peeters	1692	McLaughlin
(Missa In Honorem Reginae Pacis)				
Little Lamb Who Made Thee	M	Roff	E 8	Shawnee
Lo, My Shepherd's Hand Divine from (Mass in G)	MD	Haydn-Barthleson	5013	
Lord Bless You, The	D	Bach-Bunjes	98-1474	Concordia
May Day Carol	MD	Taylor	4873	J. Fischer
My Shepherd	E	Bach-Hirt	W 3683	Witmark
Now All The Woods Are Sleeping	E	Bach-Isaak	ECS 1567	E.C. Schirmer
Now Sing We and Chant It (Cantata 208)	M	Bach-Diack		Paterson's
Oh, Hold Thou Me Up	MD	Marcello-Weinhorst	98-1046	Concordia
One Thing Have I Desired	EM	Schuetz-Leupold	98-1369	Concordia
Panis Angelicus (O Lord Most Holy)	EM	Franck-Kjelson	1971	Belwin
(Also TB — can be found in collections)				

TITLE	GRADE	COMPOSER AND/OR ARR.	NUMBER	PUBLISHER
Three Excerpts from "Peasant Cantata"	M	Bach-Campbell-Watson	W 3427	Witmark
(select two also SSA)				
Sanctus: Holy, Holy, Holy	D	Fauré	5017	Flammer
Simple Gifts (Also TB.)	EM	Copland-Fine	1903	Boosey
Six Children's Choruses (pub. separately)		Bartok		Boosey
Hussar 2-part	E			
Only Tell Me 3part	M			
Loafer 3-part	M			
Bread Baking 3-part	E			
Don't Leave Me 3-part	E			
Teasing Song 3-part	D			
Sound The Trumpet	MD	Purcell-Erb	LG 787	G. Schirmer
These Things Shall Be from (Psalmodia Evangelica)	EM	Krones		Kjos
Three Folk Songs (Also TB.)	M	Brahms-Ehret	4116	Marks
Three Hungarian Folk Songs (select one)	M	Arr. Seiber	10826	G. Schirmer
Three Love Songs Opus 52 (with violin obligato)	D	Brahms	1055	E.C. Schirmer
Like the Sunset's Crimson Splendor				
Bird in Air Will Stray Afar				
Seat Thyself, My Dearest Heart				
Tum-Balalaika (Also TB)	EM	Arr. Suchoff	4167	Marks
Two Elizabethian Madrigals (select one)	MD	Morley & Bennett-		Shapiro
Sing We and Chant It		Fellowes		
Since First Disdain Began to Rise				
We Hasten With Eager But Faltering Footsteps	MD	Bach	2506	E.C. Schirmer
When Jesus Wept (with opt. 3rd voice or solo also TB)	E	Billings-Kjelson	1972	Belwin
Ye Sons and Daughters	M	Arr. Kjelson	2025	Belwin

SSA unless otherwise indicated

TITLE	GRADE	COMPOSER AND/OR ARR.	NUMBER	PUBLISHER
All The Pretty Little Horses	E	Arr. Owen	312-40518	Presser
Alleluia from Cantata "For Us a Child Is Born"	M	Bach	1012	Galaxy
Alleluia from Motet "Exsultate, Jubilate"	D	Mozart-Rieggar	89024	Flammer
At The Gate of Heaven	E	Arr. Allen	B 1570	Summy
Ava Maria	M	Schubert-Reigger		
Ave Maria (A cappella)	D	Vittoria-Scott	R 106	Choral Art
Ave Verum	D	de Pres-G.W.W.	816	E.C. Schirmer
Birch Tree, The	D	Arr. Stone & MacLean	2W3404	Witmark
Candu	E	Arr. DeCesare	L 8101	
Cantate Domino (Latin)	M	Pitoni-Greyson	ES 47	Bourne
Canticle of Praise (opt. orchestra)	E	Arr. Jurey	676	Mills
Cantiga de Ninar	E	Mignone	4112	Summy
Carnations Grew In My Garden	D	R. Schumann	1999	E.C. Schirmer
Celebration of Spring	MD	Franz-Skiles	312-40-425	Presser
Come Let us Start a Joyful Song (A cappella)	M	Hassler-Greyson	ES 31	Bourne
Dona Nobis Pacem	E	any arr. Latin only		
Echo Song	D	di Lasso	ES 25	Bourne
Evening Rondeau (A cappella)	D	Purcell-Jacques	OM 6	Oxford
Every Night When The Sun Goes In	EM	Arr. Owen	312-40524	Presser
For The Beauty of The Earth	E	Kocher-K. K. Davis	R 3268	
Glorious Apollo	EM	Webb	1970	E.C. Schirmer
Gute Nacht (German & English)	D	Schumann-G.W.W.	819	E.C. Schirmer
Hansel & Gretel, selections	MD	Humperdinck-Krone		Kjos
Susie Little Susie			1218	
Dance in the Cottage			1219	
Little Man in the Wood			1220	
Prayer			1221	
Song of the Dew Fairy			1222	
Come Sing and Dance			1223	
He's Gone Away	E	Arr. E. Jurey	312-40418	Presser
How Sweet I Roam'd	MD	Blake-Thomas	667	Gray
I Gave My Love a Pretty Little Ring	E	Arr. K. K. Davis	B 140	Summy
Il Court, Le Fuert (The Ferret of the Woods)	MD	Arr. Biggs	312-40525	Presser
(French or English)				
In a Cottage by the Green (A cappella)	D	Purcell-Moffat	640	Mills
In Natali Domini	M	Praetorius-Glaser	1993	E.C. Schirmer
In Paradisum from (The Requiem)	M	Fauré	W 3574	Witmark
In Silent Night (violin obligato)	D	Brahms-Rieger	83089	Flammer
In the Bamboo Wood	MD	Graham	312-40552	Presser
Jesu, Joy of Man's Desiring	M	Bach-Campbell-Watson	G 1552	Remick
(any 2-3-or 4 part arrangement)				
Jesu, Priceless Treasure	M	Arr. Perry	1045	Belwin
Keep an Eye on Me	M	Gustafson	312-40349	Presser
Laud We the Name from (Cantata #142)	D	Bach-K. K. Davis	2054	Galaxy
Let Our Gladness Know No End	M	Arr. K. K. Davis		E.C. Schirmer
Lift Thine Eyes (also found in collections)	M	Mendelssohn	26	G. Schirmer
Lo, How a Rose E'er Blooming	M	Praetorius	157	E.C. Schirmer
Lullaby, My Sweet Little Baby	M	Byrd-Greyson	ES 10	Bourne
Madrigal for Spring	M	Roff	5183	Boosey
May Day Carol	D	Taylor	4872	J. Fischer
Miserere Mei (Latin)	M	Lotti-Wilson	5232	Boosey
Mom'Zell Zizi	E	Arr. Schillio	312-40495	Presser
Morning Song	MD	Mozart	622	Boston
Morning Star, The	M	Praetorius-Shand	8593	G. Schirmer
My Lord, What a Mornin' (SSAA)	M	Arr. Turner	312-40544	Presser
My True Love Hath My Heart	D	Kirk	5012	Summy
Night-Herding Song (string bass ad lib)	EM	Arr. Owen	312-40522	Presser
Now I Lay Me Down to Sleep	MD	Thompson	1985	E.C. Schirmer
O Domini Jesu Christi	M	Palestrina-Harris	89161	Flammer

TITLE	GRADE	COMPOSER AND/OR ARR.	NUMBER	PUBLISHER
Oh! Cordelia Brown (instruments opt.)	M	Arr. Schillio	312-40446	Presser
O Filii et Filiae	MD	Liszt-Gevaert	868	E.C. Schirmer
On the Shores of Kineret	MD	Arr. Karczevski & Freed	TCL 308	Transcontinental
Pavan (A cappella)	D	Byrd-Bell	576	Mills
Popcorn Carnival	EM	Gustafson	312-40282	Presser
Peace Comes to Me	D	Murray	1726	Boosey
Preach Not Me Your Musty Rules (A Cappella)	M	Arne-Kraft	2071	Schmitt
Air from "Comus"				
Recordata	D	Palestrina-Castellazzi-Vené	NY 2-33	Ricordi
Red Rosey Bush	D	Arr. Young-Breck	CM 5282	C. Fischer
Rejoice in God O Ye Righteous (SSAA a cappella)	EM	Bach-Coleman	312-40556	Presser
Riddle, The	E	Arr. Owen	312-40884	Presser
Rolling Hills	EM	Arr. Gustafson	312-40345	Presser
Sacred Songs for the Night (select two of four)	D	Bright	B 190	Shawnee
Sakura, Sakura	E	Arr. Hairston	J 1	Bourne
Shoheen (Cradle Song)	M	Starr-Wells	2121	Schmitt
Silent Worship (A cappella)	MD	Handel-Jacobsson	9976	G. Schirmer
Silver Swan, The	M	Arr. Gibbons	284	Wood
Sleep Little One	M	Nelson	5262	Boosey
Sleep of The Child Jesus		Arr. Crowell	312-40569	Presser
Spruce Tree Carol (divisi)	M	Warner	B 1612	Summy
Stars, The	EM	Arr. K. K. Davis	1998	E.C. Schirmer
Thanks Be to Thee	EM	Handel-McKinney	8952	J. Fischer
Three Excerpts from "Peasant Cantata" (select two)	M	Bach-Sister Elaine	W 3445	Witmark
Three Folk Songs (select two)	EM	Brahms-Ehret	4017	Marks
To Music (instruments optional)	MD	Schubert-Wilson	2083	Schmitt
Turtle Dove, The	MD	Arr. Ahrold	312-40542	Presser
Tutu Maramba	EM	Arr. Erb	637	Lawson-Gould
Water Is Wide, The	M	Adapted Zaninelli		Shawnee
Weep, O Mine Eyes	M	Wilbye-G.W.W.	841	E.C. Schirmer
We Strolled One Day	M	Brahms-Gibb	3500	Walton's Galleries
Woodland Journey, A	M	Arr. Hartshorne	2W3423	Witmark

TREBLE VOICES (OR *BOYS' VOICES)

SA unless otherwise indicated

Children of the Heavenly Father	E	Arr. Ehret		Boosey
FOUR INNOCENT AIRS (pub. separately)				
A Cradle Song	M	Bacon	708	Lawson-Gould
The Schoolboy	MD		707	
*Hark the Vesper Hymn (SA TB or SAB or double alto)	E	arr. Kjelson	Bel 2063	Belwin
*Jesus Walked This Lonesome Valley	E	arr. Kjelson		Belwin
I Go Before, My Charmer (SA or TB)	M	Morley	ECS 824	E. C. Schirmer
See! Lovely Day Is Dawning	M	Morley	ECS 1994	E. C. Schirmer
Sing Unto the Lord A New Song	E	Couperin	98-1709	Concordia
Sugar and Cinnamon	M	Cromie	312-40520	Presser
THREE TWO-PART SONGS (pub. separately)				Oxford
Rainbow, The	M	Britten	OCS 169	
Ride-by-Nights, The	D		OCS 168	
*Ships of Rio, The	M		OCS 170	
*What Do We Plant	D	Copland	1639	Boosey
Younger Generation	E	Copland-Swift	5506	Boosey

SSA unless otherwise indicated

*Angelus ad Pastores est (also TBB)	D	Monteverdi-Field	5545	Boosey
FOUR INNOCENT AIRS (pub. separately)				
Return of Spring	M	Bacon	705	Lawson-Gould
Where Go the Boats?	M		706	
Hodie Christus Natus Est (also TBB)	D	Monteverdi-Field	5545	Boosey
I Think!	D	Bonnell	306	Staff
Mother, I Will Have A Husband	D	Vautor	ES 11	Bourne
O Can Ye Sew Cushions?	MD	arr. Holst	5213	Boosey
Prayer of St. Francis	MD	Nieland	ESA 513-3	World Library
Tantum Ergo	D	Faure	ECS 861	E. C. Schirmer
To Make A Prairie	M	Owen	312-40613	Presser
Welcome Sweet Pleasure	D	Weelkes-Harris	738	Wood
Young Lubin	D	Hook-Rowley	663	Mills

MIXED OR BOYS' VOICES

SAB unless otherwise indicated

Title		Arranger/Composer	No.	Publisher	Price
Away For Rio	M	Arr. Christy	5002	Schmitt	.18
Bells of Aberdovey, The	E	Arr. B. Krone	1402	Kjos	.22
Campfire Blues	EM	Gustafson	CM 6864	C. Fischer	.20
Come Sing This Round With Me	M	Martin	ES 32	Bourne	
Glory to God in The Highest	E	Whitford	5518	Schmitt	.22
I Gave My Love a Pretty Little Ring	E	Arr. K. K. Davis	5548	Summy	.35
Keep An Eye On Me	M	Gustafson	312-40452	Presser	.22
Kum Ba Yah	E	Arr. Ehret	4000	Marks	.30
Maiden Fair	M	Haydn	W 2733	Witmark	.20
Popcorn Carnival	EM	Gustafson	312-40459	Presser	.25
Rolling Hills	EM	Gustafson	312-40451	Presser	.25
Sleep of The Child Jesus	E	Arr. Crowell	312-40447	Presser	.20
Sun Don't Set in the Morning	E	Arr. Papp	312-40574	Presser	.25
Three Folk Songs (A cappella)	M	Brahms-Ehret	4096	Marks	.20
To Music	M	Schubert-Wilson	5011	Schmitt	.18
Who Chopped Down the Cherry Tree?	E	Gustafson	312-40450	Presser	.22

SATB unless otherwise indicated

Title		Arranger/Composer	No.	Publisher
Alleluia from Cantata "For Us A Child Is Born"	M	Bach	1010	Galaxy
Almighty and Everlasting God	D	Gibbons-Greyson	ES 35	Bourne
Anthem on "Marion"	MD	Willan	6063	Peters
Ave Verum Corpus	D	Byrd	520	Galaxy
Banana Boat Song, The	MD	Darling, Carey, Arkin, Simeone	A 433	Shawnee
Bonnie Blue Flag, The	M	Arr. Nightingale	2011	Gillman
Boonie Wood of Craigielea	M	Arr. Nightingale	2000	Gillman
Brother James' Air	EM	Arr. Jacob	94P316	Oxford
Cantate Domino	M	Pitoni-Greyson	ES 5	Bourne
Canticle of Peace, A	M	Clokey	B 340	Summy
Canticle of Praise (opt. orchestra)	E	Arr. E. Jurey	416	Mills
Campfire Blues	EM	Gustafson	CM 6863	C. Fischer
Chester	M	Billings	LG 501	G. Schirmer
Cicirinella (English text)	E	Arr. Krone	5-W2952	Witmark
Climbin' Up the Mountain	M	Arr. Smith	1001	Kjos
Colorado Trail, The	EM	Arr. Nightingale	2003	Gillman
Dance A Cachucha	E	Gilbert & Sullivan-Weaver	135	Mills
Deaf Old Woman, The	E	Arr. K. K. Davis	1262	Galaxy
Dear Evelina, Sweet Evelina	EM	Arr. Nightingale	2014	Gillman
De Profundis (O, I Cry Unto Thee) (Latin & English)	D	Gluck-Mason	6007	Walton
Dimmi, dolce Maria	D			
O Maria Diana Stella	EM	Laude of 15th Century	2222	G. Schirmer
Dona Nobis Pacem (Latin only)	E	Anv arrangement		
Don't Delay	M	Liadov-Mason	7004	Walton
Ezekiel Saw de Wheel	E	Arr. H. R. Wilson	1610	Schmitt
Every Night When the Sun Goes In	M	Arr. Owen	312-40523	Presser
Faithful Cross	D	King John IV of Portugal	87502	Flammer
Forward March	E	Arr. Schillio	312-40497	Presser
Geborn ist Gottes Sohnelein (God's Infant Son)	EM	Praetorius-Beveridge	9640	G. Schirmer
Gloria Patri (Glory to God) (Double Chorus)	MD	Palestrina-Greyson	ES 46	Bourne
Good-Day, My Dear	D	di Lasso-Greyson	ES 49	E.C. Schirmer
Good News!	MD	Arr. L. Kjelson	CM 7194	C. Fischer
Gonna Ride Up In The Chariot	M	Arr. Rhea	3013	Bourne
Hallelujah, Amen from "Judas Maccabeus"	MD	Handel-Brooks	C.C.7	Plymouth
I Feel Like My Time Ain't Long	E	Arr. W.G. Still	312-40304	Presser
If Ye Love Me Keep My Commandments	D	Tallis-H. Clough-Leighter	2269	E.C. Schirmer
I Know a Young Maiden	M	di Lasso-Hirt	CM 7039	C. Fischer
I'm Just a Poor Wayfarin' Stranger	M	Arr. L. Kjelson	2027	Belwin
In Thee O Lord, Have I Trusted	E	Handel-Ehret	MC 361	Mercury
I Saw a Pretty Girl	E	Arr. Nightingale	2001	Gillman
Jesu, Word of God Incarnate (Ave Verum)	M	Mozart	6813	G. Schirmer
Keep An Eye On Me	E	Gustafson	312-40284	Presser
Laud We Thy Name	MD	Bach-K. K. Davis	2054	Galaxy
Lolly Too-Dum	EM	Arr. Nightingale	2015	Gillman
Lorena	EM	Arr. Nightingale	2016	Gillman
Love Somebody, Yes I Do	M	Arr. Smale	2235	Summy
Mailied (May Song)	D	Mendelssohn	5348	Summy

TITLE	GRADE	COMPOSER AND/OR ARR.	NUMBER	PUBLISHER
Matona, Lovely Maiden	D	di Lasso	G.S. 2421	G. Schirmer
Michael Finnigin	M	Arr. Cooper	C 505	Bourne
Miserere Mei (Latin)	D	Lotti-Ehret & Wilson	1938	Boosey
My Heart Doth Beg You'll Not Forget	D	di Lasso	ESC 1145	E.C. Schirmer
My Redeemer	E	Bilings-Sanders	2112	Galaxy
Night-Herding Song	M	Arr. Owen	312-40521	Presser
O Bone Jesu (Latin)	D	Palestrina-Deis	10022	G. Schirmer
O Eyes Of My Beloved	D	di Lasso	ECS 1146	E.C. Schirmer
Oh! Cordelia Brown	D	Arr. Schillio	312-40551	Presser
O How My Heart Rejoices	D	Obrecht-Mason	7011	Walton
Oh, How My Heart Rejoices	MD	Praetorius-Mason	7012	Walton
Olympic Hymn	D	Linn-Swift	4502	Gillman
On the Way To My Sweetheart	M	Brahms-Matesky	4007	Gillman
Pick a Bale o' Cotton	EM	Arr. Nightingale	2018	Gillman
Poor Wayfaring Stranger	E	Arr. Vree	312-40341	Presser
Popcorn Carnival	M	Gustafson	312-40415	Presser
Psallite (Now We Sing)	EM	Praetorius-Greyson	ES 21	Bourne
Resonet In Laudibus (double chorus)	MD	Gallus Handel-Greyson	ES 6	Bourne
Riddle, The	M	Arr. Owen	312-40568	Presser
Rolling Hills	M	Gustafson	312-40283	Presser
Sadly I Recall Thy Vow	D	Mikolai of Cracow	2143	Fro Art
She Is So Dear	M	Praetorius	332-14558	Ditson
Six Folk Songs (select any two of first four songs)	M	Brahms	AJ 9	Marks
Sleep, Baby, Sleep	EM	Bell-Shaw		Shawnee
Song Of Galilee	D	Arr. Chajes	TCL 214	Transcontinental
Three Folk Songs	M	Brahms-Ehret	4017	Marks
To Music	M	Schubert-Wilson	1070	Schmitt
Tum-Balalaika	E	Arr. Suchoff	4143	Marks
When Allen-A-Dale Went A-Hunting	D	DePearsall-Mason	7018	Walton
When Jesus Wept	MD	Billings-Gustafson	11145	G. Schirmer
Who Chopped Down the Cherry Tree?	EM	Gustafson	312-40340	Presser
Wondrous Love	EM	Arr. Christiansen	1140	Augsburg
Ye Sons and Daughters Now Shall Sing	M	Arr. L. Kjelson	2025	Belwin

MIXED (OR *BOYS' VOICES)

*Agnus Dei (Latin)	M	Hassler	ES1	Bourne
*All Ye Who Music Love	D	Donato	ES 63	Bourne
*Alleluia from Cantata "For Us A Child Is Born"	M	J. S. Bach	1010	Galaxy
Boll Weevil Song	M	arr. Schillio	312-40612	Presser
*Campfire Blues	E	Gustafson		Fischer
*Cantate Domino	M	Pitoni-Greyson	ES 5	Bourne
*Cicirinella (Italian)	E	arr. Krone	5-W2952	Witmark
*Climbin' Up the Mountain	M	arr. Smith	1001	Kjos
*Come Comrades, Let Us Begin Our Joyful Singing	MD	Hassler	2066	Belwin
*David's Lamentation	M	Billings	CM 6572	C. Fischer
*Deaf Old Women, The	E	arr. K. K. Davis	1262	Galaxy
*Dear Love, Be Not Unkind	M	Dering	F484	Frank
*Ezekiel Saw de Wheel	E	arr. H. R. Wilson	1610	Schmitt
*Goin' Home On A Cloud	E	arr. E. M. Turner	312-40545	Presser
*Good News!	MD	arr. Kjelson	CM 7194	C. Fischer
Hammerin'	MD	arr. Gardner	486	Staff
I Am A Pilgrim	D	arr. Gardner	490	Staff
*I Feel Like My Time Ain't Long	E	arr. W. G. Still	312-40304	Presser
*I Walk The Unfrequented Road	E	arr. Kjelson	Bel 2062	Belwin
Lacrymosa	M	Cherubini	545	Staff
*Now Spring In All Her Glory	D	Arcadelt	A200	Mills
*O Bone Jesu (Latin)	D	Palestrina-Deis	10022	G. Schirmer
O Music, Thou Most Lovely Art	D	Jeep	F483	Frank
*Pater Noster (Latin)	M	Stravinsky	1833	Boosey
*She Is So Dear	M	Praetorius	332-14558	Ditson
Six Folk Songs (select any two of first four songs)	M	Brahms	AJ9	Marks
So Far Away	M	arr. Owen	312-40614	Presser
Swallows	M	Nixon	312-40611	Presser
Three Madrigals	EM	Diemer	5417	Boosey
Waillee, Waillee	MD	arr. Murray	237	Staff
Weep O Mine Eyes	D	Bennet-Greyson	ES 30	Bourne

BOYS VOICES

See SA List for other arrangements that could be sung TB.

TB unless otherwise indicated

May God Smile On You	D	Bach	6079	Peters
O Lord Most Holy (Panis Angelicus)	EM	Arr. L. Kjelson	1971	Belwin
Simple Gifts	EM	Copland-Fine	1903	Boosey
When Jesus Wept (with opt. 3rd, voice or solo)	E	Billings-Kjelson	1972	Belwin
Zion, Hears the Watchmen Singing	MD	Buxtehude-Winkworth	ECS 538	E.C. Schirmer

TTB unless otherwise indicated

Alleluia from the Cantata "For Us A Child Is Born"	M	Bach	1012	Galaxy
Benedictus	M	Vittoria	NY 2040	Ricordi
Come Let Us Start A Joyful Song (A Cappella)	M	Hassler-Greyson	ES 31	Bourne
Recordata	D	Palestrina-Castellazzi-Vené	NY 2-33	Ricordi
Shepherd, The (TTB)	M	Kennedy	5556	Boosey
To Be Or Not To Be (TTB)	M	Kennedy	5557	Boosey

TTBB unless otherwise indicated

Hiking Song (also ATBB)	E	Arr. Krones	4300	Kjos	.20
Rolling Hills	M	Gustafson	312-40414	Presser	.25

COLLECTIONS

NOTE: Inasmuch as some collections listed below do not have specific numbers indicated, it will be assumed that each director will use his discretion and will select music comparable in quality to that listed in the foregoing pages.

Anthology of Polyphonic Masters of 15th, 16th and 17th Century		Georgian Inst. of America	7 Sacred Masterpieces
Art Of Polyphonic Song, The	David	G. Schirmer	23 compositions of 16th & 17th Century compositions for 2-8 parts Sacred and Secular
Belles and Beaus	Gearhart	Shawnee	SA & Boys
Book Of Canons	Wolff	Chantry	2,3,4,5,6 parts (21 rounds)
Book of Spirituals	Smith-Krone	Kjos	
BOW STREET BOOK, The — Summy	SSA		
I Gave My Love A Pretty Little Ring			
Suscepit Israeli			
Hey, Ho, to the Greenwood			
Non Nobis Domine			
Lament			
Catches for Three, Four or Five Voices	Lawton	Mercury	
Catch That Catch Can	Taylor-Simpson	E.C. Schirmer	
Classic Canons	Reichenbach	Mercury	2-6 equal or mixed
Concord Book For Women's Voices	Davison & Surette	E.C. Schirmer	Folk, Art, Hymns, Motets, Carols, Unison 2,3, and 4 parts
	Zanzig		
Concord Junior Song and Chorus Book		E.C. Schirmer	Folks, Madrigals, Art Songs, Hymns and Choruses
Descants and Easy Basses	Krones	Kjos	
Descants to Trios	Krones	Kjos	
Easy Canons	Reichenbach	Mercury	2-6 equal or mixed
Elizabethian Two-Part Songs (Bennett Collection)	Arr. Fellowes	Galaxy	10 2-part songs of English Madrigals
English Song Book, An	Arr. Greenberg	Anchor	Sacred and Secular collection of English music from chant to 16th century
Fair Haven (Junior Choir and Duet Book)	Arr. Warren	E.C. Schirmer	
Folks Songs and Ballads of Great Composers (Set I-unison)	Zanzig	E.C. Schirmer	10 songs from Europe

FRONT 'N CENTER for THREE PART BOYS CHORUS
  —C. Fischer
  Madrigal
  My Lord What A Morning
  Erie Canal
  Lo, the Earth Is Risen Again
  Surely He Hath Bourne Our Burdens
GLEE MUSIC FOR BOYS — Morgan & Gibb   SATB
       Summy
  Passing By
  Ave Maria
  From Ill Do Thou Defend Me
  The Ash Grove
  Lullaby

Great Songs Of Faith	Krones	Kjos	
Green Hill (Junior Choir and Duet)	Arr. K. K. Davis	E.C. Schirmer	
Laudate Pueri	Lassus-Tovey	E.C. Schirmer	2,3,4,5 voices — collection of 34 Sacred Choruses
Mills First Chorus Album	E. Jurey	Mills	
More Descants and Easy Basses	Krones	Kjos	
Music Americans Sing	H. R. Wilson	Silver Burdett	Four parts

PATTERNS IN SONG—Richardson & Frackenpohl   Witmark

All Through the Night	SATB	
*Soldier Soldier	SATB	
*Non Nobis Domine	Canon	
*Dona Nobis Pacem	Canon	

Round and Round and Round They Go	Daniel	Summy	Rounds of all periods and composers
Rounds For Everyone From Everywhere	Terri	Lawson-Gould	2-8 parts All periods and composers
Rounds From Many Countries	Anderson	G. Schirmer	A collection of fifty canons for singing and recorder playing
Sacred Rounds and Canons	Boyce & Webbe	Stainer	Rounds of 17th & 18th Centuries
Salute To Music	Wilson-Ehret	Boosey	SA and SAB

SHAKESPEARE SONG BOOK — Mills
  The Willow Song   unison
  When That I Was and A Little Tiny Boy   SATB
  Take, O, Take These Lips Away   unison
SINGING IN SCHOOLS — Oxford
  Ten Songs—choose anyone of the ten songs   unison & 2-part
SOLO VOICE OR UNISON VOICE FROM ORATORIOS
       Vol. II — Belwin

Songs For Young Glee Men	Morgan	Schmitt	2,3,4, parts

SONGS FROM MANY LANDS —   Kjos
  *Just As the Tide Was Flowing
  *Song of Hope
  * Drill, Ye Tarriers, Drill   especially for boys voices

Songs From The Four Corners	Krones	Kjos	All voicing
Troubadours	Nightingale	C. Fischer	In two volumes and in one complete edition

Adoramus Te
All Through the Night
Awake My Soul
Break Forth, O Beauteous, Heavenly Light
Calm Is the Night
Coasts of High Barbara, The
Come Ye Thankful People Come
Drink To Me Only With Thine Eyes
From Ill Do Thou Defend Me
Integer Vitae
Now The Day Is Over
Pilgrim's Chorus
Send Out Thy Light
Stars of the Summer Night

Thirty-Five Sacred Rounds and Canons from Four Centuries	Bristol	Canyon	
Thomas Morely's Canzonets For Two Voices	Arr. Fellowes	Galaxy	12 2 part conzonets
Vocal Duets Vol. I and II	Phanomen-Brahms		
To the Evening Star	Schuman		
When the Cuckoo Sings	Dvorak		
Youth Sings	Simeone	Shawnee	SB and SAB

STATE MUSIC TEXTS

TITLE	VOICING & SATB MIXED OR BOYS	PAGE NO.
BIRCHARD MUSIC SERIES—Book Seven		
At The Gate Of Heaven	SA	152
Dona Nobis Pacem	Canon	201
Drill, Ye Tarriers, Drill	SAB	112
Ezekial Saw The Wheel	SATB	124
Mystic Number, The	SSA	148
Nightingale, The	SATB	246
O Rest In The Lord	Unison	190
Panis Angelicus (O Lord Most Holy)	SA	193
Praise and Adore	SATB	187
Round-Up Lullaby	SA	141
So Far Away	SSA	109
Stars of the Summer Night	SATB	145
Thanks Be To Thee	Unison	202
Through All The Year	Unison or SATB	235
Turtle Dove, The	Unison or SATB	160
Turn Ye To Me	SATB	96
Winter Is Over, The	SA	131
BIRCHARD MUSIC SERIES—Book Eight		
Aura Lee	SATB	160
Balm In Gilead	SATB	152
Bendemeer's Stream	SAB	70
Charlottown	SATB	246
Commit Thy Ways Unto Him	SATB	144
Hunter, The	3-part round	193
Joseph Dearest	Unison	235
Joshua Fit The Battle Of Jericho	SATB	134
Kye Song Of St. Bride	SATB	243
Let All The Seas and Earth Around	SAB	140
Let Us Break Bread Together	SAB	154
Mary's Lullaby To The Infant King	SA—Christmas Setting "Gute Nacht"	232
My Bonnie Lass She Smileth	SATB	244
My Lord, What A Mornin'	SATB	148
Over The Meadows	SAB	14
Rock-A My Soul	SATB	136
Tallis Canon	Unison	138
This Day Do We Honor	SATB	240

SUPPLEMENTARY MUSIC TEXTS

AMERICAN MUSIC HORIZONS—Silver Burdett Company

Adoramus Te	SATB	141
Alleluia	SATB	136
Break Forth, O Beauteous, Heavenly Light	SATB	232
Greetings	SSA	176

In The Woods	SSA	170
Lift Thine Eyes	SSA	228
Lord Of Mercy (O Bone Jesu)	SATB	140
Prayer	Unison	184
Request (Bitte)	SATB	7
Sheep May Safely Graze	Unison	148
Ye Watchers and Ye Holy Ones	SATB	12

WORLD MUSIC HORIZONS—Silver Burdett Company

Alleluia	SSA	202
Greensleeves	SAB	62
Linden Tree, The	SAB	61
On Winds Of Song	SA	226
Three Little Maids	SSA	159
Where'er You Walk	Unison	199

SINGING JUNIORS—Ginn and Company

Indian Flute, The	Unison	210
Lo How A Rose	SAB	170
O Silent Night	SAB	184
Sender Of Dreams	SSA	119
Sweet Music Enchanting	SATB	226
This Is My Father's World	SSA	141

SINGING TEEN-AGERS—Ginn and Company

Break Forth, O Beauteous, Heavenly Light	Unison	183
Cockles and Mussels	SATB	86
Dear Evelina, Sweet Evelina	SAB	110
Ezekial Saw The Wheel	SATB	176
Integer Vitae	SATB	126
Silver Sea, The	SATB	80
Time Is Never Weary, The	Canon	215
Wondrous Love	SAB	164

SING OUT—C. C. Birchard

Break Forth, O Beauteous, Heavenly Light	SA	192
Flowing River	SSA	63
Greeting	SA	194
Hymn For The Nations (Ode To Joy)	SSA	162
Music In The Air	SATB	26
Nocturne	SA with opt. descant for instruments or voices	189
O Lord Most Holy (Panis Angelicus)	Unison—SA	140
Peddlar, The	SA	95
Sing To The Lord	SSA	145

LET MUSIC RING—C. C. Birchard

Aura Lee	SATB	148
Ave Maria		
Cast Thy Burden Upon The Lord	SATB	126
Dona Nobis Pacem	SATB	203
Glory Now To Thee Be Given	Canon	223
Integer Vitae	SATB	95
Jesu, Joy Of Man's Desiring	SATB	133
O Bone Jesu	SATB	196
O Western Wind	SATB	92
Passing By	SAB	168
Sanctus	SAB	127
We Who Love Music	SATB	96

MUSIC FOR EVERYONE — Prentice-Hall   SATB

Alleluia	Unison/descant	97
Eternal Father, Strong to Save	SATB	88
Come, Come Ye Saints	SATB	86
O Bone Jesu	Unison	96
Rest in the Lord	SATB	77
Soldiers Chorus		39

TIME FOR MUSIC — Prentice-Hall

Cast Thy Burden Upon the Lord	SAT opt. bar.	38
Dona Nobis	round	46
Let Us Break Bread	SATB	31
Spacious Firmament on High	SATB	43

CONTEST REHEARSAL SUGGESTIONS

The director who is still "pushing for notes" the day before contest is headed for serious trouble. Pieces should be memorized, every note in place, at least 2 weeks before performance time so that the last 5 rehearsals can be reserved for final polishing.

1. Study each piece thoroughly yourself before placing it in the choir folders. A good school choral conductor does very little *conducting*, but a great deal of *teaching*. Decide where the trouble spots are likely to be and plan your solutions carefully.
2. Distribute the music and read through the entire piece to get an overall picture. Deal with the problems in a methodical, business-like manner, but avoid the demoralizing effect of working on one particular problem spot throughout an entire rehearsal. Spend only 5-10 minutes on the most difficult phrases every day; they will fall into place as the group improves.
3. 2 or 3 weeks before contest, sit down, all alone, with a pencil and choral adjudication form, and listen to that day's recording of your group. Put yourself in the place of the judge and prepare a full criticism sheet. Play the recording for your students, read your comments, and point out specifically what you are talking about, since their ears and minds are not as accustomed to really critical listening as yours.

PSYCHOLOGICAL PREPARATION

The director and every member of the group should be prepared to put forth maximum effort at every performance throughout the school year ... and contest is simply one appearance in that series.

It is extremely dangerous to convey to students, by either word or action, a feeling that their "life depends" on a superior rating, or to allow the feeling to persist that if they are not awarded a first division "the world will come to an end" promptly on their return to school.

Do impress on your students (and yourself!) that the most important thing about the contest/festival is the opportunity it affords students and directors to hear choirs from other schools of comparable size, as an aid to evaluating their own progress.

TRIP PREPARATION

The director must plan the details of the contest/festival trip very carefully, so that students can afford to be somewhat leisurely in their preparation for performance. The last minute panic of rushing from a bus to the stage while pulling on a robe is certainly not conducive to a secure performance. Of course, a tremendous amount of time with nothing to do often leads to bad cases of nerves, too. A sort of "relaxed efficiency" seems to work best.

Duties should be delegated by the director to responsible students within the organization. Be sure to maintain a close check on their progress. Hotel/motel or private home accommodations should be arranged well in advance. Reservations can be made with reliable restaurants if mealtime will occur while on the road.

Short concerts for other schools along the way or in the contest city can often be scheduled. The total transportation cost for 2 or 3 appearances is about the same as a single contest performance; the school will gain some fame and prestige (if your performance is good!); the choir members will enjoy visiting other schools and meeting other students; and, the pressure of the one "all-important" contest performance will be lessened.

PHYSICAL PREPARATIONS

Contest/Festival managers should provide a quick, efficient method for choirs to move on and off stage, including plans to return the students to the auditorium as soon after the performance as possible, so that they may hear the other groups.

The following rooms should be provided, if space permits:

1. Dressing Rooms — where clothes are changed and rest room facilities are available. (Two rooms, with groups alternating, is most efficient.)
2. Warm-up room — where final musical preparations are made before entering the stage.
3. The stage — with adequate riser space, and freshly tuned piano.

WHAT CONTEST JUDGES LOOK FOR

Every contest judge has a certain definite standard in his mind's ear which any group he labels "superior" must achieve. Guided by the items on the adjudication sheet, he checks, sometimes methodically, but usually almost intuitively, in mixed order, the fundamentals of *tone, intonation, diction, technique, balance, interpretation, musical effect,* and *other factors.*

Regardless of how a judge may feel after a long day of trying to make not only a fair evaluation of choral groups, but also attempting to offer some constructive criticism as well . . . and in spite of what

disgruntled directors may say ... *contest judges are human beings!*
Therefore their musical decisions are affected by a number of non-
musical, but very human factors. The first impression the judge
receives from the performing group arrives through the eye, not
the ear. He sees the students standing, ready to sing. Either he ob-
serves a group, which through its careful attention to details of
physical arrangement, and tasteful (possibly unique) uniform attire,
offers the impression of competency; or he sees a group, which, by
a careless, drab and lifeless appearance, tacitly suggests that the
music may have been approached in the same manner. An unfair
assumption ... one which has nothing to do with musical values?
Possibly. But even though every judge tries to confine this impression to the *other factors* section of the form, what he sees is bound
to put him in a certain frame of mind. He already has the impression
(even though entirely visual, so far) that this director does or does
not know what he is doing

Tone. The first aural impression is the overall sound of the group.
An experienced person can (and does) make a judgment of the tone
quality in the very first phrase of the opening selection which is
seldom changed throughout the following 15 minutes. Naturally, if
the sound is pleasant, this human being serving as judge will enjoy
his task of filling in scores for the other items on the adjudication
form ... obviously this cannot hurt your final standing.

Choice of music. The pieces must not only fit the general medium
but should also be chosen with the choir's own particular qualities
in mind. Most judges are very critical of performing adaptations
from other media, in preference to programming works in their
original settings (a girl's choir singing an SSA version of Handel's
Hallelujah Chorus, for instance).

The choir with a serious pitch problem should certainly work on
a capella pieces throughout the year. When it comes to contest performances, however, only those with strong accompaniment would
be used.

A very large group can sing some of the heavier pieces with great
success, but when a smaller choir attempts the same music, the demands on the voices can cause almost complete loss of blend, balance,
and tone quality.

A really "superior" choir will be able to perform music of quality
from many different musical periods, in good taste, with the proper
stylistic mannerisms. The wise director will suggest to the judges
that his group has this quality by scheduling 3 pieces using 3 different styles (the 3 he does best, of course!).

Musical qualities. I find that I often ask myself many of the following questions when listening critically to a group:

1. Blend — can individual voices be heard?
2. Characteristic sound — do the altos sound warm, rather than pushed and hard; have tenors been shifted over to the head voice (falsetto) rather than allowed to push along, just barely producing a sound?
3. Balance — has the weakest section been matched? Do the sopranos (often the largest number in many schools) overpower the others?
4. Relative dynamics — does the group understand this principle? The choir which cannot produce a real *fortissimo* can make their *forte* sound relatively as loud by singing the *piano* overly soft.
5. Rhythmical flow — does this performance include a free flow of phrases, within the rhythmical framework of the piece? Even in the most legato Bach Chorale, for instance, there is a strong rhythmical pattern set up, and everything must fall into the scope of that plan. This is not to say that parts should be "punched out," but rather that every singer should feel, and convey to the listener, the rhythmical context in which all music is written.
6. Confident humility — does the group convey that certain degree of humility which is so necessary to every artistic communicative effort? There is a great deal of difference between the performance of a choir with sensible self-assurance, and the singing of a group of students whose egos have been so inflated that the musical values in the piece cannot possibly survive in such a cocky, smug atmosphere.

RATING THE CHOIR

In order to evaluate his efforts, a director must know, honestly, how his product compares with that from other schools of similar size. Therefore, contests and festivals lose their value when (in order to make directors "happy") judges use only the top of the scale, i.e. most choirs are rated either I or II, and no IV's or V's are ever given.

The system of contests now generally used allows judges to name as many choirs "Superior—I" as are worthy of the designation. This is far better than the plan which requires adjudicators to pick groups in "1, 2, 3" order.

A good adjudicator will address his comments to specific points, rather than write obscure philosophical prose filled with "isms" which no one really understands. Some judges use a typewriter for comments, which at least guarantees legibility, if nothing else. A competent judge learns to use words and descriptive phrases which convey the greatest meaning in the shortest possible space. Even so, performance schedules should be planned to allow adequate time for the judges to prepare sheets which can be of practical value to the director and his students. Some judges have been provided with a tape recorder. The tape of the spoken comments, made during the contest performance (which is heard in the background), is given to the director. Festival managers with large budgets are sometimes able to hire two sets of judges in order to allow one set to speak directly with the conductor as the other set is listening to the next group.

Regardless of the method, each director and each group of students should not only understand completely why the particular rating was given, but should also learn something specific which will improve the next performance. Flattering as the comment, "Good job!" may be, it is really not too helpful to a conductor who has traveled many miles seeking ways to develop better teaching and performing techniques.

Solos and Ensembles

Directors should be very selective in their choice of solo and ensemble entries, sending students only when they are musically and emotionally mature enough to perform virtually "on their own." Often young singers compete too soon, simply because there is space on the form and they have the fee. The experience does them more harm than good at that stage of development.

Most student soloists and ensembles worthy of contest entry can be trusted to learn the notes by themselves, with the attention of the director reserved for artistic guidance and final polishing.

Massed Choral Groups

Whatever is done in connection with all-district, all-state, or other festival choruses must be aimed toward the creation of beautiful music which can provide the participants (not just the audience) with a meaningful experience.

Most states ask the conductor to choose a program. The music is then ordered, often bound together, and sent out to the schools well in advance of the first mass rehearsal. The local chorus directors teach the individual parts at home, and the guest conductor attempts to fashion a finished performance after one or two days of concentrated rehearsal. The success of this type chorus depends on the amount of enthusiasm which that state's choral people have generated in preparing the music.

Determining the method of choosing students for any select group often involves a clash of theories. The name *All-State Chorus,* for example, indicates that students from the entire state are participating, but it also implies that these are the best ("all-star") of the state. Many methods have been used, ranging all the way from an open invitation to choral directors to "send those who are qualified" (or sometimes just "send 10, quick") to a very complicated quota system based on school and/or performing group populations.

The members of the Oklahoma All-State Chorus are carefully selected by audition, and the music is distributed (for the first time!) at the opening rehearsal. It was a pleasure for me, as guest conductor, to work for blend and balance, notes and nuance from the very beginning ... everyone at the same stage of familiarity with the music ... and the concert on the evening of the 3rd day was an exciting testimonial to the value of this plan. Contrasted with this extremely pleasant experience is another which I shall never forget— a nightmare masquerading as a one day festival for 3,000 unselected, totally unprepared students. It was a disaster!

Oklahoma All-State Chorus Audition System [2]

A chorus numbering between 200-240 is chosen from the approximately 1,200 students who normally apply. Music is not mailed out in advance, but distributed at the first rehearsal. Those who have worked with this system for a number of years find that it has increased the prestige of the event, caused choral teachers to place greater emphasis on music fundamentals, and, most important, they feel that the entire project has a good deal more true musical value for everyone concerned than is possible under alternative plans which are available.

1. Adjudicators (outstanding choral directors within the state) are appointed for a period of 3 years. Terms are staggered by district.
2. Every applicant is auditioned by one of these specialists, sched-

---

[2] Based on information supplied by Russell Mathis, University of Oklahoma, Chairman of Oklahoma All-State Chorus.

uled so that no judge hears students from his own district.

3. Since those chosen as chorus members will not see the perform-
    ance music prior to rehearsal, the primary goal of the audition
    is to determine the youngster's vocal quality, basic music and
    technical skills, and ability to take directions under an emotional
    strain. Original sight-reading material is prepared annually for
    use throughout the state.

4. A numerical score is recorded for each student who auditions.
    No fewer than 200, nor more than 240 with the highest scores
    (regardless of geographical location) are notified of their selec-
    tion. In case of ties, seniors are given preference.

The program should be well balanced, consisting of easy, medium
and difficult pieces of the finest quality selected from various historical periods and compositional styles. If the music appeals to the
young people even as it provides a strong challenge for their abilities, the guest conductor will undoubtedly have an easier time with
the very essential task of selling both the music and himself to the
singers.

A wise visiting conductor will check into the level and type of
music being done in the state before he chooses a program; a
thoughtful manager will send him the last 3 or 4 programs, as well
as brief him (honestly) on the performance level of most schools
in the state, in order to provide the best background for an appropriate choice of music.

The budgeting of time (both the student's and the director's) is
important to the success of any rehearsal, but is crucial in preparing
a massed chorus. Every rehearsal must be carefully planned, and
executed with no waste of time. Routine tasks of seating, music distribution, etc. should be handled by the staff of the organizing chairman. The guest conductor's time is valuable (fees are approximately
$50-$100 per day, plus expenses, for a state-wide event) and should
be used wisely.

PITFALLS OF CONTESTS AND FESTIVALS

While contests and festivals may generally be labeled "good,"
there are also some very serious problems to be considered. I have
become most concerned about the following:

1. Undue emphasis on the preparation of this particular music to
    the exclusion of other important parts of the choral music pro-
    gram in the school. I would like to observe the entire choral

music program of the choir which I rate "superior," or the one which places many students in the all-state chorus. In most cases the program would probably rate "I" also, but many schools get out of balance.

2. Choosing music that is "far out," in order to impress colleagues, rather than performing a more balanced program which will aid in the musical education of the students.

3. Concentrating so exclusively on learning the notes perfectly that the musical aspects are neglected. Too many times I hear good clean sounding groups (the tone quality is good, the balance is pleasing), but they just "miss the boat" musically. Conductors, themselves, must first understand the musical message and then convey it to the students. Together they project it to the listener.

Conductor's Testing Ground

The fact that a person has received a degree from an accredited institution does not necessarily make him a good choral conductor. The contest gives each person a chance to evaluate his own ability to prepare a performance group by comparing his results with those achieved by other directors in other localities. Such factors as school location, student population, age of the program, attitude of the administration, etc. will affect the quality of work being done, but generally, *a choir is only as good as its conductor.*

While the practice of hiring and firing choral directors solely on the basis of contest ratings will almost certainly create a music program which is far out of balance, some directors who receive poor ratings year after year leave the field, and those who earn consistently acceptable scores over a period of time, not only remain, but are inspired to even greater achievements based on their increased self-confidence.

Regardless of the rating, every conductor, after his yearly trip to the "testing ground" is usually better able to understand his own strengths and weaknesses. By planning around the weaknesses and emphasizing the strengths (as he works to increase his knowledge and skills) each director can help to improve the quality of his own group and to raise the musical standards of the entire music education profession.

8

The Summer Choral Workshop

by the officers of the
North Carolina Summer
Choral Workshop

**the officers of the
Choral Workshop**

*Paul B. Fry, Maxine Blackwell, Robert H. Ellis, Joel Carter, shown here
with Lara Hoggard (seated), Permanent Musical Director, are the officers
of the North Carolina Summer Choral Workshop, held annually on the
campus of the University of North Carolina at Chapel Hill. The workshop
was begun in 1953, and is unique in that it is sponsored by the choral
section of the state music educators conference.*

*Maxine Blackwell (Mrs. J. R., Jr.), who is the Permanent Chairman,
teaches at Kernersville. Paul B. Fry, the Registrar, teaches in the Albe-
marle schools, and is state chairman for the American Choral Directors
Association. Both he and Mrs. Blackwell have served as President of the
North Carolina Music Educators Conference. Robert H. Ellis, Page High
School, Greensboro, is chairman of the choral section of the NCMEC.
He serves as Head Counselor for the Workshop. Dr. Joel Carter, of the
Music Department, University of North Carolina at Chapel Hill, is
responsible for coordination of efforts between the workshop and the
University.*

"Now you do that at home," heard innumerable times during rehearsal sessions at summer camps and workshops throughout the country, is a very short phrase, yet it does much to summarize both the purposes for, and the advantages of, this growing movement.

When even a limited number of students and their directors can spend time investigating the glorious choral literature of our musical heritage ("rubbing shoulders with greatness", Lara Hoggard, Permanent Conductor of the North Carolina Summer Choral Workshop, calls it), the inspiration is quickly transmitted to other students in the home town choral program. Of course, students who witness the work of a conductor of national reputation will demand more from you in rehearsals back home, but after the same experience, you (with the advantage of maturity, a musical education, and high personal and professional standards) will probably demand even more of yourself.

During a concentrated period of summer study away from the responsibilities and tensions of the regular school season, there is often time, as well as inclination, to investigate fresh approaches to problems. Unfortunately, the challenge of a new idea is sometimes frightening in the midst of a busy (but firmly established, and at least workable) routine of school rehearsals and performances.

Inspiration, Fellowship, and Love

Too many times choral directors see each other only at the state contest when their attitude is liable to be much more competitive than cooperative. Through a week's close association at a summer workshop, however, a strong sense of sharing can be developed.

Inspired by a conductor who, through great insight and years of meaningful experience, can demonstrate effective choral techniques as he probes life's deepest meanings; and surrounded by a spirit of fellowship resulting from the free sharing of ideas among colleagues, even the most overworked and temporarily discouraged choral director is almost bound to find a renewal of strength and the capacity to expand his love for students, colleagues, and the entire profession.

Choosing the Place For You

The choice of location—college or commercial, comprehensive or specialized, small or large, national or local, near or far—depends on many factors, and is best determined by an examination of your own students and how they can best be served.

Some sessions have been organized only to provide summer employment for 10 month contract school teachers; others may be purely a college public relation man's idea of how to attract students. While these and other personal advantages may be important fringe benefits, fortunately most concentrate on teaching music under conditions which are physically pleasant and educationally effective.

Camp? Clinic? Workshop?

There are several names for the various summertime sessions in every part of the country. Three terms—camp, clinic, and workshop —sometimes used almost interchangeably, seem to have certain specific connotations.

Summer Camp usually brings to mind visions of living in cabins by the lake, rehearsing under the trees, and participating in outdoor recreation. There are large camps, like the National Music Camp at Interlochen, Michigan, which offer a comprehensive, full-summer course in all of the arts, or there are many small camps which can be reserved for private use during the summer. Local directors, with the help of parents' organizations, often schedule a week's work in the wilderness away from the distractions of the home town drive-ins and car-hops.

Clinic, probably because of the medical definitions (1. a place for the treatment of non-resident patients. 2. the instruction of medical students by examining or treating patients in their presence), usually indicates a shorter session of correctional, or at least instructional nature, designed either to solve current problems, or to prevent future ones.

Workshop (a place where work is carried on) seems to indicate a cooperative effort of people (workers) actively participating in the pursuit of some specific goal. One of the particular strengths of the North Carolina Workshop is the joint participation of both teachers and students. They share the same experiences: singing, studying, and working side by side under the direction of an inspiring conductor.

The North Carolina Plan

The North Carolina Summer Choral Workshop was organized in 1953 by a group of choral directors. Early leaders were Miss Eula

Tuttle, and the first chairman, Dr. Charles Taylor. The beginning years were spent at various colleges and church camp grounds before the move to the campus of the University of North Carolina at Chapel Hill. It is a non-profit organization whose annual workshop is sponsored and supervised by the choral section of the North Carolina Music Educators Conference, and administered by the University of North Carolina Department of Music in cooperation with the University Extension Division.[1]

While good work can often be done in less than ideal surroundings, the large air-conditioned rehearsal room, comfortable seats, quality piano, and proper acoustics of the University's Department of Music have eliminated many problems and increased learning. Thus the complete human and physical resources of a modern department are readily available for all musical needs and the facilities of a large and beautiful campus are open to students and directors who attend the workshop.

Preliminary Planning

The first planning session for each summer is held on the last day of the current season, while problems and their possible solutions are still fresh in the minds of the staff. During the fall meeting of the North Carolina Music Educators Conference, a full critique of the previous workshop is presented, and improvements suggested. A Spring meeting, during the choral festival, is concerned mostly with the distribution of assignments for the summer.

Because this is virtually a year-round project, other details of operation are supervised by the workshop officers through letters, phone calls, and much individual work. Time is extremely important and none can be wasted if optimum results from the week are expected. Everything must be considered in advance.

Officers and Staff

The Workshop Chairman is finally responsible for all phases of the project's operation.

The Registrar supervises the enrollment of students and teachers and is responsible for the collection of all fees.

---

[1]*Editor's note*: Since they have always felt the need for a specialized choral workshop to serve as a laboratory for both teachers and students, based on sound educational principles, with costs held within reasonable limits, the authors of this chapter have put their best efforts into the expansion and refinement of a program which has been founded on the unselfish cooperative efforts of a group of dedicated music educators. The information is shared freely with the hope that other state organizations may be encouraged to sponsor similar projects.

Fig. 8-1

**The Modern Facilities of a University Music Department
Are Ideal for Workshop Rehearsals**
(University of North Carolina Photo Lab)

The Head Counselor supervises the activities of 10-15 adult counselors.

The Coordinator for the University Department of Music, and the *Head, Bureau of Residential Adult Education,* implement the spirit of fullest cooperation expressed by their respective departments.

The Dean and the *Assistant Dean* supervise the activities of the students during their stay on the campus.

The Workshop Nurse is responsible for the medical needs of the students and staff.

The Musical Director selects the music and conducts all rehearsals.

The Accompanist provides every possible assistance to the conductor during rehearsals, often anticipating his rehearsal technique so as to be ready with the proper pitch, isolated part, or the like.

THE CONDUCTOR

The choice of conductor is the most crucial single factor in the success or failure of a choral workshop. No matter how well organized the week's activities may be, or how many capable and interested directors and students are in attendance—both of these points are extremely important—only the right director can inspire students and expand director's horizons, whereas the wrong one can very quickly spread insecurity and doubt.

In addition to the usual professional requirements, which include a thorough grasp of vocal and choral fundamentals, superb rehearsal technique, and a reasonable perfectionist's pride demanding maximum quality while still considering the physical limitations of each and every singer; the outstanding workshop conductor must have that peculiar, almost electric contact with young people which leads them to great musical achievements and builds lasting aesthetic appreciation.

A few thoughts, gleaned from workshop sessions with Lara Hoggard, permanent conductor of the North Carolina Choral Workshop, will indicate the depth of understanding which a conductor of this stature can impart in rehearsal sessions:

"Do not waste the time of other human beings—you don't have the right."

"Art is discipline. Most people do not like the discipline of drill, but the great scientists searching for the right combinations go through many thousands of possibilities before they come up with the one which will work . . . drill. Nearly everything in life is *refinement through repetition.*"

"The unprepared people are the 'have-nots.' Don't be too hard on them; they are not necessarily the 'don't-cares' . . . they simply *have not* the notes."

"Don't force a youngster into music if he does not have the necessary qualifications. Music is just *one* of the arts. A child with a poor ear may have a great sense of color balance, a feel for sculpture, or an ability with words."

THE SCHEDULE

Youngsters must be kept busy in order to stay out of mischief, but still need ever-increasing opportunities for individual choices in order to build character. Based on observation of this somewhat paradoxical fact, the workshop staff has set up a full rehearsal schedule which places the emphasis on the *work* portion of workshop, but also allows ample time to enjoy the many fringe benefits of a week away from home, with new friends, on the campus of a large university.

Daily Schedule — North Carolina Summer Choral Workshop

7:15 A.M.	Breakfast
8:00-8:45 A.M.	Ensemble rehearsals or other special choral/vocal activities for select groups.
9:00-11:00 A.M.	The Morning Rehearsal
11:15 A.M.	Lunch
12:30-1:00 P.M.	Ensemble rehearsals or other special choral/vocal activities for select groups.
1:15-2:45 P.M.	The Afternoon Rehearsal
2:45-5:00 P.M.	Free time–for rest or recreation
5:15 P.M.	Dinner
6:30-8:00 P.M.	The Evening Rehearsal
8:00 P.M.	Evening entertainment–a daily special feature.
11:00 P.M.	Lights out.

FINANCIAL ARRANGEMENTS

Major expenses for a choral workshop include housing, music, conductor, and accompanist. University dormitories, plus a fee for use of other campus facilities, costs about $10 per person, per week. The price of a week's meal ticket may be added, or students may be allowed to buy their own food at any one of the many cafeterias or restaurants in the area. Bound music, with one copy for each singer, costs approximately $5 per booklet. Conductor's fees will vary, depending on experience, reputation, the number of rehearsals, etc. Those of national reputation usually receive a minimum of $100 per day, plus expenses. As experienced, professional accompanist often charges $50 per day. If a low fee per participant is to be maintained, many people obviously must be willing to donate their time, with only room and board furnished.

After totaling the anticipated expenses for the week long North Carolina session, the staff finds that a fee of $25 per student will allow them to organize the type of experience they desire. Schools sending six or more students must provide an adult chaperone who will remain for the duration of the workshop. These counselors are furnished a room and given a stipend to cover food. Civic clubs from many communities provide scholarships to cover enrollment fees for their local students, and often pay travel expenses as well.

The cost per participant may be determined by the following method:

1. Add the cost, per person, of
   a. housing   _____
   b. student activity _____
   c. meals   _____
   d. music   _____
   e. miscellaneous _____
      Sub-total "A" _____

2. Add the total cost of
   a. conductor   _____
   b. accompanist   _____
   c. other staff   _____
   d. rehearsal facilities _____
   e. administration cost _____
      Sub-total "B" _____

3. Divide Sub-total "B" by the number of students expected to attend your camp or workshop; add this figure to Sub-total "A". This is the grand total, per person.

WORKSHOP INFORMATION

Directors, students, and parents must receive clear, concise, and appealing information about the summer activity well in advance. Definite dates should be set and published early so that family

vacations and other summer programs under local control may be
scheduled without conflict.

Information brochures that are colorful and illustrated should be
sent to every high school choral director in the state. Often the
University Public Information Office will help with this, since ultimately a great deal of attention will be focused on the University's
role of service to the people of the state. Date and place, name of
conductor, a brief resumé of musical and recreational activities,
housing information, fees, and application instructions should be
included.

Every person who receives these advance materials should sense
that this is a thoroughly organized and competently operated undertaking which has the best interests of the student as its ultimate
goal.

Application forms should be uniform, easily handled, and separate (or detachable), so that the registrant may keep the essential
information in the rest of the material. Instructions for payment of
fees and mailing of forms should be clear. Cut-off dates for both
acceptance of applications and cancellation refund requests should
be stated, and observed. Distribution must be well ahead of deadlines. A stock form (*see* Fig. 8-2), printed on a 6 x 4 note card may
be adapted for local use.

Fig. 8-2
Application Form—6x4 Note Card

Please mail before _____ to _____	
Type or print	Circle one:
(Name)	Student or Adult
(No., Street, PO Box, RFD, etc.)	Auditor or Regular
(City, State)	Commuter or Resident
(Father's name - Phone)	Female or Male
(Name of roommate preferred)	Fee enclosed $_____
CHORAL DIRECTOR PLEASE COMPLETE: I recommend that this student be permitted to register for the annual summer choral workshop. (signed)_____ (school)_____	Voice: S1 T1 / S2 T2 / A1 B1 / A2 B2 / Ability: I (best) / II / III

Welcoming letters should be sent to students, once they are officially enrolled. All the essential information concerning their week away from home must be related, including:

1. Date and time of checking in.
2. Necessary fees (late penalty, room key, swimming, parking, activity, others?)
3. Name of dormitory, with mailing address, phone numbers.
4. Meal arrangements, with approximate cost, if individual.
5. Daily schedule.
6. Check list of necessary clothing and equipment (linens, pillows, dress clothes), including specific campus dress rules, rehearsal/performance attire.
7. Medical care available, injections required, request for unique personal history, including allergic reactions.
8. Assurances to parents of excellent care for their youngsters.
9. Special regulations for swimming, automobiles, dating.
10. Visitors policy, including an invitation to the final rehearsal.

RECREATION

Even though the North Carolina Workshop staff has never represented the summer choral workshop as a "vacation" for either students or directors, they do plan recreational activities as a very necessary complement to the vigorous daily rehearsals.[2]

Teen-agers want to make their own decisions, but really prefer that adults set some rather clearly defined limits within which they can operate. Since the varied facilities of the University allow the young people this freedom of choice, at least 3 possibilities for each "free" period are scheduled. These include planetarium shows, art gallery visits, student union lounging and dancing, softball, tennis, swimming, movies, concerts, and variety shows. The entire group participates in the annual picnic (*see* Fig. 8-3), and the popular "let-your-hair-down" highlight, *Workshop Gaities* which is a variety show and stunt night held on the eve of the final day of the weeklong session.

---

[2] *Editor's note:* It has been their experience that since the work sessions are especially satisfying, the purely entertaining events are less popular, because the rehearsals themselves are so much fun.

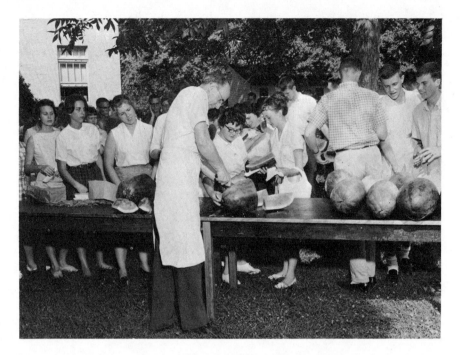

Fig. 8-3

There Is Fun for All at the Annual Picnic
(University of North Carolina Photo Lab)

Rigid rules have been adopted to help each workshopper maintain a high level of personal conduct. For instance, high school singers are not allowed to date any college students who are not also enrolled in the workshop, nor can they ride in an automobile unless a counselor is also in the car. Those students who have brought their own cars are required to deposit the keys with the dean of the workshop.

STUDENT COUNCIL

The staff has been very pleased to observe the development of a student council which has gradually assumed important responsibilities in the conduct of a successful workshop. Led by a president, vice-president, and secretary, approximately 15-20 junior counselors (one for every 15-20 workshoppers) check attendance, plan the variety show, and generally keep the schedule running smoothly. House meetings are held immediately preceding "lights out", when junior counselors conduct a short devotional service, outline plans for the following day, and allow students to freely discuss any topics of interest to the overall welfare of the group.

Student council representatives are elected at the first of these nightly meetings. An election at the end of the week names the student council president who returns (on scholarship) to serve the following summer.

At first the student council was merely another non-musical "fringe-benefit," but this group has now become a sort of "sub-workshop" . . . in democratic action. It is extremely gratifying to watch young people learn the techniques of self-government through this experience.

WORKSHOP PHOTOGRAPHS

Photographs are made of each student and each director, grouped by school, along with the workshop conductor. Through the cooperation of the University Photo Lab, a top-quality print which will reproduce beautifully in the local newspaper, is sent to each student's home town. All choral activities (both rehearsal and recreational) are photographed, and the prints are available for individual purchase, as well as for publicity use by the University.

THE FINAL REHEARSAL

A summer choral workshop should be designed to provide a vital educational experience for students and directors, rather than to produce an impressive concert program for colleagues. Intimidated by the pressure of a potentially poor performance, a conductor (who, after all, gets the credit or the blame for the group's efforts) has time only to say, "Do it!", with the implied reason, "because I am the Authority and I say so" rather than the more permanently valuable, but initially time-consuming explanation of why it should be done.

For these reasons, the staff of the North Carolina Workshop is very much opposed to the scheduling of a formal concert as the culmination of activities. It prefers to invite parents, friends, relatives, and directors to the final "open" rehearsal of the workshop chorus. In this way the conductor and the students may sing beautiful music without the restrictions of a formal concert, as they share with the audience—both vocally and verbally—some of the wonderful experiences of their time together.

Do It Yourself

A summer choral workshop similar to the North Carolina session can be organized anywhere in the country. From our experience the necessary ingredients seem to be:

A small group of people who are willing to work hard . . . together . . . in order to create and sustain this unique means of assistance to others. The state music education association's choral section chairman could be a natural beginning for such a dedicated nucleus.

An outstanding conductor who can provide a pleasantly memorable experience for every student, director, administrator, and parent who attends the rehearsals. Choose carefully, and do not hesitate to change if this seems necessary. While the use of different conductors each year gives regular workshoppers an opportunity to compare approaches and consider various techniques, the steady progress and depth of understanding which can be achieved through the continuing work of one man can be far more valuable.

A college or university with adequate facilities and the personnel to implement a stated philosophy of cooperation and service. Although many locations are ideal, the state university is a logical first choice, because there are so many excellent facilities which are immediately available. Since money, extra hours, advance planning, and physical adjustments are involved, your area college may be hesitant to embark on such a project. However, persistence, and an occasional reference to both academic obligations and potential public relations value, usually will result in the beginning of a mutually satisfying and beneficial experience.

SATISFACTION GUARANTEED

So, consider organizing a summer choral workshop. You will have problems (without which there can never be the wonderful fellowship of cooperative solution), and you will work hard (name one significant choral director who does not), but you will receive great and lasting joy from participation in a project which can cause the performance level of choral music in your state to rise to an overwhelming flood stage of achievement.

Jump in. The water is fine . . . and the flood is just beginning.

9

Junior High School--
the Pivotal Point

by Robert Knauf

Fort Thomas. Kentucky

Robert Knauf

serves the Northern Kentucky-Cincinnati area in a number of important positions. He is Director of Choral Music for Highlands High School (Ft. Thomas, Ky.), Chorusmaster for the May Festival (Cincinnati), Director of Music at the University of Kentucky Northern Center (Covington, Ky.), Choral Director of the High School Music Institute (Cincinnati College-Conservatory), and Choir Director at the Ft. Thomas First Presbyterian Church.

Mr. Knauf received his B.S. from the University of Cincinnati Conservatory of Music, and the M.M. from the University of Kentucky. He has done advanced work at both the Cincinnati College-Conservatory and Boston University.

Since 1952 he has prepared choruses annually for the Cincinnati Symphony Orchestra and the Cincinnati May Festival, serving as Chorusmaster for Robert Shaw, Max Rudolf, Stanislaw Skrowaczewski, and Thor Johnson. He has been guest conductor, adjudicator, and clinician on every level of music education.

Under his direction the schools in Fort Thomas, Ky. supply a thorough choral training program for the many students (an unusually large percentage, when compared with national averages) who have been attracted to the music program. Students may perform with a 5th, 6th, 7th, 8th, or High School Chorus, in addition to their regular music classes.

Because of his experience and success at many levels of professional music and music education, and because of his understanding of the particular problems of junior high (he works with these students every day), Mr. Knauf is uniquely qualified to discuss this crucial area of choral music education.

A good choral music teacher, working with reasonably talented youngsters in a musically conscious community, choosing palatable pieces with care, can produce a rather amazing senior high school chorus in a relatively short period of time and perform to the apparent satisfaction of most of the adult community. Why then should anyone concern himself with the problems of the junior high, or the even more remote elementary classroom music teaching situation? Why not just concentrate on the high school?

While the "almost instant" chorus is often used to gain support for the beginning of choral efforts in a school, most directors recognize that you can never upgrade any program by starting at the top.

A real music program—one which is completely honest in its attempted implementation of the "music for every child" theme — must be based on actual participation. Those adults who announce, "I can't sing a note, don't play an instrument, but I just *love* music," have merely erected a facade. Possibly because they never had, or never took, the opportunity to learn to play or sing, they do not know what they are missing, and thus have absolutely no idea what the *love* of music really is!

The gift of musical talent has been dispensed in unequal shares to be sure, but even those who have received the smallest measure can still acquire skills to an amazing degree. It is a matter of exposure. Wait until high school to introduce choral activity and you may, with hard work, be able to serve 1 out of 4 students; but, with a complete program of competent musical instruction throughout the school system, easily 3 out of 4 can, through active participation, enter into a love affair with music which can bring a lifetime of satisfaction.

GRADUATED LEVELS OF ACCOMPLISHMENT

No high school literature class spends its time reciting in unison, "Run, Dick, Run," and no secondary school mathematics instructor lectures on the concept "$2 + 2 = 4$," yet many choral directors find they must teach elementary music reading, and explain the 2:1 relationship of eighth and quarter notes.

In order to produce a teen-age youngster who not only considers music an important part of his life, but who also has acquired the skills necessary for true enjoyment of the art, the elementary school music program must consist of certain graduated levels of accomplishment ... all vocal centered.

The Primary Grades (1, 2, 3) should be concerned with finding the singing voice. While many songs are taught, and some instrumental activity (rhythm bands, bells, etc.) can be started, the main objective is to turn the non-singers and the near-singers into singers.

The Intermediate Grades (4, 5, 6) should learn to read music. Two part harmony should be accomplished by late 4th or early 5th grade, 3 part singing in the 6th grade. Elementary theory, modes, and solfeggio can be introduced.

The Junior High School (7, 8, 9 or 7, 8 depending on school plan) students must sing 4 part harmony — SATB. The wide range of changed and unchanged voices, plus the necessity for boys to acquire the "feel" and the "sound" of a real tenor or bass line (not any hybrid) dictate this. Everyone should be permitted to participate, regardless of natural ability or current stage of development.

The Senior High School (10, 11, 12 or 9-12 depending on school plan) students with this kind of background can proceed to an unrestricted height of choral accomplishment . . . and equally unlimited depth of musical understanding.

ELEMENTARY SCHOOL MUSIC

I have great respect for elementary classroom teachers. As a group they are probably the most competent *instructors* in the entire educational system.

The classroom teacher is responsible for teaching all subjects to every child in the room. Since only this teacher, who spends the entire day throughout one full school year with the children, knows the most favorable conditions and times when music can become an integral part of the core situation, the final responsibility for the daily teaching of music is logically also placed on this individual. Music should be taught every day, but it is not the type of subject which lends itself to a "10:15 - 10:30" type of schedule. Often there is a 2:30 (in the middle of Geography class) which can be just right for "Alouette," for example.

Most classroom teachers need the help of a "special" music teacher or a music "supervisor," although I continue to be amazed at the number of elementary teachers (with their 3-6 hours of music) who do a better job of teaching the songs to their students than many of us can with a major in music. They should be required to remain in the room during the music class, so that they know exactly what needs to be done between visits of the music specialist.

I remember a second grade teacher in our system who listened, but never sang, throughout one entire year of my weekly instructional periods in her room. The next year when I came prepared to spend 25 minutes teaching several new songs, I found that after 3-4 minutes I was "out of soap" — her students already knew the songs! Since this happened every class period throughout the entire year, we had a wonderful time doing a wide variety of pieces from the supplementary texts. The girl has never sung a note in my presence, and there was no piano in the room, yet somehow she taught them every song, and taught them well!

Another teacher—this one taught sixth grade and claimed to know "absolutely nothing" about music — would invariably greet my weekly visit with something like, "Now here on page 106, the third line down, on the words, 'we lift our voices . . .', the firsts and seconds are OK, but the thirds are getting off. I know it sounds wrong, but I don't know what to do to get it right."

Although she lacked the technical solution for that one spot (as the music specialist, I knew it was my job to provide this), her daily singing sessions had already produced a fine sounding number.

Anyone who can teach, can teach music, although some must be convinced of this fact.[1] Those teachers who feel "completely unqualified" should probably be reminded of their affirmative answer to the question which appears on many applications for teaching positions, "Can you teach music in the .... grade?"

There are several things a music teacher can do to help classroom teachers, so that together they can further the musical education of each student.

1. Leave enough undone after each class so that there is a real need (and thus motivation) for the class to accomplish something before your next visit. For example, one-half of a song can be taught and the group told to learn the other half by the following class. Or, if today's song was about a rabbit, you can suggest they learn the song on page 68 which is about a fox.
2. The children should be supplied with a standard text, but teachers should have desk copies of books from every publisher. Too many times the same songs are sung over and over, in Kindergarten, Sunday School, Brownie and Cub Scouts, 4H Club, and throughout the elementary school. Students enjoy singing new songs, and teachers have fun teaching them.

---

[1] *Editor's note*: In Mr. Knauf's very effective Northern Kentucky Community College course in Public School Music, the emphasis is never placed on *how to teach* music (these are in-service educators), but rather on learning enough *about music* so that fear of the subject is eliminated and the teacher can begin teaching.

3. Since good teachers write out a lesson plan anyway, it can be put on a master sheet and dittoed for each classroom teacher. Even if sketchy and in brief "shorthand" form, it will provide a reminder of what you have done, and what you would like to have accomplished before your next class.

The Feeder System

Young people are won or lost to music during the formative junior high school years. Those who remain active participants and make progress during this crucial period usually proceed naturally into a satisfying high school experience, but those who "vacation" for a couple of years (until their "voice settles down" or they feel "refreshed and more physically able to perform") seldom return.

Junior high music should be a required course for all students. Young people are seldom capable of selecting those experiences which will be of permanent value to them — a brief glance back through our own lives will verify this — but they must be presented with a broad base of interests and skills from which they can develop the ability to discriminate when specialization becomes necessary. Requiring the course, however, will not accomplish anything by itself. The important thing is how effectively the introduction to choral music is handled.

A strong junior high teacher can practically assure the success of a high school chorus (even though the older group may be directed by someone of only reasonably good ability), but one who is not uniquely qualified to solve the problems of the junior high level can not only completely compromise the effectiveness of a secondary program, but virtually neutralize the accomplishments of a thorough elementary system.

Junior High Materials

I can now get good solid 4 part harmony from seventh and eighth graders in a very short time ... but it took me 5 or 6 years to find out what to do. In those first years of teaching I used the standard materials, but publishers then (as now) insisted upon loading 60-75% of most textbooks with unison and SA arrangements, even though it is physically impossible for these students to sing unison! There are some boys in the alto-tenor range, others with completely changed voices; some girls retain a crystal clear soprano and others have developed a maturing, "husky" sound (girls' voices change too, of course).

Most of the music I was trying to use not only was impossible to sing, but the occasional unison or 2 part piece I could use after adjusting the key and rewriting the parts, did *nothing* to prepare the boys for the SATB arrangements they would meet in high school (if I could hold them that long with that kind of music).

CREATE YOUR OWN

Strictly in self-defense, I began to write simple 4 part harmonizations of tune in public domain (not copyrighted compositions). The first one, which the youngsters sang from the chalkboard, gave them such a pleasant sensation of success — they "sounded like" a chorus —that I have had no problem with literature since (*see* Fig. 9-1).

Fig. 9-1

"The Cowboy's Lament": an Example of Mr. Knauf's Very Simple 4 Part Arranging Style

The arrangements adhere to just a few basic principles:

1. All parts, especially boys, should sing as high as they can, until the actual change puts them in a completely different range (most baritones are lazy tenors). The bulk of published junior high music is pitched too low. (*see* Fig. 9-2 for best ranges)
2. In order to build legitimate part singing, the tenor must be written rather simply, but it must sound like tenor. No hybrid form which permits the tenor to sing the melody in the old alto-tenor range should be used.
3. The bass should be kept very fundamental — roots and fifths,

with an occasional first inversion, but *never the melody* (that was all right for the little boy in the primary grades, but this is a maturing young man who will soon join the bass section of your high school choir).

4. Soprano and alto remain very much like the first and second parts in elementary songs, but should be more complicated than the boy's parts. Descants can be used to develop the upper register and provide a greater challenge for the more talented girls.

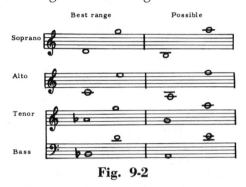

Fig. 9-2

Best Written Ranges for Junior High School 4 Part Music

How to Teach SATB Junior High Music

Generally the procedure I use involves teaching the least melodic part first . . . to all singers. Then, after the melody and other parts have been learned separately, they are sung in various combinations. Finally the entire song is assembled. Although students love to learn pieces they have heard before, musically it is better to start with unfamiliar songs so that knowing the tune will not interfere with hearing and learning the other parts.

1. The whole class learns the bass part.
2. Basses sing their part alone.
3. Sopranos learn the melody.
4. Bass and Soprano sing together.
5. Tenors learn their part (alto may learn this too).
6. Tenor and Soprano sing together.
7. Soprano, Tenor, and Bass sing together.
8. Altos learn their part.
9. Soprano and Alto sing together.
10. Soprano, Alto, and Tenor sing together.
11. Soprano, Alto, Tenor, and Bass sing together.

OTHER TEACHING TECHNIQUES

Good teaching techniques at the junior high level are essentially the same as those at any other level, that is, they are those ways of imparting knowledge, expanding understanding, and developing skills which produce the most desirable, lasting results. Effective teachers evolve their own methods early in their careers, and a "style" begins to emerge. An introverted, quiet, almost diffident person can be just as effective as the aggressive, strong-willed extrovert, if the techniques he employs are a natural outgrowth of his own particular personality.

Although the unique combinations which lead to success seem to be as individual, numerous, and varied as people themselves, *great enthusiasm* is undoubtedly a universal requirement. On the other hand, a common cause of failure is the blind attempt by one person to adopt the techniques of another which may not be at all consistent with his own personality.

My own best avenue to rapport with young people has always been through a sort of "delineated informality" which I learned at home. My father ran our family in a very relaxed manner, but he also made it clear where the line was, and no one ventured beyond that point (more than once, anyway!).

Regardless of your own teaching style — and every person has one, fully developed or not — I have found the following techniques to be useful in the junior high school:

1. For changing voices, especially the boys', establish the general rule that the lower the pitch, the softer it will be sung. The one certain way to injure a young voice is to allow students to sing loudly, too low. Otherwise it is doubtful if a voice can be injured by any singing activity in the junior high school.

2. Make certain that all girls who have completed the eighth grade have sung both soprano and alto for at least a full semester. Sopranos who can only sing the "tune" greatly restrict the potential of any group.

3. When the class is unsuccessful initially, try re-seating. Often the "chemistry" is incorrect. Sitting by the right person instead of the wrong one can often make the difference.

4. When a section has difficulty learning its part as a group, ask the most talented students in that section to sing it as a solo, or (with talented students from other sections) as a duet, or even a small

ensemble. Work the entire section back into the group by adding
a few persons at a time. The newer or more difficult the material
is, the more talented the students should be who sing it initially.

5. The better the singer, the farther he sits from the teacher. Those
who need the most help should be closer, and *in front* of the very
best singers. This way no one hears any other whose ability
is less than his own. In performance this is reversed. The poor
singers should be placed on the edges of the group where the
lack of solid singing from the rear will help to suppress the exu-
berance which creates a tendency to over-sing.

Junior High "Music Appreciation"

Teachers sometimes attempt to circumvent junior high vocal problems by playing records, making notebooks, studying composers —
doing almost anything in the name of "music appreciation" *instead*
of facing up to the challenge of teaching these youngsters how to
sing. Listening, creativity, and directed rhythmic activities play an
important part in the program; even a limited number of peripheral
activities are beneficial when pursued *in addition* to direct participation in music. But always remember that students should experience
the joys of actually doing it themselves. We must attempt to develop
firsthand love, not secondhand "appreciation."

Individual Singing

Students must sing individually from the first grade through the
twelfth if there is to be any real musical development. In addition
to keeping you posted on the exact vocal capabilities of each student
at any given time, there are other benefits. I use these techniques:

1. Each student sings one phrase in rotation with the other members of his group, moving in order right down the row. Elements
of form are established very quickly this way.
2. Students from different sections sing their own parts, in order.
A 16 measure tune may be sung 4 measures of tenor, next 4
measures bass, then alto, and finally the melody in the soprano.
The order should be varied.
3. One student begins singing his part. Just as he is finishing the
phrase, the name of another student is called out. He must then
pick up the rhythm and continue with his own part throughout
the next phrase, when the name of still another is called.

Through these frequent opportunities to compare his results with others, the student learns self-criticism. Individual singing is readily accepted by all, even those at the "very sensitive" junior high level, if it is made a part of the daily routine, and the youngsters can see that "everybody is doing it."

SMALL ENSEMBLES

The logical extension of individual singing is to assemble small, balanced groups of singers, preferably one to a part. After the entire class has learned a piece, I will pick 4 students (SATB) who will sing it as a quartet. Often it does not work out, and, after they have finished, I will say, "The balance is bad; what's wrong?"

"Well . . . I can't hear Margie," will come from the back of the room.

"What's Margie singing? . . . alto . . . OK, let's get some help for Margie."

Eventually, holding a part against several others becomes a normal and personally satisfying experience.

JUNIOR HIGH VOICE TESTING

With such strong emphasis on individual singing in all classes, the director can easily detect changes in quality which may indicate that a shift of sections is necessary.

It is not range alone that determines voice classification, but rather the range in which the beauty of the voice lies. A good bass can sing just as high as a tenor, and a mezzo soprano can hit "high C", but who would want to listen to them?

TEENAGE PSYCHOLOGY

The junior high students represent a phenomenon unlike anything else in captivity today—and I love every one of them! They are just as cute as can be, full of the "Old Ned," and literally glowing with health. Their enthusiasm is so great that after 20 minutes with them I get a feeling of power and elation that the "Pied Piper of Hamlin" must have felt. I am certain they would march right off the bridge into the Ohio River . . . if we did it in a happy way!

But my first few years with this age group was the nightmare which every junior high teacher can relate in vivid detail—they do not come through the door to your classroom, they crawl out of the woodwork! Make a mistake and they will tell you about it, in rather blunt terms. Lose control for just a few seconds and a chain reaction of adolescent hyperactive volatility turns your classroom into what could pass for an anthill which has just been kicked over.

Today I honestly enjoy teaching these students. My appreciation of them might have developed a little sooner had I known in the early years what I have since observed:

1. The program must be varied, in order to cope with the hyperactivity of the age. Rhythmic pieces are very popular. Techniques should be numerous, and flexible. The teacher must be acutely sensitive to the reactions of the class, and be able to change the pace exactly when it is necessary. The full hour rehearsal devoted to careful preparation of one piece for an important performance—often necessary and usually effective in college, sometimes in high school—is a complete disaster in junior high chorus.

2. Since rapid physical changes create a somewhat chaotic emotional state, the teenager seems to react favorably to established routines on which he can depend for some measure of stability in his life. Even though there is tremendous variation within the form, my junior high classes follow the same pattern:
   a. opening—vocalizing, breathing exercises, other fundamentals.
   b. middle—the new work planned for this class period.
   c. close—a recapitulation of previous learning, from other class periods.

3. The "easy" director will not find junior high friends, since students are honestly disappointed if you do not control them. The misbehaving student is actually saying, "Look, I'm wrong; you stop me or you're not a very good teacher."

4. Teenagers are very susceptible to social pressure (from their own group). They want to "belong." Sometimes in a general music class I will ask for singing only from "the peasants"—these are the students who did not make the select choir. The group is large enough that no student is embarrassed by being the only one singled out, but it does motivate many to more serious effort. Students love this kind of "name calling" and the identification with some group (even if it is the peasants), but it must always be handled with care, growing out of honest affection.[3]

---

[3] *Editor's note*: While Bob Knauf, Chorusmaster for many a "name" conductor, recognizes many of these suggestions as "a little on the cornball side" for print, Mr. Knauf, the personable junior high teacher, make very effective use of them — in person.

5. Students jump at an excuse for an evening "out of the house" at this age. Occasionally I will call a night rehearsal.
6. Girls follow the boys in whatever they do (alright "chase" if you prefer). By concentrating on teaching the boys how to sing in junior high (real men's parts, tenor and bass) they will remain active in high school chorus, and you can select the best singers from crowds of eager girls anxious to join the group.
7. These youngsters can spot a "phony" very quickly. You must be honest, admit mistakes easily, and avoid putting on airs.
8. They love to correct errors. If you have not been wrong for a while, let a mistake slide by. It keeps them alert and humanizes the teacher's "infallible" image, which many students resent.
9. Teachers and students can, and should be "friends." In fact, I often say to an erring group, jokingly, "Now you be careful, I'm the only friend you have." However the relationship cannot be equal, but rather is one in which the student knows he can always depend on the teacher as a reliable source of assistance.
10. Reactions are more violent at the junior high level. They are quicker to praise, but also quicker to blame and thus less tolerant of poor instruction than other age groups. You must avoid things which are completely unexpected—they will simply go into orbit! Detailed planning of every class is absolutely essential. If there is ever even a *moment* that you cannot fill, believe me, *they will!*

Two Problems—One Solution

Two major problems appear to stand in the way of significant progress in junior high music, and thus seriously hamper the effectiveness of any feeder system which is developed.

First, most published music for junior high school is abominable. Composers and arrangers must sell manuscripts to publishers, who must sell music to teachers, and many teachers do not know, do not care, or are just content to "get by," so they continue to buy the music which the publishers continue to request from the composers and arrangers. It is a very vicious circle. The high school director and the students he watches drift away from the choral music program during this crucial junior high period are the ones caught in the middle.

Secondly, the vast majority of present-day junior high music teachers seem to fall into 2 major categories:

1. Former elementary school teachers who are trying to get into high school.
2. Former high school teachers who are trying to stay out of elementary school.

This is at least partly due to the lack of attention which teacher training institutions have focused on the preparation of junior high school specialists.

Music departments in colleges and universities could do a great deal to correct both of these unfortunate situations by:

1. Restructuring their public school thinking to include 3 distinct areas (rather than merely elementary and secondary).
2. Offering courses which thoroughly investigate the problems of the changing voice, beginning part singing, applied teenage psychology, SATB arranging for changing voices, etc.
3. Considering the establishment of a degree with major emphasis on junior high school music teaching.

Because of the pivotal nature of these important years in the musical lives of our young people, the junior high school demands *the best* our profession has to offer. The battle for future musical participation is won or lost in the junior high school, and we are in great danger of losing it.

10

Physical Facilities and Equipment

by Wayne S. Hertz

Central Washington State College

Wayne S. Hertz

is Chairman of the Department of Music, Central Washington State College, in Ellensburg. He holds the Ed.D. in Music Education from New York University, M.M. from Northwestern University, and the B.S. in Music Education from the University of Illinois.

In 1933 he began his teaching career as vocal music supervisor for the West Aurora (Illinois) Public Schools. Since 1938 he has been chairman of the music department and director of the "Central Singers" (the concert choir) at Central Washington State College.

Dr. Hertz has served in many professional positions of responsibility, including presidencies of the Illinois School Vocal Association (1936-38), Northwest Division MENC (1943-45), and the Washington Music Educators Association (1950-52). He has been on the Editorial Board of the Music Educators Journal (1960-64) and was National Chairman of MENC Commission VI (1955-59) which published "Music in the Senior High School" under his editorship. Since 1963 he has been a member of the Academic Music Panel, Office of Cultural Presentation, U.S. State Department. He is very active as a guest conductor, having directed over 100 music festivals.

During an intensive period of research preceding the construction of new facilities in Ellensburg, Dr. Hertz visited most of the music buildings in the Northeast U.S. and many in other sections of the country.

As school student bodies continue to overflow their present structures and communities become more willing to provide new buildings and equipment, the choral director has an ever-increasing opportunity to ask for, and get, modern facilities which will aid in the development of a truly outstanding program.

Although the school board and the administration will decide when and where construction will take place, *you*, the expert on the needs of the choral department, must be ready with the facts and figures, the authoritative advice on what is best... and why!

This Takes Time

The $1,100,000 Central Washington State College Music Building[1] is the result of detailed planning over a long period of time. Even when all parties concerned are anxious to proceed as rapidly as possible, certain delays and disappointments must be expected. Our experience is typical:

1. A ten year waiting period during which we were asked to "get along" in the old structure while construction with a higher priority was taking place on the campus.
2. 18 months of staff meetings to determine precise recommendations for room sizes and equipment specifications.
3. The elimination of about $200,000 in features and equipment through the swift movement of the Governor's red pencil.

Selling the Need

We have all heard fine music produced in the most limited space, with only a bare minimum of equipment. But we have also seen how much can be accomplished when there are acoustically satisfying rehearsal rooms, adequate storage areas, sound-isolated practice rooms, and equipment which reflects the latest scientific advances of our age.

Unlike the instrumental music program, which requires a great amount of school-owned equipment and large personal expenditures for instruments, the choral director needs students, he needs music, and he needs space. Thus the choral music department can serve a very high number of students at a very low cost per pupil.

---

[1] *Editor's note:* Author Hertz is too modest. It is the *Wayne S. Hertz Music Building,* dedicated to the man who has served with great distinction as chairman of the music department, since 1938.

A competent director can often involve at least 50% of the entire student body in some phase of his program.

We, as music teachers, know these things to be true, but often we must remind administrators, mentioning not only what we feel our function to be and how effectively we have been accomplishing our goals, but also calling attention to our needs—those things which will enable us to do an even better job in the future.

Preparing A "Brief"

As part of the justification for our request of a new music building, we prepared a rather thorough, but straightforward, paper, entitled "Tentative Estimate of Needs for a New Music Building." In it we quoted (directly from the college catalog) the philosophy, functions, and general objectives of the college, and then showed how the music department applies these principles to its own more specific objectives and functions.

The first 2 paragraphs of the cover letter summarized the work being done by the music department and referred to the recognition already received. The third and fourth paragraphs arrived at the meat of the matter:

"We have been doing our job handicapped by physical facilities which were originally intended for most anything but the teaching of music. We do have space. But the space is not conducive to the best teaching of our subject. Acoustically, the building is atrocious. Floors are sagging, the heating is archaic, ventilation means opening or closing a window. In spite of the physical surroundings, the Department of Music has been recognized as outstanding. In other words, we have progressed because of staff and staff alone.

"Now combine a fine staff with adequate facilities and there is unlimited opportunity in our effectiveness."

Other sections of the paper, which might serve as a model (or at least an idea-springboard) for public school choral directors in search of new facilities, are reproduced below:

The Music Department serves:

A. The student
   1. Helps him to meet situations effectively by developing value-judgments.
   2. Helps him to understand himself. Since music is an expressive art, the student must clarify his own ideas before he can successfully communicate them to others.
   3. Helps him to understand other people by offering wide ac-

quaintance with the folk and art music of all countries.
4. Helps him to understand the inter-relationship of music with all other branches of learning.
5. Teaches him how to apply what he knows to the new and unfamiliar.
6. Teaches him the recognition of and respect for competence.
7. Provides opportunity for development of leadership.
8. Encourages him to put forth his best effort.
9. Acquaints him with the music that constitutes a large part of the world's cultural heritage.
10. Encourages the constructive use of leisure time.
11. Provides courses for vocational preparation in music and music education.
12. Provides individual practice rooms and instruments.
13. Provides a materials laboratory, recordings, and listening facilities for both music students and others.

B. The School
1. Provides instruction in one aspect of the curriculum directly concerned with Man — one of the Humanities.
2. Provides an area of study closely related to that part of the curriculum dealing with Human Relations. Music is a communicative art, which expresses and contributes to the physical and spiritual environment.
3. Provides performing organizations in which all students may participate.
4. Provides music for assemblies, sports, and special events.

THE PRELIMINARY SUGGESTIONS

Although most architects have never conducted a mixed chorus, they can be very expert in designing facilities for a choral program —if you tell them what you need! Our staff prepared the following list of music building requirements:

Recital Hall — 7200 sq. ft.

Stage	35 x 60
Organ installation	6 x 50
Toilet facilities — 2	100 sq. ft.
Off-stage area	35 x 5 x 2
Foyer areas	10 x 600
Seating for 400	3750 sq. ft.

Teaching Studios — 5208 sq. ft.

12 rooms	15 x 22
3 rooms	16 x 26

Class Rooms — 6900 sq. ft.

2 rooms	30 x 48
4 rooms	30 x 35

Rehearsal Rooms — 4200 sq. ft.

Band	40 x 50
Band Instrument storage	4 x 50
Choral	40 x 50

Practice Rooms — 2720 sq. ft.

22 rooms	8 x 10
8 rooms	10 x 12

Organ Practice Room — 320 sq. ft.

Administration Office — 1240 sq. ft.

Reception, with coat	16 x 25
Office	16 x 20
Studio	16 x 20
Work room	10 x 20

Store Rooms — 2300 sq. ft.

Band instruments	40 x 27½
Music (Library)	20 x 30
Uniforms	20 x 30

Research and Listening Area — 1200 sq. ft.

Conference Room — 1100 sq. ft.

General Toilet Facilities – 4 – 1000 sq. ft.

Corridors and Circulation — 9850 sq. ft.

Custodial and Maintenance — 600 sq. ft.

Service and Mechanical Spaces — 2000 sq. ft.

TOTAL – 45,838 sq. ft.

SPECIFIC ROOM REQUIREMENTS

Suggestions for each individual area were also included to help the architect to understand the function of the rooms, and to note the specific requirements of each. No attempt was made to itemize every detail, but rather to call attention to those things which might be unique in a music building, as opposed to the requirements of the architect's "normal" clients.

Recital Hall

Seating area for about 400. European type, sloping floor. Cork tile in aisle. Asphalt tile under seats. Variable light levels. Carefully designed acoustics paramount. Provision for portable risers on stage. Double doors at sides of stage. Organ installation behind stage, pipes must be exposed in hall, integrate into design. Exact installation and space requirements from organ maunfacturer. Location of console optional. Minimum circulation space behind stage. Toilet facilities for both men and women backstage. Some practice rooms should be placed in backstage area so that they can be used as dressing rooms. Basic high illumination for stage lights. Disappearing type footlights. Arrangement for adjustable spotlights. Provision for originating and receiving radio and TV programs. Consider connecting this with classroom TV closed circuit system. Wood floor on stage (parquet type desirable).

Teaching Studios

Arrangement suitable for 1 grand piano in 15 x 22 rooms, suitable for 2 grands in 16 x 26 rooms. Desk and chair plus 5 additional guest chairs. Storage facilities to include coat closet; book case, adjustable shelves 12' x 7', some open, others with doors; 2 file cabinets; music storage cabinet for sheet music. Provision for use of tape recorder. Relatively high level of uniform light. Full length mirror in voice studios. Acoustical treatment in brass studio relatively dead, but live in 4 voice studios. 12 lineal feet of portable tack or chalk board (instructor to select relative amounts). Carpeted floors. Homelike, rather than institutional, atmosphere. Space for work table.

Class Rooms

Teacher's closet and storage cabinet. Coat racks, Adjustable chalk and tack boards. Provision for use of audio-visual material (opaque projector, exact type of equipment should be studied, must be built-in and able to lock it up). Closed circuit TV connection. Conventional style classrooms.

Rehearsal Rooms

BAND AND ORCHESTRA: storage for drums, large instruments, other equipment. Floor stepped (size suitable for instrumental). Should be on ground floor, accessible to outdoors, with loading dock. Accessible to instrument storage room, adjacent to student's instrument storage. In and out circulation through storage areas. Large (double width) doors.

CHORAL: floor stepped (size suitable for choral). Room used for choir only. In and out circulation.

BOTH ROOMS: Music storage cabinets — 100 cubicles for current use. Tack and chalk boards. Double or soundproof doors, with closers. Provide high level of light and hookup with closed TV circuit. Drinking fountains.

Individual Practice Rooms

Adequate lighting, ventilation and sound control paramount. Should not be too dead. Prevent sound from escaping — sound proof doors. One way glass panels in doors. These are 8 x 10 rooms.

Ensemble Practice Rooms

Requirements same as individual practice rooms. Can be used as seminar rooms. These are 10 x 12 rooms.

Organ Practice Room

See existing organ which will be reused. Measure console, box, blower. This is practice room only — no space for audience. Must be large enough to take care of sound. Sound absorptive walls. Must be humidified, verify percentage. Sound proof doors.

Administrative Offices

RECEPTION ROOM: reception desk, work counter, work space, typewriter. Supply storage above, also reference books. Coat closet.

WORK ROOM: 2 work tables — long, for mailing. Desk for student help. Duplicating equipment. Should be able to see into reception room.

Office and studio connected. Studio requirements same as teaching studio.

Storage Areas

Humidity control. Verify exact requirements. One area for students' personal instruments and equipment, arranged for continuous circulation through area by students picking up or returning equipment. Flexible for variation in number of instruments. Accessible at all times. Individual locks on each compartment.

STANDARD LOCKERS: either 12 x 12 or 18 x 18—arranged along corridors or in separate locker area — 150 now, 300 ultimate.

Locked storage area for school-owned property: see separate list for permanent storage requirements. Should be adjacent to band and orchestra rehearsal room.

ROTC band instrument storage—separated from school-owned equipment. Size requirements could double in future.

Instrument repair space (in school-owned storage room)—work bench, vise, storage for materials and tools, Bunsen burner connections.

MUSIC STORAGE: for permanent storage, in general vicinity of rehearsal area. Sorting racks for 60 folders. Repair table. Card file. Sink space for black and white copy machine. Space for ditto machine. Storage racks, vertical or horizontal.

UNIFORM STORAGE: drawers for handkerchiefs, belts, braids, capes. 125 uniforms, 30 pep band coats, 100 choral robes. Provision for issuing uniforms, including check-out counter, uniform file card system. Separate storage for coats and pants. Fitting room.

Research and Listening Room

Supplementary, since new college library will provide facilities for entire school. Storage for materials borrowed from main library. Storage for permanent materials (pamphlets, books, scores). Provision for small booths for 8–10 listening, with headsets.

Conference Room

For use of student and faculty organizations. Could serve as a classroom. Provision for kitchenette adjacent.

Corridors and Stairways

8 ft. wide, terrazzo if possible. Non-slip treads on stairways. Probably wider in areas of possible congestion (lobby). Lobby display for announcements of coming events. Building directory at main entrance. Provide seating areas where students can congregate. Lockers may be in corridors. Some coat racks in corridors. Small ticket booth, if possible. Protective wainscot. Bulletin boards near administration area. Provide freight elevator for moving heavy equipment (including grand pianos).

Toilet Facilities

1 set men's and women's each floor (assuming 2 story building). Numbers, fixtures, etc. determined by code. Wall hung fixtures. Ceramic tile floors and wainscot. Mirrors, soap dispenser, towel holders. Metal toilet stalls. Rest room and lounge in women's toilet area.

Miscellaneous Notes

Must provide humidifiers where required. Verify humidity percent. Storage for specialized equipment. Storage for expendable materials. General dead storage, near receiving area for uncrating shipments of supplies. Refuse disposal. One-way communication from practice rooms. Two-way communication with studios. Phone (to main switchboard) in each studio. Chair rail in all studios, practice and rehearsal areas. Lockers for individual students. Prefer 2 story building. Proper adequate ventilation essential in all practice and rehearsal rooms. Acoustical control is essential. No transoms. Space somewhere for one good recording set-up, not accessible to students. Must have adequate space, no matter how shiny. What to do about small classes? — there are quite a few — psychological effect of small classes in a large room. Study may indicate that storage areas and research and listening room area can be reduced. Question listening area in our building, since it is provided in main library.

Acoustical Control is Basic

Since music, as either art or science, is communicated through the medium of sound, obviously the sound conditions in a music building are of paramount importance. Each room must, in itself, provide a satisfactory acoustic environment consistent with its function, but also the sound from one room must not intrude on the activities in any other area. Accordingly, our objective was not to *absorb* sound, but rather to *contain* it.

In the contract with the architect there should be a clause which requires him to hire an acoustical engineer. Too much acoustic treatment in the past has been done by those who were merely guessing. We were very fortunate to have Robin Towne Associates, of Seattle, who went to great lengths to measure the sound output of individual instruments and voices, as well as the volume level of various sizes of ensembles, including the largest chorus. By this method they were able to recommend construction which could contain these sounds.

The rehearsal rooms and the recital hall have been treated, individually according to size and function, with "pyramids"—alternating patterns of pegboard, wallboard, and acoustical tile—to provide the sort of acoustic atmosphere which is pleasant for the listener and comfortable, even flattering, for the performer.

Separation of sound has been achieved through the use of double

Fig. 10-1

The Recital Hall, Showing the Alternating Patterns of Pegboard, Wallboard, and Acoustical Tile

Fig. 10-2

llways Have Been Used to
ieve Separation of Sound

walls and intervening dead spaces (closets, hallways, storage areas, etc.). No cement floor is common to any 2 rooms, but has been poured separately. The second floor consists of one 4 inch layer of cement, a 2 inch piece of felt, and another 2 inches of cement. The first floor ceilings are "free hanging", i.e. they are suspended on wires and special springs which eliminate any transmission of sound—expensive, but effective. No window can be opened, and wherever there is a possibility of sound leakage, double windows have been installed.

The Choral Rehearsal Room

The Central Washington State College choral rehearsal room is approximately 40 x 50 feet, with a 22 foot ceiling. It has been our experience that low ceilings in rehearsal rooms deaden the sound, but high ceilings allow the director to hear more exactly what each singer is producing. The floor is cement with vinyl covering. Walls are cement block, with multiple pyramids extending from the walls. The ceiling is a combination of plaster and acoustic board.

Four levels of permanent, built-in risers extend in a curve for the entire 50 foot length of the room. Ample space (45 in.) has been allowed on each level for chairs and ease of movement when the chairs are occupied. With the first row on the floor, the 5 levels will accomodate 175 singers. With a second row on the floor, 35 more students can be added without crowding either the director, or the accompanist who sits at a 9 foot grand piano.

Coat and book racks line one entire wall. In the front of the room there are 2 bulletin boards, chalk board, and filing cabinets for 300 folders. Chairs, manufactured by Heywood-Wakefield, were selected after extensive search for a comfortable chair which does not invite a slumping posture.

Lighting is fluorescent, suspended from the ceiling. A forced air heating system provides for a complete change of air every 2 minutes. Even when filled to capacity, the atmosphere in the room has never become uncomfortable.

Two loudspeakers are permanently installed on the front wall for both hi-fi or stereo playback of either tapes or discs. The *Viking* tape deck is used regularly to record rehearsals. Two *Shure* microphones are suspended from the ceiling, but may be moved to other positions easily. Additional microphones are used on flood level through an *Ampex* 4 channel mixer.

The rehearsal room (as well as other rooms) is wired to send and receive closed-circuit TV broadcasts to and from classrooms in the local public schools. In this way actual educational situations can be observed by prospective teachers, and young students can enjoy college originated programs.

We have experimented with providing a music rack for each 2 singers, in order to develop better posture, and to allow for more concentration on the conductor. The music, not being handled so often, remains in much better condition.

THE DIRECTOR'S OFFICE

The person who is directing the choral activities of a large percentage of the total school population has many administrative responsibilities. While he may be able to operate from a coat pocket, or a clip board, his leadership can be much more efficient and his relationships with the public much more effective, if a separate office is provided.

A desk, telephone, and filing cabinet are minimum equipment, but space and furniture for confidential student, parent, and business conferences should be considered. Depending on the scope of his activities, the following equipment and supplies may be of use:[2]

Typewriter	Calendar
Adding machine	Binder covers
Desk letter trays	Clip boards
Rotary telephone index	Pencil sharpener
Desk spindle	Steel cash box
Cellophane tape dispenser	3 hole punch
Desk nameplate	Paper punch
Memo pad	Magnifying glass
Desk organizer	Shears
Desk set	Tubular coin wrappers
Stationery rack for desk drawer	Currency wrappers
Sponge moistener	Rubber stamps
4 x 6 cards	Bond typing paper
4 x 6 file guides	Bond envelopes
Filing folders	Onion skin
Letter size file guides	Carbon paper
File folder labels (color coded)	Address labels
Ledger	Metal clasp envelopes
Dictionary	Rubber cement

---

[2] Kenneth L. Neidig, *Band Director's Guide*, Englewood Cliffs, N.J., Prentice-Hall, Inc., 1964.

All-purpose glue   Ruler
Rubber bands   Eraser
Paper clips   Gummed reinforcements
Staples   Duplicator master units–plain
Thumbtacks   Duplicator master units–music lined

PRACTICE ROOMS

A minimum of 4 individual practice rooms should be constructed as a part of new facilities in every school. Many students have some time available during the school day, and, if practice rooms are available, they will make good use of them. One person may work in a room 6 x 8 feet, but one or more larger rooms for small ensembles or sectional rehearsals should be considered. Adjoining rooms must be separated by a double wall in order to isolate sound.

STORAGE AREAS

The large amount of money which is often invested in equipment must be protected by providing adequate storage facilities. The life expectancy of robes, sheet music, or any other material used by the choral music department can be very short, indeed, if not cared for properly. Humidity should be controlled. Moth proofing must be considered when storing garments.

The music storage room, or library, should include these items:

1. Adequate filing. Either built in, or steel filing cases for all music, a card index file for cross reference (title, composer, classification).
2. Work space. Including sorting racks, table and chairs for general work, and a sink, with running water.
3. Library supplies. Including rehearsal folders, transparent tape for mending music, heavy tape for repairing folders, rubber stamps for identifying music and numbering copies, manuscript paper, and filing envelopes.

We also use both multilith and spirit duplicator machines.

PORTABLE RISERS

Risers for both seated and standing chorus are available, in both wood and metal. Only the standing type are used by most schools, since permanent, built-in risers are available for seated rehearsals. We have used folding wooden risers with satisfaction through many seasons of active touring, but now are carrying the more expensive aluminum riser. We have found that the higher cost, and the slightly increased noise when they are assembled or moved is more than compensated for by their lightness.

THE ACOUSTICAL SHELL

We have found the portable acoustical shell to be very helpful in mixing and projecting sound, especially in concerts by a relatively small group performing on a large stage. Panels, which weigh 116 pounds each, can be folded to 4' x 6' x 5". Standards weigh 22 pounds each and fold to 5" x 7" x 8'. Although they are easily moved, especially with the casters, on stage and even within the building, the size and weight of the number we require prohibits us from using them while on a tightly scheduled, many-stop tour.

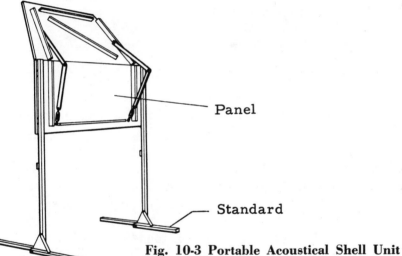

Panel

Standard

Fig. 10-3 Portable Acoustical Shell Unit
(Wenger Music Equipment Co., Owatonna, Minnesota)

PIANOS

Whenever students are asked to sing with a fixed pitch instrument, it is essential that the instrument be in tune. The differences between *a capella*, pure temperament singing and adherance to the tempered scale of a keyboard instrument are great enough, without also adding the confusion of an "ill-tempered clavichord."

Our instruments are tuned regularly 4 times per year. A local tuner is on call for additional work whenever necessary. Since the temperature in the building now remains exactly the same 24 hours a day, we find that the pitch is holding better than ever before. Our bill for the care of 54 pianos (10 grand and 44 upright) averages in excess of $1500 per year, but we feel this to be an absolute necessity to create a proper ear-training environment for the students.

Reliable piano manufacturers make the following recommendations for the care of your piano: [3]

1. Use a slightly dampened cloth for thorough cleaning, followed by a soft, clean cloth (also used for frequent dusting). Use high quality cream wax occasionally, but never use oiled or "treated" dust clothes.
2. Clean the keys by rubbing front to back (never across—it will darken the sides) with a slightly moistened, soft, lint-free cheese cloth. A very limited amount of the mildest soap may be added, but rubbing must be very gentle.
3. Extreme temperature or humidity changes have a damaging effect. Do not place your piano over a heated register or near an open window. Although sometimes impossible to maintain in a school building, 75–80 degrees, with 35% relative humidity, is ideal.
4. Moth damage can be serious. Hanging a bag of camphor inside the piano, or having a service man spray every year or two will be helpful, although there is no known permanent mothproofing suitable for pianos.
5. In addition to regular tunings at least twice per year, the action should be adjusted and other mechanical items checked. The average piano contains over 7,000 parts in the keys and action alone. Over 200 strings are stretched to an average tension of 150–200 pounds each, putting a stress of 18–20 tons on the metal plate and its support. This is a complicated mechanism. Since proper maintenance demands considerable knowledge and experience, your tuner/technician must be chosen with utmost care.

ROBES AND OTHER ATTIRE

The trend of many school choirs seems to be toward blazers, or formal dress, and away from the sacred-associated choir robe. However, groups often present a formal, serious, sometimes sacred, opening portion of the program in robes, then change during intermission into a more casual, although still uniform attire (*see* Figs. 10-4, 10-5).

---

[3] Adapted from *Care of Your Piano*, Baldwin Piano and Organ Company, Cincinnatti, Ohio. Used by permission.

Fig. 10-4

Traditional Choir Apparel: The Very Formal Robe and Surplice (Left) and the Standard Robe with Collar (Right)

(De Moulin Bros. & Co., Greenville, Ill.)

De Moulin Bros. & Co.

Fig. 10-5

Other Popular Choir Apparel: Blazers with Contrasting Trousers or Skirt, Tie and Tails with Long Black Dresses for the Girls

The Central Washington Music Department owns a set of robes. Also, the men have a red blazer and black trouser outfit (the school's colors), and the women make their own black, sheath-type dresses. On our tours we have found it best to hold each person responsible for his own clothing, rather than to use large robe carriers, which are difficult to get on and off busses.

Fig. 10-6 shows a number of the standard accessories most commonly used with choir robes.

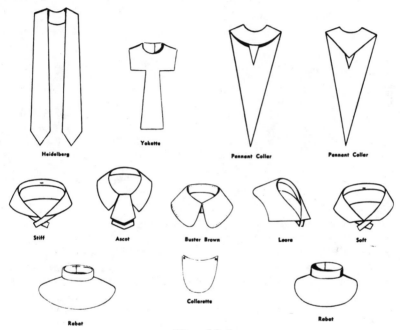

Fig. 10-6

Choir Accessories Guide
(Collegiate Cap and Gown Co.)

MAGNETIC RECORDING TAPE[4]

Your intended use should determine the magnetic tape you buy. To select the "right" tape you must be familiar with its 2 basic parts:

1. *The backing* (the shiny side) supplies physical strength: *cellulose acetate* for economy, *polyester* for immunity to humidity, and added strength which reduces the danger of breaks and

---

[4] This and the following 2 sections are based on materials provided by the Magnetic Products Division of Minnesota Mining and Manufacturing Company (3M), St. Paul, Minn., makers of "Scotch" brand tapes and accessories.

allows the very thin double and triple lengths to be wound on standard size reels.

2. *The oxide coating* (the dull side) does the actual recording: *standard* for general recording, *high output* for greater dynamic range and freedom from distortion on signal peaks, *high potency* for complete purity of sound, and *low print* to reduce "print through" (signal transfer from layer to layer).

Use the following chart to determine recording time for your machine and the particular tape you want to use.

TAPE CHART

Recording One Direction — Single Track Monaural, Dual Track Stereo

TAPE LENGTH	1 7/8 I.P.S.	3 3/4 I.P.S.	7 1/2 I.P.S.
150 ft.	15 min.	7 1/2 min.	3 3/4 min.
225 ft.	24 min.	12 min.	6 min.
300 ft.	30 min.	15 min.	7 1/2 min.
600 ft.	1 hr.	30 min.	15 min.
900 ft.	1 1/2 hrs.	45 min.	22 1/2 min.
1200 ft. (standard 7")	2 hrs.	1 hr.	30 min.
1800 ft.	3 hrs.	1 1/2 hrs.	45 min.
2400 ft. ("double")	4 hrs.	2 hrs.	1 hr.
3600 ft. ("triple")	6 hrs.	3 hrs.	1 1/2 hrs.

Recording Both Directions — Dual Track Monaural, 4 Track Stereo
(Double These Times for 4 Track Monaural Recordings)

TAPE LENGTH	1 7/8 I.P.S.	3 3/4 I.P.S.	7 1/2 I.P.S.
150 ft.	30 min.	15 min.	7 1/2 min.
225 ft.	45 min.	24 min.	12 min.
300 ft.	1 hr.	30 min.	15 min.
600 ft.	2 hrs.	1 hr.	30 min.
900 ft.	3 hrs.	1 1/2 hrs.	45 min.
1200 ft. (standard 7")	4 hrs.	2 hrs.	1 hr.
1800 ft.	6 hrs.	3 hrs.	1 1/2 hrs.
2400 ft. ("double")	8 hrs.	4 hrs.	2 hrs.
3600 ft. ("triple")	12 hrs.	6 hrs.	3 hrs.

TAPE HANDLING PRINCIPLES

1. Avoid storing unboxed reels of tape. The original box protects tape from dust and physical damage to its edges.
2. Wind reels of tape loosely. Store "on edge" or flat on individual shelves. Avoid stacking as the weight may distort the plastic reels or damage the edges of the tape.

3. Where there are wide variations in humidity (40–60% is ideal), tape storage in sealed containers is recommended. The use of drying or humidifying agents is not recommended because of difficulty in controlling the results.

4. Avoid extremes of temperature (70–75°F. is ideal). If tape is subjected to extreme temperatures, such as in shipment, allow 16 to 24 hours for it to return to room temperature before using.

5. Occasional use of the tape improves storage characteristics. Playing the tape releases strains and adhesions.

6. Avoid excessive tensions in rewinding tape for storage. The tape may become stretched or permanently distorted if wound too tightly.

7. Cleaning of tape is not necessary in normal operation. If dust is excessive, the tape may be cleaned by wiping with a clean, dry, lint-free cloth while re-winding.

8. If tape has been stored 6 months or longer, it's a good idea to rewind it once before using. For storing 5 years or longer, it should be in sealed containers.

USEFUL TAPE ACCESSORIES

1. *End-of-reel tape clips* prevent spilling or tangling. They fit inside the reel, thus work equally well on partial or full spools, and will not warp the reels during long periods of storage.

2. *Empty reels and boxes* (3, 4, 5 and 7 inches) are a must for editing and for extra take-up reel use.

3. *Splicing tape,* pressure-sensitive, made especially for magnetized recording tape will not become gummy or sticky, ooze adhesive under tension, or harden and crack, but actually increase in strength with age. (*see* Fig. 10-7 How to Splice Recording Tape.)

Fig. 10-7

How to Splice Recording Tape
(Courtesy Scotch Brand Tapes)

| 1. Hold overlapped ends of magnetic tape securely between fingers and cut at shallow angle —about 45 degrees —for maximum strength and flexibility of splice. | 2. Butt the cut ends of the tape in a splicing block without overlapping them. Make sure you apply the splicing tape to the shiny side of the magnetic tape. | 3. Apply small section of splicing tape. Use the 7/32″ size and apply it parallel with the magnetic tape as shown. Rub splicing tape firmly with fingernail to iron out air pockets for positive adhesion. | 4. If a splicing block is not available, lay magnetic tape on a flat surface. Butt the cut edges carefully and hold in position with index and forefinger. Apply short strip of ½″ or ¼″ wide splicing tape diagonally across splice and rub firmly to remove all air pockets. | 5. If splicing tape is wider than the magnetic tape used, trim off excess, cutting into magnetic tape very slightly. This eliminates danger of exposed adhesive gumming up recording head or sticking to adjacent layer of magnetic tape. |

4. *Leader and timing tape* protects the ends against repeated damage, allows for more recording space since leader (not tape) is used for thread-up. It provides an area for labeling (thus avoiding the problem of tape in the wrong box), and can be used to identify selections in the middle of the tape, since the colored leader contrasts with the dark magnetic tape. Markings placed exactly 7½ inches apart allow for precise timing or cueing between selections. At a tape speed of 7½ i.p.s. (inches per second) this means that one 7½ " section of tape passes the recording head every second, or at 3¾ i.p.s., it will take 2 seconds for the section to pass.

5. *Tape library labels,* self-sticking, with tear-off tabs to mark the reels, wrap around the box hinges to give both front and edge identification and to reinforce the hinge. Information may be typed or written in ball-point pen.

How to Make Better Tapes[5]

1. Make a test recording before performance, then play it back. Listen for hum and equipment noises due to defective recorder, microphone, or connections. Determine the correct volume level. Too high causes distortion; too low brings out tape or amplifier hiss.

2. For clarity, presence, diction and best over-all sound, microphones should be located overhead, a few feet behind the conductor. Get as close to the performers as possible while still spanning the group. Avoid placing the microphone in the audience or at the rear of the hall.

3. After corrections, make another test before the performance.

4. Use full track tape or record on one track only. Avoid "bargain" tape. Do not use ½ mil, extra thin tape.

If you plan to have phonograph records made from your tapes:

1. Program your selections (by cutting and splicing if necessary) in the same order you wish them to appear on each side of the record. Leave 5 seconds of blank or leader tape between each selection.

2. Furnish the record manufacturer with timing in minutes and seconds for each selection. Do not use the index counter on the

---

[5] Adapted from materials supplied by Recorded Publications Company, 1558 Pierce Avenue, Camden, New Jersey.

tape recorder as these readings do not correlate with professional equipment.

3. Always use special splicing tape. Only tape which is recorded on one side can be spliced without loss to the other side, of course.

4. Consider maximum playing times when planning your continuity of pieces for each side of the record:

12 in. LP—22 min. per side (44 min. total)

10 in. LP—15 min. per side (30 min. total)

7 in. LP— 6 min. per side (12 min. total)

or 45 RPM

If you want visible bands between selections, deduct 20 seconds for each band.

THE MUSIC FILING SYSTEM

Obviously music must be cared for properly if it is expected to serve the long-term needs of a permanently established choral music program; however, to be most useful, an effective filing and card index system must also be established. Filing envelopes and Title—Composer—Classification cards, such as those shown in Fig. 10-8 can be used for this purpose.

FORM 4			TITLE CARD										

Fig. 10-8

4x6 Index Cards. Title (White), Composer (Blue),
Classification (Salmon)
(Southern Music Co., San Antonio, Tex.)

As music is purchased, essential information about it should be recorded on the title card, the composer card, and on as many classification cards as may be necessary for complete cross-reference. Information is then recorded on the front of the filing envelope and the music placed inside.

Title cards and composer's cards are filed alphabetically in separate card file boxes. Classification cards are grouped according to classification in a third file box. They are separated by blank index guides on which you can write the name of the classification. There are many possible subdivisions. The ones you use will depend somewhat on your own personal tastes and background, and on the activities of your choir. Some possibilities are:

1. By period (like Renaissance, Baroque, etc.)
2. By type (like madrigal, folk, etc.)
3. By country (Russian, German)
4. By use (Commencement)
5. By season (Christmas, spring)

Filing envelopes are numbered from "1" on, as the music is purchased, then placed either on shelves or in cabinets in that same numerical order. All pieces in choral collections can also be indexed with this system by using "C1", "C2", etc., as the library numbers.

If you also note *where* on the "when used" lines of the choral filing envelope (*see* Fig. 10-9) this will help you to avoid repetition when planning programs.

Fig. 10-9

9x12 Choral Filing Envelope
(*Southern Music Co.*)

CHORAL FILING ENVELOPE

| No. Copies.................... | Library No....................... |

Title......
Composer.......... Arranger..........
Publisher.......... Catalogue No..........

Arr. Voice:
UNISON........ SA........ SSA........ SSAA........ SATB........
SATB 5-8 Pts........ SAB........ TB........ TTB........ TBB........
TTBB........ Boys ( )........ ☐ Sacred........ ☐ Secular........

WHEN USED

Southern MUSIC COMPANY
SAN ANTONIO 6, TEXAS
NATION-WIDE SHEET MUSIC SERVICE

QUALITY COSTS—BUT WILL LAST

When making any purchase for the music program of a school, from a $1.1 million building down to a new needle for the phonograph, the best procedure is:

1. Find out all you can about the subject, through both personal observation and liberal use of consultants.
2. Contact the many reliable companies who sell the product you desire.
3. Make the best selection, based on quality, not just cost alone.

Occasionally an unscrupulous or over-anxious businessman will offer a chroal director a commission ("kick back") or other large favors in exchange for particular contracts. In addition to being illegal and immoral, the acceptance of such offers (even if they are successfully concealed from others) can place the director in an impossible bargaining position with the company making the under-the-table payments. The wonderful American system of competition and free enterprise, coupled with the "sealed bid" technique, will protect you in this respect.

Remember that quality usually costs more, but it will last. Cheap robe materials, for instance, may look beautiful immediately after delivery, but will not take the abuse which repeated wearing, cleaning, and pressing give a garment. "Bargain" tapes may produce an acceptable recording of a conversation or speech, but miss the high frequency peaks of your best choral performance. An "unknown" piano may cost less, but the cheaper construction could be a constant source of pitch and maintenance problems. A fly-by-night contractor, or cut-rate architect can create many varieties of headaches.

Becoming, and remaining, well-informed in this vital area of physical facilities and equipment is a demanding, time-consuming, and sometimes almost overwhelming task. New products are being developed every day. Since these non-musical considerations can have such a direct influence on the entire choral music program, they, of necessity, become an important part of every director's responsibility.

II

Practical Rehearsal Techniques

by Warner Lawson

Howard University

Warner Lawson

is Dean of the College of Fine Arts and School of Music, Howard University, Washington, D.C., where he is also director of the University Choir. The Eastern Division of the MENC elected him President for 1965-67.

Born into a musical family (his father an outstanding pianist and teacher; his mother soprano soloist with the famous Fisk Jubilee Singers), he completed college with a major in music at Fisk University, took a Bachelor's degree in music literature under Bruce Simonds at Yale, and went to Berlin in 1930 to study with Arthur Schnabel. Four years (2 as department head) on the Fisk faculty preceded a Master of Arts in music and conducing with Professor Archibald Davison at Harvard University. In 1936 he turned his attention to the development of the choir and music department at A&T College in Greensboro, N.C. In 1942 he moved to Howard University, where he enlarged the staff, expanded the curriculum, tightened the standards, won full accreditation in the National Association of Schools of Music (NASM), and developed the University Choir into a first-rate, internationally-acclaimed organization.

Dean Lawson has been a repeat guest conductor with the National Symphony (debut Jan. '55, Orff's Carmina Burana). He led the choir on a highly successful 80 city State Department Latin American tour. Many sections of the U.S. have enjoyed his services as guest conductor and workshop instructor. His counsel and advice are often sought and graciously given as a member of arts committees for the Kennedy Cultural Center, U.S. Information Center, Department of State, and the President's National Council on the Arts.

244

If this chapter only concerned a *philosophy* of rehearsal technique, and terms were universally accepted and understood, it could be a very short one, indeed.

"The word is the tone."

I have based my whole approach to the development of a workable rehearsal technique on this one statement. A thorough discussion of the many practical applications of this principle would require volumes. The intention of this single chapter, therefore, is to suggest a basic skeleton on which each director can allow those specific techniques which work best for him to attach themselves and to become a part of his own rehearsal personality.

PERSONAL REHEARSAL CONCEPTS

Effective rehearsal techniques are developed over a period of years, through study, observation of successful conductors, and the trial and error of daily experimentation. They become a very personal possession, although the source can sometimes be positively identified. My entire career as a choral conductor, for instance, stems from the wonderful experience I had with Dr. Archibald Davison at Harvard.[1]

These concepts are basic to my personal rehearsal technique:

The word is the tone. When the word is enunciated, articulated, and pronounced properly, the whole singing apparatus is automatically prepared for proper projection, placement, and tonal resonance. A great deal of time, therefore, need *not* be spent on elaborate lectures to students concerning the functions of diaphragm, larynx, pharynx, etc. If the word is pronounced correctly and enunciated properly, resonance, focus, projection, and position will all be proper. An over-all quality and homogeneity of tone is achieved when everyone says the same word in the same way. Dr. Davison expresses this fundamental precept when he says, "pronunciation is the key to impressive choral singing, the root from which all the choral virtues spring."

For some time it was fashionable to concentrate on the singing of vowels and the production of a beautiful tone with a minimum

---

[1] *Editor's note*: Warner Lawson, a very gifted pianist, studied with Arthur Schnabel and began a promising career as a concert artist. However, during his first course with Dr. Archibald Davison at Harvard, he became so impressed with the man and what he had to offer musically that he soon began to enroll for every course which had Davison listed as the instructor. Since these were primarily choral-centered, this led Warner Lawson away from the piano and straight to choral conducting.

of interruption from the consonants (which were practically banished). I have always felt that the consonants actually provide the vitality, excitement, the emotional impact, to the word itself. For instance, if "glory" is sung "gu-lory", the "u" acts like the vaulter's fibreblass pole: it is a springboard for the word. This extra "u" should be added to all words with a double consonant, just as a word with a vowel needs the aspirate "h" to open the throat and thus prevent the glottal stroke ("click") which mars over-all tone quality.

Singing must make sense, conversationally. We Americans are quite careless with our diction when we speak, dropping word endings and sliding through syllables. Our ears have become accustomed to this sound and will accept it in conversation, but not in musical speech—thus most conductors, very correctly, teach precise diction (often exaggerating pronunciation in order to insure a natural sound by the time it reaches the audience).

In festival choruses that I have conducted in recent years I have found diction basically good, whereas just a few years ago nearly every word uttered was the signal to start massive repair work. This indicates that conductors are giving rather careful attention to the problems of diction. Too often, however, the end result is *artificial* sound.

Choral speech must flow naturally, with the same stresses and relaxations of normal conversation. Just as we speak in groups of words, we must also sing in phrases which are at the same time characteristic of both the music and the sense of the text.

Improper singing of the half step is the basis of most pitch problems. When singers see an approaching minor seventh or augmented fourth, they realize that it is a difficult interval and they are alerted by their intelligence and experience to be careful. But as a result of overconfidence, they are extremely careless with the half step. When descending, they drop too far, and do not stretch far enough when moving upwards.

Much has been written about the relationship of pitch to the temperature of the rehearsal room, to the mental and physical condition of the singers, and to numerous other factors. The older I become and the more experience with choirs I accumulate, the more I begin to realize that (1) until students have been made acutely aware of how you have to *squeeze* the half step when singing "do-ti-do", and (2) how you must overcome the temptation to be lazy and thus undershoot when ascending one half step, your pitch problems will never be solved.

I use a warm-up exercise in which everyone must sing a chromatic scale through one octave, ascending and descending—the object being for every singer to return to the exact pitch from which he started. The voices are spread to a dominant seventh chord, primarily to avoid parallel octaves, but also to provide added color (B-root, T-5th, A-7th, S-3rd). All sing "lah-loh-lay-lee-loo." They must be conscious of raising the pitch a full half step each time; the basses, especially, often become lazy when they reach the G below middle C.

The use of the five vowel sounds in this exercise, designed primarily to achieve fundamental pitch security, simultaneously serves another important purpose. It allows the director to work also for pure vowel sound. Homogeneity of pronunciation (particularly of the vowels) is a must for every chorus. In this way provincialism or regional speech characteristics can be eliminated.

The interval of the major third is also a problem. Often I ask my choir to sing "c,d,e," listening very carefully. Then I ask them to sing "c,d,F,e." This second "e" is more apt to represent the pure major third because the pitch is achieved from above rather than below—on "top" of the tone, as it were.

Basic Rehearsal Goals

Rehearsal goals may range from the idealistic and ultra-sophisticated desire to assemble just to enjoy making music together, all the way to the practical and ultra-expedient necessity to prepare an appealing number for the PTA meeting tomorrow night that you were just told about yesterday by the president, a close friend of the superintendent.

All of us need the stimulus of an impending public performance to call forth our best efforts—the young people who are your students are no exception to this basic element of human nature. However, these very important short term goals should be balanced with equally important long term goals, in order to create well-rounded musicians, not just trained singers of parts.

Music should be chosen and the year's work planned so that each student has the opportunity to learn of balance, blend, tone, intonation, diction, etc. as he sings a varied repertoire of high quality literature.

TIME IS PRECIOUS

Imagine being able to say to your group, "Take this music home with you and learn it; when you come back we will spend our school rehearsal time working on interpretation, balance, and final polishing."

Of course this idealistic phantasy is completely impractical. Today's student has many interests which make demands on his time. Because the work must be done by the director—struggling, in many cases, under the handicap of a full performance schedule with too little rehearsal time—it is imperative that he make full use of every moment.

The conductor must plan every rehearsal in much the same manner as he would plan his most important concert, i.e. balanced, with climax points, diversionary pauses, and a pleasant ending.

The time in one class period often will not allow you to achieve all that you might hope for, and experienced conductors realize that the definite accomplishments of any one rehearsal are apt to be very limited. What ever is achieved, must be very secure, so that more can be added in subsequent sessions.

Even though the school choral conductor has educational objectives which go beyond the usual professional goal of preparing music for the next concert, he can learn a great deal from his commercial colleagues, who know that "time is money," and thus must be used wisely.

TIME-SAVING DEVICES

The following suggestions may help you to save time without sacrificing results:

Before the rehearsal

1. Thorough planning has been the key to efficiency and success in most undertakings throughout the history of the world—choral rehearsals are no exception.
2. Plan to use different methods of learning:
   a. *Project.* Learning a specific piece for a specific purpose in the shortest possible time.
   b. *Lecture.* Gaining basic skills for later use. For example, learning to read music is very time consuming in the beginning, but certainly is better than learning every piece by

rote throughout the entire choir life of each non-reading member.

   c. *Discussion.* Contributions from students, led by the director. This type can be used to convey text meaning, discover likes and dislikes, teach appreciation, etc.

3. Plan to use different rehearsal approaches:

   a. *Whole Method.* Sing throughout, refining a little each time.

   b. *Detail Method.* Work throughout the piece, measure-by-measure, doing repair work.

   c. *Common Problem Method.* Work throughout one rehearsal on a problem common to several different pieces, lightness of eighth notes, for example, in both Bach: *Glory in Excelsis,* and Calypso Carol: *The Virgin Mary Had a Baby Boy.*

4. Consider planned teaching units (like the first 6 weeks on tone, second on diction, etc.). Do not completely neglect the other elements, but concentrate on one during the unit.

5. Consider possible coordination of efforts with other departments (like Physics: acoustics, or Physiology: voice production apparatus).

6. Students cannot rehearse several compositions in succession with a high tessitura, and other demanding musical factors. Pace your rehearsal by inserting familiar pieces, or older numbers which you want to retain in the repertoire, between these very difficult pieces.

7. Plan some very short term and very attainable goals for every rehearsal. This can be a good psychological boost for both the students and the director.

8. Keep the room arranged in an orderly manner. The atmosphere of efficiency will cause students to be more business-like in their approach to the work for the day.

9. To begin the rehearsal quickly and to put students in the proper frame of mind, develop an opening routine which includes rapid folder distribution, immediate roll check (the "vacant chair" method) and brief warm-up.

10. Prepare a written lesson plan for each rehearsal: a brief outline form, allowing for flexibility, is adequate. Include announcements you want to make to the students that day. Place it on your music stand. Copy on the chalkboard the order of pieces to be rehearsed so that the students will have music ready as well as sense that you are an organized, efficient person who will not waste their time.

11. Write down exactly what you want to accomplish when you plan each rehearsal. List the measure numbers of places which need work, and the rehearsal technique you will use to solve the problem. (*see* Fig. 11–1 Rehearsal Work Sheet)
12. Each measure of every piece should be numbered for quick reference. A student librarian and staff can take care of this.
13. Be sure that all music for the current unit of work has been placed in the choir folders.
14. Prepare visual aids (note value charts, statements from choral technique books, consonant and vowel charts, etc.) well in advance of the class in which they will be needed.
15. Mark important spots in the score. Some conductors use a color-code system (blue for dynamics, red for tempos, etc.).
16. Schedule a rest period for yourself immediately preceding a rehearsal, whenever possible. If you are fresh and alert, the singers (even though they may be tired) will receive inspiration and strength from your energy.
17. Go to the rehearsal only after you have first completed a *thorough* study of every piece to be rehearsed.

Fig. 11-1

Rehearsal Work Sheet

Piece	Measure	Voices	Problem	Solution
"Song of Democracy" by Howard Hanson	p.11-12	SATB	"choppy-ness" as parts alternate on the word "building"	① hold second ♩ for full value, so female voices end their tone at same time male voices enter (also vice versa) ② accent on first ♩ (1st syllable) – less accent and extension of second ♩ (2nd syllable)
	p.27	Bass	loss of low C♯ as part alternates on the octave	less accent on top (doubled by tenors) – more strength on low C♯

During the Rehearsal

1. Begin on time, with an attitude of enthusiastic anticipation of the results which this session of work will achieve.

2. Keep the rehearsal moving by proceeding, without interruption, through the logical sequence you have planned. Answer irrelevant questions with, "See me after class."

3. Always remain sensitive to the reaction of the singers, and, like a good lecturer or successful comedian, change the pace if you feel their attention span reaching the breaking point. The choir must be "with you" at all times.

4. You may want to allow a student to conduct the warm-up so that you can "float around" through the rows of singers. This warm-up period should be prolonged only long enough to prepare the body to sing. Just as soon as this is accomplished, proceed directly to work on the compositions.

5. Begin work on the most difficult problems immediately after warm-up, when students are fresh and can make the most efficient use of the time.

6. Sing pieces all the way from beginning to end *only* in early readings when you are trying to get the "feel" of the music, or in the last stages of preparation. Otherwise, save time by working on trouble spots only.

7. Do not start "at the top of page 3" if the problem is actually on "page 3, measure 8."

8. Routine yourself to give starting places in the same logical sequence each time: "page ......, line ......, measure ......, beat ...." Time your directions so that you give the next item *just* as the singers are ready for it.

9. Always explain, specifically, what you want improved when you ask students to repeat a section they have just sung. Never say, merely, "All right, let's go back to the beginning and try that again."

10. Develop your diagnostic technique so that you can recognize the exact reason for the problem—is it the rhythm? the text? the interval? Don't waste time treating the wrong ill.

11. Prevent unnecessary stops by calling out directions to the students which will warn them of what to expect in the following phrase.

12. Teach all sections to accomplish a smooth re-entry after rest by mentally singing another part during the time their part is absent.

13. Do not waste time by leaving most of the chorus idle. Individual voice part repair work should be done very quickly, even if not as thoroughly as might be desired. If a great deal of correction is necessary, call section rehearsals.

14. To keep all students occupied and learning during short individual section drills, ask them to:
    a. Keep quiet and listen carefully.
    b. Watch the music to see the relationship of their part.
    c. Hum their own part along with the part being checked.
    d. Hum or sing the part being checked, in their own range.

15. Say the words as you conduct. This maintains sensitivity for the phrase as well as reflects the meaning and mood of the text as a whole.

16. If you need an illustration, sing it—no matter what kind of voice you have. This is faster and more effective than long descriptive monologues filled with picturesque adjectives.

17. When you do explain, choose language carefully. Develop a vocabulary of single words which sum up paragraphs of prose. For example, I use "squeeze" to indicate a tightening of the interval (certainly not meaning to squeeze the tone or the throats—the students understand this and know the difference) so that the choir sings *on top* of the pitch.

18. Tape record trouble sections and play them back immediately for the students. This is often more effective than trying to explain to them want they are doing wrong.

19. Do not allow side comments, rustling around, "whew, that's over", etc. when the choir has finished one section. Think while they sing and be ready with immediate instructions for the next phase of learning.

20. Save fatigue, which costs time, by allowing those parts written in a difficult range (especially the soprano) to be sung an octave lower when doing repeated drill.

21. Rehearse slowly at first, to insure accuracy, then increase to the proper speed.

22. For quick reference, memorize all possible rehearsal combinations:
    for 2 parts (SATB): S-A, S-T, S-B, A-T, A-B, T-B
    for 3 parts (SATB): S-A-T, S-A-B, S-T-B, A-T-B

23. Try changing keys both up and down. Often the parts will fall into place immediately and save hours of rehearsal designed to hold the pitch level in the original key.

24. End on time, with a "rouser." Be sure the students know what gains they have made during the rehearsal period just ending.

After the Rehearsal

1. Objectively evaluate the rehearsal just completed. Determine its strengths and weaknesses. Write down suggestions for improvement.
2. Make a note, immediately following the session, of rehearsal techniques you may have developed "on the spot" which were particularly effective. File for future reference.
3. Write an occasional full criticism of your rehearsal technique. Analyze what you are doing and attempt to evaluate its effectiveness.
4. Constantly check yourself in front of a mirror for clarity, accuracy and economy of motion. Don't hesitate to ask colleagues for evaluative criticism.
5. Make tape recordings of complete rehearsals. Check effort vs. results. Determine how you can be more efficient.
6. Develop a vocabulary of *action* words. The advertising industry uses words which cause people to *do* things. Make your own list of words which have worked best for you.
7. Develop a reasonable balance of intellect and emotion which allows you to be proud of accomplishments and thus gain in self-confidence, even as you retain your ability to be objective and realize that there is still ample room for improvement.

THE ACCOMPANIST

Whenever the director must interrupt his work with the choir to give full and complete directions to the accompanist, not only is time lost, but more important, the attention of the singers wanders. A first rate accompanist who knows almost intuitively what the director is going to do next, the pitches needed, the exact tempo to be used, can be of tremendous value. The director should always confer with the accompanist before the rehearsal in order to minimize misunderstandings and save time.

Suggestions to Accompanists

1. Practicing the piano as an accompanist differs from preparing to be a soloist. Remember that in choral music the piano is

used first as a *tool* and second as a producer of music, therefore:

    a. Learn to play all vocal lines independently, or in various combinations.

    b. Be prepared to begin playing on any beat of any measure.

    c. Memorize all warm-up exercises.

    d. Learn to count measures forwards and backwards in order to find the place the conductor wishes to start—as quickly as possible.

2. Learn the score as thoroughly as possible before the first rehearsal.

3. If your part is an orchestral reduction, listen to a recording and learn to "fake" the proper orchestral *effect*: many times it is impossible to play every note written in such scores.

4. Arrive at the rehearsal before the singers, with all music in hand.

5. Follow the conductor very carefully at all times.

6. Listen carefully to the singers. If one part falters, play that line *fff* until they recover.

7. Never stop playing—even if you play only the first and third beats of a measure, keep going.

8. In early stages of learning, play the accompaniment at a higher volume level than normal, so that the chorus has maximum support. Gradually reduce volume to the proper level as the chorus becomes more secure.

9. If the accompaniment is completely independent of the voices, play the vocal score during the early rehearsals, then add the regular part when the singers have become more secure.

10. Pitches are heard better when struck in octaves.

11. Do not hesitate to improvise a substitute accompaniment which will help the choir through a problem spot—especially in the early stages of rehearsals.

12. Mark your score on the basis of the director's comments.

13. Singers must breathe; the piano does not, but the accompanist should think in phrases (along with the conductor) and "breathe" with the piano part as well.

14. Never give your views on interpretation during a rehearsal, unless asked, specifically by the conductor, but (after the rehearsal) do point out weaknesses in certain sections you have noticed from your position which may have escaped the conductor's notice.

15. Put paper clips on the page needed in a collection so that you can turn to the individual selection quickly.
16. A really first-rate accompanist must have a thorough knowledge of style and form.
17. Work assiduously to develop your sight reading ability.

Physical Arrangement of Voices

Never hesitate to experiment. Students are able to adapt very quickly to a new arrangement, even if first introduced during the warm-up for a concert. On a Latin American tour for the State Department, we had the opportunity to sing in a marvelous new outdoor shell. Late in the Brazilian afternoon, during a brief rehearsal period for the evening concert, I discovered that our regular placement was not working well at all. We began to make adjustments, then found that certain voice relationships in the compositions we had programmed were not right. Finally we arrived at a totally new arrangement—the one that was best for our choir in that particular acoustical situation, performing those particular pieces.

Too many directors will endure a sound which leaves much to be desired rather than move students. They say, "Jane has been singing next to Mary all this year, and I'm afraid she would feel strange next to Sally." Today's teen-agers are extremely adaptable —give them a chance to prove it.

Some Possible "Seating" Plans

In the many school choruses which contain fewer boys than girls, I prefer to place the tenors and basses front and center, surrounding them with the sopranos and altos.

Pitch problems and an over-all feeling of tension often develops in an extremely large group (250 and up) simply because of the great physical distances between singers. I have found that by placing the students in the position of a double chorus (even though they may never sing antiphonally) will do much to solve the problem.

By grouping in quartets the blend is improved greatly. This arrangement demands (but also helps to teach) security of individual parts.

By rehearsing in a complete circle, with piano and conductor in the center, each singer can hear every other singer very clearly.

There are many possible arrangements for mixed chorus. Fig. 11–2 offers several more suggestions.

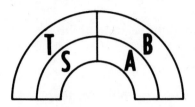

Effective when all sections are strong.

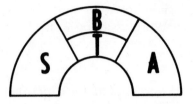

Works well when male voices are weak.

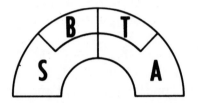

Achieves unity between the female voices.

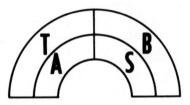

Extremes being next to each other aid tuning and blending - useful for contrapuntal pieces.

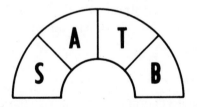

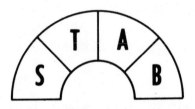

Either of these arrangements can be very helpful in a large hall where the basses would be lost if placed to the rear of the other singer.

Fig. 11-2

Suggested "Seating" Plans

Dividing the chorus into the 4 main sections in order to go through the parts separately often will save a great deal of the full choir rehearsal period. Section leaders can be trained to help the individual parts gain a fair amount of security.

The danger is in keeping the groups separate too long. A number of students will become irritated very quickly, especially if they can read most of the part fairly well at sight. If you have the facilities, it is very effective to break quickly into sections when the group hits a troublesome section, solve the problems, and return to the full rehearsal immediately.

It is best to allow the group to struggle with the problem in full rehearsal long enough for them to be convinced that they really *do* have a problem. This realization usually assures complete cooperation, increases the efficiency of the sectional rehearsal, and allows the students to appreciate the results more fully.

PREPARING A NEW PIECE

When introducing a piece the choir has not seen before, I generally follow the same pattern:

1. Sing the entire piece, disregarding mistakes in an attempt to proceed, non-stop, to an over-all concept of the composition.
2. Solve problems, using innumerable practical techniques. Some have been accumulated through many years of experience and observation, but others are invented, under pressure, to solve particular problems in a special situation.
3. Check very carefully on the results of the problem solving phase. I try to avoid being fooled into thinking that a whole chorus has mastered the difficulty, when it is actually only a few students, singing correctly, who allow the spot to "slide by" . . . while half or two-thirds of the group is still making the same mistake.

DESIRABLE QUALITIES OF REHEARSAL CONDUCTORS

The physical aspects of conducting are relatively simple. The beat must be clear, cues reassuringly obvious, with attacks and releases precise. Diagrams and other basic techniques which have become accepted over a period of many years should be used.[2] Employing non-standard movements, known only to the local group, makes it difficult for your students to adapt to the other conductors they will meet. Within a traditional framework there is still much opportunity for personal expression. I say the words to myself (singing does not allow me to hear the choir properly), and my emotional reaction to these words determines and develops the meaningful gestures I use to convey the full meaning of the phrase to the singers. (Later these same movements can also help the audience to understand.)

---

[2] *Editor's note: The Modern Conductor*, by Elizabeth A.H. Green, Prentice-Hall, Inc., 1961, explains this very clearly.

Most people can learn the mechanical manipulations of conducting; however, the really significant aspects of the art go far beyond this technical fringe. There are many desirable qualities of a conductor which could be listed, on both the technical and the psychological level. The following seem to be basic:

1. A specific choral concept, preconceived and fully-formed in the mind's ear, readily available for comparison with what is being produced currently by the choir, but never diluted by it.
2. The ability to diagnose specific flaws which prohibit the product from matching the model in his ear, coupled with an efficient rehearsal technique which drives to the heart of the problem without wasting time on irrelevant side effects.
3. An instinctive creative talent which allows for adaption of the original concept as the exciting interaction of composer, conductor, and singers begins to take place in the rehearsal hall.
4. The ability to recognize, and then crystallize, the complete work of art—the combination of so many volatile forces—at the moment it is ready for display.

THE TEMPERAMENTAL CONDUCTOR

In my early days as a conductor I was a real dictator who blew up regularly, threw chalk, etc., but I have since discovered that such temperamental behavior merely develops fear and insecurity among the group.

Those who sing in school choirs certainly are not required to be there, and would not give their time at all unless they really wanted to be members of the group. The mistakes they make are honest ones—because they do not *know*, not because they do not *care*. Why should they be ridiculed and condemned for that? I do not berate my youngsters anymore—but it took me some little time to learn this.

TRAINING THE CONDUCTOR

Only relatively few people possess the desirable qualities necessary for an outstanding choral conductor. It is no wonder that professional music schools often have difficulty, not only in producing graduates who approach this goal, but in discovering the special kind of talent—the raw material—they should look for when seeking the best students for their programs.

How does one teach, or even recognize, artistic sensibility, innate creativity, organizational ability, and economy of effort, all as applied to choral conducting? No one is certain. I do know from personal experience, however, that becoming a choral conductor is the *result* of all of the knowledge and training, formal and informal, one has been able to acquire in a lifetime of searching. For this reason I cannot recommend a major in choral conducting as the best means of training young conductors, but prefer a sort of "liberal arts of music" approach, with courses in both choral and instrumental literature, history of both music and related arts, theory, composition, conducting ... everything!

Becoming a choral conductor is somewhat like becoming head of the corporation, or even President of the United States. Few Americans spend their lives consciously preparing for the position, but are guided there by circumstances growing out of their total experience with all aspects of life.[3]

Some Practical, Proven Techniques

So many of us do our work almost instinctively and find it difficult to remember—off the podium—the many techniques which come from our subconscious very quickly when activated by the desire to improve the sound of groups of students in our rehearsal halls.

The following proven, practical rehearsal techniques have been contributed by colleagues who have used them successfully with student groups. Young directors may want to use these examples as the beginning of a notebook of practical rehearsal techniques (*see* form, Fig. 11–3), to be filled during the coming years of experimentation in rehearsal and the observation of other conductors at work.

Tone

1. AN OPEN THROAT IS NECESSARY FOR GOOD TONE. 6–8 minutes per rehearsal during the first 6 weeks, periodically after. I ask students to:
   a. Place 2 fingers in the mouth (index and third) with the thumb down, in order to keep the head down.
   b. Sing vowel *oo* or *oh* on an octave run, plus the 9th.
   c. Vocalize all voices to the top of their range.

---

[3] *Editor's note*: The wisdom of this concept is borne out not only by Dean Lawson's personal background, but also by the lives of most other chapter contributors as well.

Practical Rehearsal Technique

from _Warner Lawson_, position _Howard U._
source _personal conversation_ – NASM – St. Louis

Primary goal: _better 1st reading of new piece_

"Fringe benefits": _rhythmic security – precision_

Principle involved: _separation of elements speeds understanding_

Time spent – when : _few minutes – 1st reading_

Mechanics of solution:

1. _say words only – in strict rhythm_
2. _clap hands in rhythm of words_
3. _Hum or "la-la" the melody_
4. _Sing words and music together_

Fig. 11-3

Practical Rehearsal Technique Notebook Form

   d. To provide the necessary carry-over from exercise to actual use, do this on a Bach *chorale* or similar piece of music. Call attention to the improved tone quality.

  from Gordon H. Lamb, Choral Director, Sac Community High School, Sac City, Iowa

2. RESONANCE IS THE KEY TO GOOD TONE. 20 minutes per rehearsal, first 6 weeks. I ask students to sing the following:

   a. *Ming.* Sing through the *m* and go on to the *ng.*

   b. Unison exercises.

   c. Chordal exercises (voiced B–Ab, T–Eb, A–Ab, S–C), the alto and bass are doubled on the root because I want the same type of round tone from these two sections, in order to give the choir the color I desire. Sing 5 *mings,* breathe, then raise one-half step and repeat.

   d. Vowel sounds preceded by *n* (not nasal, but with attention focused on the cheek bones and the sinus area).

   e. Same procedure, with *mum.*

from Dallas Draper, Choral Director, Louisiana State University, Baton Rouge

3. ALL GOOD TONE MUST HAVE FOCUS AND FREEDOM. 5 minutes daily. I establish clarity (ping) by vocalizing on *zhee* (*zee* or *thee*), and establish fullness (freedom) by vocalizing on *zhah* (*zah* or *thah*). These 2 properties of good tone can be correlated by proceeding from *zhee* (bright vowel) to *zhoo* (dark vowel). Using scale steps 1 through 5, the process is as follows:

Steps:	1 2 3 4	5 4 3 2	1
	zhee	zhee	zhee
	zhee	zhay	zhay
	zhee	*zhah*	*zhah*
	zhee	zho	zho
	zhee	zhoo	zhoo

Caution: Continuous use of the *zhee* approach may result in a thin, tight tone. Vary the approach by beginning with *zhay* or even *zhah* until a sense of freedom and body has been established. Then proceed towards *zhee* through *zho* and *zhoo.*

from Bernard W. Regier, Director of Choral Activities, Western Washington State College, Bellingham

4. TO IMPROVE RESONANCE. 3–5 minutes. Using the rhythm of four eighth notes-quarter note-pause, sing the syllables "mae-me-maw-me-maw." Voice the chord in 8 parts (B2–Bb, B1–F; T2–Bb, T1–D; A2–F, A1–Bb; S2–D, S1–F). Begin by building the chord, from the bottom up, in strict rhythm. You can also hold the chord as long as necessary to evaluate the success of the resonance. Move higher by half-steps.

from Irving Bunton, Chairman Music Department, Englewood High School, Chicago, Illinois

5. THROUGH THE USE OF RESONANCE AND CORRECT VOWEL PRODUCTION MANY OTHER CHORAL PRINCIPLES CAN BE HELPED AS WELL. 10 minutes per rehearsal. Use Italian vowels (*ah, eh, ih, o, oo,* plus *e* and *ay* at times) and consonants *l, n, m, t* before vowel. Voicing a chord Bass–C, Tenor–G, Alto–C, Soprano–E, sing 5 vowels, breathe, raise one-half step, and repeat. Then chant vowels 3 times, tenors raise ½ step; chant vowels 3 more times, sopranos raise ½ step; chant 3 more times, bass and alto raise ½ step. Use both fast and slow chanting at various dynamic levels.

from William R. Trego, Coordinator of Fine Arts, El Dorado (Arkansas) High School

Diction

1. TO VITALIZE ORAL COMMUNICATION. As needed. The spacing of words and sylables not only is vital to diction but also improves freedom of tone, and adds a buoyancy of rhythmic drive which allows the choir to come alive. I often ask the choir to:
   a. Sing the line staccato, with space in between the notes. Four quarter notes, for example, would be sung as dotted eighths with sixteenth rests in between.
   b. This concept can be correlated with instrumental spacing— as a flutist, for example, must space in order to get clean attacks.
   c. Emphasize that the duration (depending on the note value and tempo) of the note must give most attention to the vowel. Consonants must be said quickly and crisply. Avoid lazy mouthing of words.

from Edward Anderson, Choral Director, Colorado State University, Fort Collins

2. TO FOCUS VOWELS AND CONTROL CONSONANTS. 5–10 minutes per rehearsal.
   a. Sing word phrases (like "Kyrie Eleison", "Hodie Christus Natus Est", "I Saw the Sea") on a full chord. Be very conscious of consonants and uniform vowel sound.
   b. Raise the last vowel one-half step and repeat.

from Starr L. Cole, Choral Director, Mt. Pleasant High School, Wilmington, Delaware

3. TO ACHIEVE A CLEAN, POWERFUL, DRAMATIC RELEASE. Ask once. For a song requiring a very dramatic ending, I ask my students

to stop the tone by taking a breath—very quickly and very quietly.

from David A. Davenport, Director of Choral Activities, Richmond (Ind.) High School

4. TO DEVELOP CLEANLY ARTICULATED PHRASES. 3–5 minutes the first 6 weeks, periodically after. Proper breathing is necessary to articulate runs cleanly. I use the following procedure:

   a. Sing staccato exercises on the vowel "oo", in a rhythmic sequence of four quarter notes, 8 eighth notes, 4 sets of triplets, and 16 sixteenth notes. Voice the chord with Bass and Alto on the root, Tenor on the 5th, and Soprano on the 3rd. Raise one-half step and repeat.

   b. Students should move the stomach muscles in on each note. Tenors may use falsetto in the upper part of their range.

   c. This exercise makes a cleanly articulated phrase possible without the use of an "h" or *aspirate* between the notes of a run.

from Gordon H. Lamb, Choral Director, Sac Community High School, Sac City, Iowa

5. TO OBTAIN COORDINATED, MUSICAL RELEASES ON FINAL CONSONANTS WHICH HAVE NO SUSTAINABLE SOUND OF THEIR OWN. A few minutes regularly during early rehearsals and spot drills as needed later.

   a. Concerning final consonants *b, d, g, j.*

   b. When singing *dig,* ask the choir to sing *di,* thinking *dig,* and add 1/100th of an inch of that vowel on *g* as you give the release signal.[4]

   c. Students are asked to see which section can get the most unison, musical, in-tune-with-the-preceding-vowel-tone release.

from Maurice R. King, Director of Choral Groups, North Florida Junior College, Madison

6. A CONCENTRATED STUDY OF VOWEL CONCEPTS AND CONSONANT PRODUCTION IN RELATION TO THE VOWEL TO WHICH IT IS ATTACHED. About 20 minutes at the beginning of each rehearsal.

   An anthem is used that does not require too much concentration on the part of the volunteer choir to sing the right pitches. Singers then center on the proper use of vowels and consonants

---

[4] This is what I call the "stopped consonant," as compared to the pronounced consonant — W.L.

in the production of a completely musical and understandable phrase. *Nothing* is allowed to "get by" during this period. Sometimes the entire time may be spent on a phrase or two, demanding that *every* choir member become conscious of every sound that is involved and that they be blended into an artistic phrase of beauty which is understandable and meaningful to both the trained and the untrained ear. With this concentrated effort, a reminder now and then during the remaining rehearsal time will be sufficient to bring into constant use the principles covered at the beginning of the period.

from James A. Berry, Minister of Music, Myers Park Baptist Church, Charlotte, North Carolina

Humming

1. PLACEMENT IS THE KEY TO PROPER, RESONANT HUMMING. 3 minutes, occasionally. I suggest that students begin humming with an open mouth. While humming, close the mouth, and if a change in sound occurs, placement is incorrect. If no change occurs, the hum will have the proper quality.

from Tom Wikstrom, Director of Research, West Virginia Department of Education, Charleston

2. NATURAL, FLOWING, RESONANT PHRASES ARE THE KEY TO SUPERIOR HUMMING. 8 minutes per rehearsal during the first 6 weeks. I ask the choir to do the following:
   a. Sing the word *humming*.
   b. Exaggerate the prolonged consonant *ing*, but do not change anything in the throat; simply continue to hum the pitch and tone of the early part of the word.
   c. Continue the process, opening the lips, mouth, and throat, but do not change the natural quality in your throat achieved when you first sang the word *humming*.
   d. Individuals, groups, entire sections alternate opening and closing lips. If done properly there will be no difference in the quality of the tone while humming, whether the mouth is open or closed.
   e. Exercises using scales, triads, all intervals, both ascending and descending while humming, over a period of time can make any chorus sound like a beautiful organ or the string section of a symphony orchestra.

from John Raymond, Director of Music, Lafayette College, Easton, Pennsylvania, Dean of Fred Waring Summer Workshops

Sight Reading

1. A FIRM KNOWLEDGE OF INTERVALS IS THE BASIS OF FINE SIGHT READING. 5 minutes daily. I use a technique which demands quick reaction from the mind, ear, and voice:
   a. Sing chord in root position (Bass-A, Tenor-E, Alto-C#, Soprano-A)
   b. Director calls out "perfect 4th higher," all voices move immediately.
   c. Director calls out other intervals—never in the same order, completely at random. This must be done quickly and regularly.

from Thomas Hilbish, University of Michigan

2. PRECISION AND IMMEDIATE ACCURACY ARE NECESSARY FOR GOOD PERFORMANCE. Time as required for solution. I often ask my choir to sing the piece as written, but using a short staccato *ah* or *lo* for each note, resting the appropriate length of time before singing the next note. This forces all members of the group to make an immediate individual commitment as to rhythm, pitch, tone quality, etc., rather than joining the group (a la community singing).

from Clarence E. Garder, Choral Director, Central State College, Edmond, Oklahoma

Intonation

1. REGULAR EAR TRAINING IS NECESSARY TO SINGING IN TUNE. 5 minutes at beginning of each rehearsal. I use an exercise which also allows the students to enjoy harmonic choral sound as they become aware of chord tuning.
   a. Sound Bb major chord (B–Bb, T–F, A–D, S–Bb), with the syllable *loo.*
   b. Use a 4 beat measure.
   c. On the third beat, alto and tenor move up one-half step, others sustain.
   d. On the first beat of the next measure, soprano and bass move up one-half step, as others sustain.
   e. The process is continued until an F major chord is reached,

then the descent is begun, inner voices moving down one-half step on the third beat of each measure, the soprano and bass on the first beat, until a Bb major chord is once again reached.

If any chord goes out of tune, the procedure should be held up until the tuning is adjusted. Soprano and bass should listen very carefully to each other in order to insure a perfect octave.

from Evalyn J. Still, Choral Director, Vandermeulen High School, Port Jefferson, New York

2. SINGING SUSTAINED NOTES, ONE-HALF AND ONE STEP APART, WILL OPEN THE EARS OF THE CHOIR TO CONTEMPORARY ATONAL SOUNDS. 3–5 minutes daily.
   a. Entire ensemble sings a unison pitch on a natural vowel (usually *o* or *ah*).
   b. One section moves to a pitch one step below and sustains this against the other sections.
   c. Another section moves to a pitch one step above and sustains this against the other 2 sections.
   d. Continue moving sections back to the unison pitch and then away again. Alternate sections.

from Henry E. Busche, Professor of Music, MacMurray College, Jacksonville, Ill

3. THE STUDY OF INTERVALS AND CHORDS WILL GIVE A CHOIR THE NECESSARY AURAL AWARENESS OF MAJOR, MINOR, AUGMENTED, AND DIMINISHED SOUNDS. 10 minutes per rehearsal, first 10 weeks. I use a procedure designed also to improve the clarity of sound, blend, and brilliance of tone. Singing *a capella:*
   a. Master the half-step, up and down from a given tonal center (sing neutral syllable or hum).
   b. Proceed to the major and minor third—both above and below a given tonal center.
   c. Add the perfect 5th and sing major and minor triads, allowing each section an opportunity to sing the root, third, and fifth.
   d. Add extended dominant harmony (7th, 9th, 11th) and resolve each, according to the strong individual tendencies of each tone.
   e. Build longer idiomatic phrases and cadences.
   f. During the rehearsal period, use phrases from the current

literature of the choir which correspond to those being studied.

This study can extend to the point that a choir can sing a series of chords (I, IV, V, etc.) voicing it themselves, and then harmonizing simple melodies.

from George E. McKinley, Director of Choral Activities, Wakefield (Mass.) High School

12

The Challenge of

Performance

by Hugh Ross

New York City

Hugh Ross

is Music Director and Conductor of the Schola Cantorum of New York, a post he has held since 1929. He was head of the Choral Department of the Berkshire Music Center from 1941 to 1962, and from 1930 to 1966 was head of the choral department at the Manhattan School of Music, where he continues to teach choral conducting and music history. Dr. Ross is recognized as the chief expert in this country on ensemble performances of chorus and orchestra, and other combinations.

He was born in 1898 in southwest England, began studying violin and piano at the age of 6, and became a Fellow of the Royal College of Organists at 17, the youngest ever admitted. He obtained his degree in Philosophy at Oxford, studied composition at the Royal College of Music with Vaughan Williams. In 1921 he became conductor of the famous Winnipeg Male Choir, touring with Percy Grainger, who composed several works for the choir. Upon the retirement of Kurt Schindler in 1929, Hugh Ross became conductor of the Schola Cantorum (founded in 1909 on the urging of Gustav Mahler). The Schola has been heard with every famous conductor to appear in New York—Walter, Koussevitzky, Rodzinski, Beecham, Mitropoulos, Stokowski, Bernstein, Krips, to mention but a few, and regularly appears with the Boston Symphony and the New York Philharmonic. For 10 years it was "Toscanini's chorus", presenting among many other works, the late maestro's first performance of Beethoven's "Missa Solemnis." It has also made numerous TV appearances. The entire responsibility for preparation of the chorus has always been in the capable hands of Hugh Ross.

270

Historically, the earliest musical "performances" were presented as a part of ancient tribal rituals. Music has a great capacity for releasing man from the burden of every-day affairs, and for allowing his soul to soar to unlimited heights of ecstasy. This is not *escapism*, but an adventure into the higher life, and it is this mesmeric quality which audiences seek, whether they sit in Lincoln Center, Covent Garden, LaScala, or the Jefferson Junior High on South Main Street, in Hometown, U.S.A.

The most effective performances, therefore, are those which take a firm, almost hypnotic hold on an audience and guide their individual and collective emotions through an exciting maze of musical experiences.

Obviously, the first requirement for any successful performance is that the music be done well. Nothing can break the magic spell so quickly as inept execution. But a thorough investigation of the aesthetic aspects of a great choral performance, and the steps which the conductor must take to achieve it, demand a lifetime of the most dedicated study. The purpose of this *single chapter*, therefore, will be to suggest some of the practical techniques which may be used to present the products of your school's choral music department in their most favorable light.[1]

THE CONCERT HALL

There is a virtual plethora of fine auditoriums in every section of the country, and, in general we are far ahead of anything which has ever existed (except for an occasional isolated masterpiece) throughout the entire history of the world. The burden of performance is on the conductor, not on the hall.

That is not to say, however, that *every* auditorium is such an ideal site for performance. In fact, during a tour involving 36 communities, we met at least 20 physical situations which would be almost impossible to remedy. One reason for this seems to be that school stages are used for non-dramatic purposes—a place for the principal to make announcements, introduce speakers, and show films. Often their original function is forgotten.

Ingenuity and technical skill can often turn seemingly hostile con-

---

[1] *Editor's note*: Dr. Ross, throughout a long and distinguished career, both in the U.S. and traveling abroad, has been directly responsible for first performances of a great deal of very important choral music. He continues his many regular activities, in addition to frequent appearances as guest conductor for large choral festivals throughout the country and engagements as visiting professor in colleges and universities.

ditions into a source of pleasure for performers and listeners alike. I remember the terrified feeling I had when my traveling group of 20 singers, 6 instrumentalists, and I walked into the very large, and empty, Raleigh, N.C. gymnasium, which seats 14,000 people! By the end of our warm-up period, though, my anxiety had changed to joy, and I had become an admirer of their clever engineering. A very heavy canvas, cutting off about 3,000 seats, was stretched across one area; a Wenger portable shell was assembled on stage; and, just one microphone, *lying on the stage* at my right hand, was relaying the sound through an extraordinary public address system to every seat in the hall. I asked my manager to conduct, and as I listened from every location in the gymnasium, I found that the sound had been so carefully scaled that even the madrigals, sometimes with only 5 voices singing very lightly, could be heard clearly and in proper balance!

ACOUSTICS

There is a good deal of music that has been written strictly for the enjoyment of the singers (madrigals being the best example), but when this music is presented in concert, the audience must have an opportunity to share the wonderful intimacy with you. So that they can hear easily, clearly, and with distinct definition, some kind of shell is essential. Whether it is especially engineered, like the Wenger product (the best I have ever seen), or merely a solid wall, some provision must be made to mix the choral sound and project it on to the audience.

There are two common causes of unfavorable acoustical conditions in auditoriums.

1. The lack of any "ceiling" directly above the singers allows sound to go directly up into the "fly" areas above the stage, where it is trapped, and bounces around from one light pipe to another until completely dissipated. Commercially manufactured boards are available to prevent this, although sometimes plywood or a type of stage "flat" can be used.

2. The beautiful velvet draperies and thick curtains which seem to be a trademark of most school auditoriums can soak up so much sound that the vibrant tone achieved in your rehearsal hall now sounds as if it has been wrapped in cotton. All of this bulky material can be gathered together and "flown" over the light pipes above the stage, thus exposing the walls, which will put some life back into the performance.

OTHER PHYSICAL PROBLEMS

Choral performances are greatly enhanced by effective lighting. Combinations of even the basic red, white, and blue bulbs found on many stages can be used to produce pleasant general lighting, and certain dramatic effects as well. However, since it does not take special lighting for the local minister to present an assembly program, or for the study hall teacher to take the roll, it is not unusual to find half of the bulbs burned out and many others in the wrong sockets. When you try for all blue lights, for example, a few white ones will come on as well. You, the choral director, may also have to turn electrician (or at least train a student), if you desire visual effects which can help, rather than hinder, the aural portion of the program.

A change of the basic stage setting, and mobility of participants can add variety and interest. A good stage should have wide entrances on both sides, with a crosswalk backstage to allow performers maximum freedom of movement. I recall a Baltimore theatre in which the only way to get from one side to the other (without crossing on the stage itself!) was to leave the building, walk around the back, and enter a door on the opposite side. We left several girls—who had to make a fast trip, through the snow, in thin gowns, after a long period under the hot stage lights—in the hospital, as a result of that architect's oversight.

THE VISUAL EFFECT

Today's audience, particularly due to the impact of television, is more visually oriented than ever before. By the very nature of the life we lead, people have become too impatient to concentrate entirely on the auditory effect; thus, on the concert circuit the ensembles, with their treats for the eye as well as the ear, have become much more popular than the soloists, whose appeal is basically limited to the sense of hearing.

Performance attire, based on simple formality, should be pleasant to look at but never distracting. I prefer white dresses for women and evening clothes for the men, since they give a sensation of artistry to the performance, and convey, visually, an image of people seriously concerned with what they are doing and who expect the audience to approach the music with the same attitude. For me, choir robes have a slightly melancholy effect, particularly when grays are used. At any rate, a definite religious connotation seems to restrict their use to church-associated groups.

Placement of singers, giving each person enough "elbow room", presents a more pleasing picture for the audience, in addition to the musical improvements accruing from increased acoustical amplitude. The optimum distance is the same as placing every chair one chair apart. Louis Diercks has experimented with great success in the use of varied formations of singers for the benefit of specific pieces (large sections for antiphonal music, balanced quartets for maximum homophonic blend, etc.). While the chorus should never appear to be doing an impersonation of "the shifting sands of the Sahara" throughout the performance, *some* changes in physical arrangement can add interesting effects to a concert.

Stage decorations are not necessary, or appropriate, whenever colorful costuming and staging become a part of the performance. When a formal concert is presented, a very limited number of ferns, plants, or flowers may be useful. Refined, conservative taste must prevail.

Planning the Program

Whenever a major work, a "full-evening" piece, is performed, the effect it will have on the public largely depends on the composer's organizational ability; but, in a miscellaneous program, it is the conductor's responsibility to arrange music of many composers into an experience for the listener which will be just as artistically satisfying.

Even a casual review of the great masterworks will reveal the unified variety which is characteristic of quality composition. They begin with orchestral preludes, go on to full choruses, and are interlaced with solos and small ensembles. No serious composer ever restricts his program to a steady stream of SATB music—why should the school choral director?

The opening section of a miscellaneous program is, traditionally, the most solid work of the evening. An "appetizer" may precede this, but if your audience can be trusted to arrive on time, the "curtain raiser" may not be necessary.

The effect which each number has on those which follow is crucial and should be tested through critical listening to tape recordings of rehearsals.

The program in Figure 12–1, performed on tour by *The Schola Cantorum*, will serve to illustrate some practical considerations of program planning.

1. This particular program, designed specifically for travel, attempts to make the best possible use of a modest-sized choral group, accompanied by a very small instrumental ensemble.[2]
2. Scoring for all accompanied pieces was determined by the instrumentation of the Singer score for *Alcottiana* (flute, clarinet, bassoon, trumpet, piano, and percussion).
3. Over-all, the six sections of the program provide both contrast and balance.
4. Balance *within* the sections of the program was determined through various approaches:
    a. Group 1. An episode from the oratorio *Solomon,* as written by Handel.
    b. Group 2. The madrigals were chosen by emotional content: first, a charming work of the early French school, with a certain delicate humor to it; then, a very serious and extremely beautiful masterpiece by Marenzio; followed by a farce of Lassus depicting a German beer hall in the Middle Ages; and, finally, a gay canzonet by Morley.
    c. Group 3. Three contrasting scenes from operas of the same period, ending with the popular and exciting Carmen . . . just before intermission.
    d. Group 4. This was conceived as an independent unit by the composer.
    e. Group 5. Here some choral sounds which may serve to broaden the scope of the listener are introduced, just before the finale.
    f. Group 6. The exciting finale—balanced internally with solos, ensembles, and contrasting moods of songs with all stops pulled for the finish.

THE CONCERT ITSELF

Warm-up, in the place of performance, is very important for professional and student groups alike. The conductor should listen to the group from various places in the hall as the pianist or student conductor takes them through certain crucial numbers. You must be sure that the balance of the voices is being properly reflected by the auditorium.

---

[2] *Editor's note:* While Dr. Ross was working strictly with a professional touring company, many select school groups are capable of this type of presentation. Without the advantages of mature singers, but with freedom from economic considerations, the home-based student group would probably be larger, although still balanced in the same proportion.

PROGRAM

1. Solomon's Invocation to Music　　　　　　　　　*Handel*
　　Five Choruses:　　　　　　　　　　　　　　　　　　1685-1759
　　1. Music, spread thy voice around
　　2. Shake the dome and pierce the sky
　　3. Draw the tear from hopeless love
　　4. Thus rolling surges rise
　　5. The Fame of the Just
　Solomon: (alto) Judith Keller
　The Queen of Sheba: (soprano) Kay Winkler

> This episode from Handel's oratorio SOLOMON occurs when
> the King welcomes the Queen of Sheba to his newly-built
> palace: he calls on his musicians to entertain her through
> the whole gamut of musical expression.
> "Where Art her utmost skill displays
> And every object claims your praise."

2. Four Madrigals
Chant des Oiseaux　　　　　　　　　　　　*Clement Jannequin*
　　　　　　　　　　　　　　　　　　　　　　　　ca. 1500-1560

> Jannequin was internationally famous in his own day. Baif
> wrote of him and of this particular madrigal as follows:
> "If he with heavy chords motets compose
> Or imitate birds' voices in design,
> Good Jannequin in all his music shows
> No mortal spirit—he is all divine."

Solo e Pensoso　　　　　　　　　　　　　　*Luca Marenzio*
　　　　　　　　　　　　　　　　　　　　　　　　1553-1599

Marenzio was a word builder in music. This madrigal with its slow, faltering semi-tones
describes the poet wandering desolately through a chromatic landscape, that even Wagner
would have admired.

Audite Nova　　　　　　　　　　　　　　　*Orlandus Lassus*
　　　　　　　　　　　　　　　　　　　　　　　　1532-1594

Roland de Lasse was Belgian by birth, Italian by training, French and German by resi-
dence, and used all languages with equal ease in the 1200 compositions which he wrote.
Despite its title, this madrigal is a German drinking song written to celebrate St. Martin's
Day.

The Nymphs in Green Arraying　　　　　　　*Thomas Morley*
　　　　　　　　　　　　　　　　　　　　　　　　1557-1603

Morley published his "Canzonets or Little Short Airs to 5 and 6 Voices" in 1597. They
are one of the first results of the influx of Italian madrigals, particularly those of Marenzio,
into Elizabethan England, and Morley excels in his contrapuntal but light and airy development of the canzonet. This (No. 4 in the series) is a description of a "catch-as-
catch-can" game called Barley-break.

3. From the Operatic Stage
Ballad from "The Girl of the Golden West"　*Giacomo Puccini*
Jake Wallace, a roving ballad singer, wanders into the "Polka," a typical canteen in the
days of the Gold Rush. The gold diggers are playing cards, but they drop their game and
join in Jake's nostalgic song of home.
　　　　　Jake Wallace: (baritone) William Wiederanders

Children's Prayer, from　　　　　　　*Engelbert Humperdinck*
"Hansel and Gretel"
　Duet: (soprano & alto) Barbara Freeman & Jane Gunter

It is night. The children are lost in the forest, which to their mind is haunted by ogres
and fairies. The sandman appears and calms them, so that they sing their evening prayer
to the fourteen angels.

Opening Chorus, Act IV, "Carmen"　　　　　*Georges Bizet*
The last act of "Carmen" opens in a plaza in Seville next to the arena where the bull
fights are held. The stage is crowded with street-vendors selling oranges, cigarettes, etc.
Later, the Toreadors enter and are greeted to the strains of their famous song.

Fig. 12-1

Schola Cantorum Program

INTERMISSION

4. Alcottiana, a scenic cantata by — *Andre Singer*
Libretto by the composer
Soloists (in order of appearance):
> *Lucy:* (soprano) Kay Winkler
> *Alcott:* (bass-baritone) William Wiederanders
> *Emma:* (alto) Jane Gunter
> *Mary:* (mezzo-soprano) Judith Keller
> *Lemuel:* (tenor) Richard McComb

> The text of "Alcottiana" is freely based on A. Bronson Alcott's "Conversations with Children on the Gospels" as published in 1837 in Boston. Bronson Alcott (1799-1888), father of Louisa May Alcott, was the transcendentalist philosopher and progressive educator whose experimental school—though short-lived—exerted a profound influence on the American scene and soon became the center of a lively controversy which did not end even with the school's eventual enforced closing.

> The libretto, as adapted by the composer, foregoes a plot in the conventional sense. It concentrates instead on the delineation of character and personality of several young people and of Alcott himself and on their emotional reactions as they are revealed in the discussion. The actual conversations were faithfully recorded at the time; Bronson Alcott's "Journals" contain in addition many fascinating references to them and to the various participants as well.

5. Two Yugoslav Songs
The Lord's Prayer (from "The Deeds of the Holy Brothers Cyril and Methodius") — *Sirola* 1883-

This setting of the Lord's Prayer appears at the climax of this oratorio where it is sung by the two Saints of the Slavic people as the decisive mark of their conversion to Christianity. It is derived from Byzantine sources and still redolent of the idiom which pervades indigenous Yugoslav folk music.

Slepacka (The Blind Beggar) — *arr. Slavenski*

Slavenski started life as a baker's apprentice and taught himself music; then studied at the Conservatory in Budapest, and like many Yugoslavs went on to finish at the Conservatory in Prague. His music is representative of nationalist Yugoslavian inspiration and is often based on folk song, as in this case. The poignant lines of the original tune are finely used in canonic imitation.

Laudes Creaturarum — *Orff*

A polychromatic setting by Carl Orff of the Hymn of St. Francis to the Sun. It is a splendid example of Orff's chordal style, written over pedal basses which are supported in this case by instruments.

6. Selected Choruses from "Candide" — *Bernstein*
> Best of all possible worlds
> I'm easily assimilated
> What's the use
> Finale

Soloists (in order of appearance):
> *Pangloss:* (bass) William Wiederanders
> *Cunegonde:* (soprano) Barbara Freeman
> *Candide:* (tenor) Richard McComb
> *Old Lady:* (alto) Judith Keller

> To many, Voltaire's "Candide" is the greatest satire ever written, as brilliant and funny today as to the 18th Century to which it was addressed. It is a satire on the philosophy that "All is for the best in this best of all possible worlds." This is what Candide learns after passing through earthquake, fire, and flood, and visiting Paris, Buenos Aires, and Eldorado, to come home at last to cultivate his own garden.

> Lillian Hellman and Leonard Bernstein have reincarnated this story in a modern musical. We have selected a few of the most striking and characteristic songs.

> "Candide" was produced at the Martin Beck Theatre on Broadway in December, 1956.

Section	Function	Appeal	Type	Period	Scoring	Visual
1	opener	general	oratorio	Baroque	accomp. choral, with solos	concert
2	contrast	chamber	madrigal	16th C.	unaccomp. sm. ensemb.	concert
3	first half close	general	light opera	Romantic	accomp. choral with solos	staged
INTERMISSION						
4	second half opener	interesting libretto	cantata	Contemp. (19C text)	acc. choral solos, ens.	staged and costumed
5	contrast	education-broaden	sacred	Contemp.	unacc. & acc. choral	concert
6	finale	general	Broadway musical	Contemp.	acc. choral solos, ens.	staged and costumed (changed colors)

Just before the concert, a few well-chosen words from the conductor can be of great value. This brief statement is sometimes just the psychological preparation your group needs.

Intermission length depends somewhat on local customs, but I personally feel that 15 minutes is about right.

Applause is intended for all participants, but it is the conductor who acknowledges it, on behalf of the chorus and himself. I feel the ability some conductors have developed to "milk" an audience completely dry is in poor taste, but, of course, not to show genuine appreciation in your recognition of their applause is also very discourteous.

When there are soloists within the choir, the conductor should single them out for applause at the end of the piece with a gesture in their direction. Visiting soloists may wish to share an ovation with the conductor through a similar gesture before leaving the stage. Whenever the conductor shares in a "curtain call," he always *follows* the soloist on and off stage.

Applause in the "wrong" place is merely the sign of an uncultivated audience, who can usually be trained over a period of time. No abrupt treatment of any kind is ever called for.

Encores are never given on the "one-evening" type of performance, but are quite proper and are usually expected for the miscellaneous concert. Obviously a touring organization will receive more demand for these extra pieces than the local group which is readily available to the listeners. Since they are mere "after-thoughts" to the program, encores should be of a light, possibly virtuoso nature, and served as the "dessert" to an otherwise complete performance.

The post-concert critique is a valuable aid to instruction. On tour, significant adjustments can be made between concerts, since basically the same program will be performed at the next stop. But even following a concert which will not be repeated, you can point out mistakes in general procedures which should be eliminated before the next performance. Some directors actually write out a full critique sheet after concerts (some even do it after rehearsals) for distribution to every member of the choir.

Unless there is something very seriously wrong which needs immediate attention, I prefer not to speak critically to the group immediately following a concert. Since each performance has its own effect on the chorus members (perhaps a feeling of uplift, or a disappointing depression), a serious evaluation session brings them "back to earth" so violently that it is never very successful, or even fair.

CHORUS IN COMBINATION

When chorus and orchestra perform together, it is *not* the chorus which should always play "second fiddle." Too many times singers will have worked very hard to prepare one of the major works to be sung with a great orchestra, only to find that the symphony conductor wants them to be able to sing *louder* than the orchestra, sometimes *softer,* but otherwise he doesn't appear to care what they do!

But all conductors are not this narrow. Consider the satisfying situation when we performed and later recorded the Bach *Magnificat* with Leonard Bernstein. He spent the larger part of the first rehearsal trying out various orchestral sections and the chorus against each other, in the context of the hall. First the woodwinds, then brass, strings and chorus. Each time he made certain that every line could be heard equally well. Not satisfied with the balance of chorus and orchestra, he sent some of the strings home. Still unhappy with the low level of volume coming from the singers, he said to me, "What's the matter with this dinky chorus?" I told him that the stage manager had not given him the correct risers; since the group was too low they were singing directly into the backs of the orchestra members and the sound was being swallowed up before it reached him. He immediately stopped the rehearsal and spent 30 minutes elevating the chorus so that they could sing *over* the heads of the orchestra. Only then was he satisfied with the balance and we proceeded with the rehearsal.

Chorus and organ combinations can create a beautiful result. There is a great deal of suitable and very wonderful literature, either actually written during, or strongly influenced by, the Baroque or Pre-Broque periods. The instrument is supposed to provide a *concealed* kind of support which allows the choral sound to predominate. When providing a contrasting type of accompaniment, the playing must be of a light and decorative nature. Unfortunately for choruses, the big modern organ has been designed primarily as a solo instrument and is not easily adaptable to this type of playing. Also, there is often great danger of a serious acoustic lag because of the distance between chorus, manual, and organ pipes.

I actually prefer a good portable electronic model to one of the grandiose 100 stop instruments, simply because it will give you what the music calls for, and can be moved to the most convenient position with very little trouble.

Small instrumental groups can add a great deal to choral performances, but we need to overcome our hesitancy to rescore works for
combinations which are available. We seem to be so tied to the
"letter of the law" as far as performance is concerned. Leonard
Bernstein has had enough spats with critics in New York over this
point that he found it quite necessary to say to an audience assembled for a *full orchestra* performance of Milhaud's *La Creation
du monde,* "I should like to explain that *we know* this work was
written for 17 instruments, but we have the composer's permission
to treat it differently."

Chorus with band is a whole fertile field which is not even beginning to be explored. There is a wealth of excellent choral music
which has never been performed by school choirs—not because they
cannot sing it, but because the 100 piece symphony orchestra called
for by the composer is not available to them. However, there *are*
many really first-rate school bands throughout the country capable
of playing the music . . . if it were re-scored.

I had never been a real admirer of bands—the music always
sounded like an outdoor athletic event or an indoor series of simple
harmony exercises—until one day I happened to overhear a summer
camp band playing Billings' beautiful chorus, "When Jesus Wept,"
rearranged by William Schuman as a fantasia for concert band. The
marvellous Gothic harmonies, attention-arresting ideas in the
orchestration, and over-all sound of the band made it one of the
most interesting things I had heard in months, and proved that the
band *can* be comfortably compatible with a choral organization.

BROADWAY SHOWS

The inexperienced, but enthusiastic, high school student may
often clamor, "Let's produce *The King and I,*" or "Why can't we do
West Side Story?" Sometimes choral directors fall into the trap and
put on a Broadway-type musical with adolescent voices, immature
instrumentalists, inexperienced actors, inept dancers, and a very
low budget. Every production I have ever seen of this type leaves
all but the most loving of parents with a very dreary impression of
musical comedy.

No school would dream of attempting an *opera* which has been
staged by the Metropolitan, but they apparently fail to realize that
the Broadway show performer must have just as much talent as any
opera star. In fact a friend of mine—a very well-known singer who

has sung in opera houses all over the world—had occasion to appear in a Rodgers & Hammerstin show. She simply could not get over how polished the productions are, and told me that the Broadway show was 100 times more professional than any opera performance.

A chorus or song from these shows makes a pleasant piece for the Junior Chamber of Commerce meeting, or for a gathering of tolerant parents, but the demands are too great, and the material too easily ruined for amateurs to try a full public performance.

STAGED CHORAL MUSIC

There is an enormous "in between" world, neither opera nor musical comedy, which *is* entirely accessible to school choral organizations. It is not a formal concert, drama, or ballet (although certain of these elements are present), but is more closely akin to the great oratorios of the late 17th and early 18th Centuries which were actually written to be staged, not to be presented in the straight concert form we hear today.

In our presentations (*see* program pp. 276-277), we have used multi-level platforms but no scenery—it is imagined. By using a simple basic costume with numerous changes of accessories, a wide variety of seemingly different outfits can be created.[3]

When staging choral music, chorus members are placed in those carefully predetermined groupings which produce the best audio and visual effects for the particular music being presented. Smooth transitions between a planned sequence of such positions are provided by individual movement and dramatic lighting. Not as rigid as a series of *tableaux vivants,* the entire process is more like stopping a motion picture film at particularly striking scenes in order to supply an appropriate setting for the performance of outstanding choral music. (*see* Fig. 12-2)

Somehow we must persuade potential audiences to abandon their everlasting dependence on television and come out to enjoy the physical presence of great music. Staged choral music, without ever compromising artistic standards, can attract these people to your concerts, thus affording you the opportunity to share with them the best our art has to offer.

---

[3] High school students are very capable of making their own costumes. A marvelous group I worked with in Lima, Ohio, once came up with some fantastic things as a result of their research and ingenuity.

Fig. 12-2

Hugh Ross and Members of *The Schola Cantorum* in a "Staged Choral Scene" from Singer's *Alcottiana*

The Printed Program

The printed program can be a very artistic tangible representation of your work in addition to serving its function as literary aid to the concert-goer. There are many acceptable printing styles. A file of programs from professional concerts you have attended can serve as a guide.

I am not personally in favor of the printing of texts, except when very important poems will be heard for the first time. I prefer a précis of the meaning of the compositions presented, in order to provide the proper atmosphere for listening. A good chorus can project a great majority of the words. Or in certain cases when a well-trained narrator is available, the words can be read to the audience before they are sung.

Judgment based on knowledge of the audience and a consideration of printing costs will determine how complete or elaborate the program should be.

Record Exchange *

There are many fine commercial recordings available of the major choral works (*The Schwann Catalog* usually lists about 8 *Messiahs*,

* Elwood Keister at the University of Florida is assembling a library of choral tapes for loan to choral directors.

4 Brahm's *Requiems*, etc.), but only a limited number of pieces which can be used by high school choirs on a miscellaneoues program. Boosey and Hawkes put the Bartok peasant songs on record for the reference of potential customers; Summy once had a series of promotional records, with score; other publishers have made similar offers from time to time.

Today more and more high schools are preserving their best efforts, on both tape and disc. Many of the groups I have worked with through the years send me very good recordings of a varied repertoire.

If performances by some of the outstanding high school choirs throughout the country could be distributed to other high school directors, they would inspire, inform, and have a significant effect on all school choral music.

Until the time some organization is able to develop a workable record exchange on a mass scale, individual directors should actively seek out opportunities to swap their recordings of usable materials with other schools.

THE MUSIC CRITIC

The critic's function is an everlastingly essential one. The fact that they are wrong on certain opinions merely becomes a necessary part of history. When criticism is entrusted to a man like Virgil Thomson, for example, certain sub-standard practices are laid so bare to public scrutiny that radical changes can be accomplished. Or when a critic (like Robert Schumann for *Zeitschrift*) gets behind a young composer (like Brahms) his rise to fame is greatly accelerated.

A good critic can point out the exact essence of a performance which each member of the audience feels, but cannot formulate. Many times the critic can put his pencil on a unique facet which has escaped the attention of everyone else. We discover the really great music largely through a process of trial and error. Generally speaking, the critic is much more representative of the trial than of the error.

Most high school directors will be concerned only with amateur "critics," that is, those who dislike pieces because they have not had the experiences necessary to understand them. While criticism should never be ignored, the source of this type must be carefully analyzed.

If the quality of performance is always kept high, and a certain amount of contemporary, even slightly shocking, music is injected into every miscellaneous program, the taste of the audience can be broadened. This is an important part of our function as musicians and teachers, and must not be neglected.

LOVE OF MUSIC IS THE FINAL RESIDUE

It is the challenge of performance which inspires choral organizations to their best efforts. Younger groups, particularly, do not take their rehearsals very seriously when no performance is imminent. On the other hand, over-performance is equally harmful. Sometimes external influences demand that the group appear in public to sing music which has nothing to do with educational objectives—in fact, may be directly opposed to them. Other times the choral director himself may be overly-enthusiastic, or too anxious to make a name for himself and move on to a better job and is pushing the organization to do more programs than they are physically and mentally capable of handling. The answer is to carefully regulate the number of appearances your group makes.[4]

There is a certain time in the lives of our students, probably between the ages of about 14 and 22, when we as choral directors have the opportunity (and as music educators the *obligation*) to provide those performance experiences which can lend meaning and direction to the life of each individual. If it does not happen while they are in school these young people may go off in any number of directions, never having sensed the deep feeling which only music can provide . . . and the opportunity is lost forever.

In 1942, Serge Koussevitzky insisted that we would go through with the Berkshire Festival, even though the Boston Symphony had told him it was impossible because the war had taken away the gasoline people needed to drive out to this country resort and they feared a financial failure. He, therefore, organized it on his own with money from some friendly foundations and an orchestra made up of graduate students.

At the garden party on Sunday afternoon, which was the traditional opening affair for the center, he said to me, "Well, we must finish the performance this year with the 9th Symphony."

"But, Maestro," I said, "how on earth do you expect to do that? There are 165 students here . . . 95 are in your orchestra . . . the rest are mostly girls . . . there are only 10 men and 6 of them are pianists

---

[4] *Editor's note*: see Louis Diercks' discussion of his performance quota, Chapter 2.

who have never sung anything in their lives . . . how are we going to perform Beethoven's 9th Symphony?"

His only reply was, "We shall perform it."

At the same party I met an old friend who provided the solution to our problem. He had just been asked to take charge of the singing at Williams College (less than 25 miles away) which had been turned into a training camp for the army engineers. I went over to the school 2 or 3 times a week in order to train the 70 men who performed with us. I still meet these men, all over the world, who were in that chorus and who will never forget the experience. You know . . . neither will I.

The opportunity of memorable performance came quite late, almost too late, for some of these young men. It is terribly important that your school choral music program be organized so that whatever else it may accomplish, it leaves a deep love of the art of music as its final residue.

13

Establishing a Program
of Permanent Value

by Thomas Hilbish

Princeton, New Jersey

Thomas Hilbish

is now Associate Professor of Music at the University of Michigan, where he moved after over 15 years of astonishing work with the Princeton (N. J.) High School Choir. His Bachelor's degree is from the University of Miami (1941), Master's from Westminster Choir College (1948). He has studied privately with Julius Herford since 1955.

Mr. Hilbish's philosophy of quality literature for music education *expressed in this chapter is supported in fact by the overwhelmingly successful Princeton High School performances of the complete* Theresa Mass *of Haydn (MENC Eastern Division, 1959),* Mass in G *by Schubert, cantatas by Bach, Honneger's* King David, The Unicorn *by Menotti, Handel's* Messiah, La Damoiselle *by Debussy,* Dido and Aeneas *by Purcell, and* Les Noces *by Stravinsky. On a State Department trip to Europe (the first high school group to be invited, in 1962) the choir's repertoire included Stravinsky's* Symphony of the Psalms, *the* Magnificat *and* B Minor Mass *of Bach,* Cantata I and II *by Anton Webern,* Magnificat *by Pachelbel, a Buxtehude cantata, and* Mass *by Roger Sessions. The music was performed, from memory, to the amazed satisfaction of audiences and music critics throughout the world. A comment from* Sovietskaya Muzyka *is typical:*

"The young singers and their director achieved complete cohesiveness of ensemble, precision of rhythm and intonation, and showed an uncommon level of vocal culture."

The truly successful school choral music program must thoroughly investigate the best literature to be found, as a part of the regular curriculum, and with the same seriousness of purpose which has characterized quality education in other fields. Students who study advanced chemistry and physics, discuss the vital political issues of our times, and read Faulkner with understanding, are capable of wrestling with problems of similar magnitude in their music classes. The conductor who continues to concentrate merely on "slick" commercial arrangements of pure "entertainment" music can neither expect to hold the interest of today's teen-ager, nor can he establish for choral music a position of permanent respect in our modern educational system.

Choose Quality Literature

When students encounter only the very predictable, cheaply melodic "ditties," they may sing, but they are not required to concentrate on the music. Their minds, understandably, are on any number of other unrelated subjects. Serious music from the permanent repertoire, however, demands and receives, the full attention of all participants.

The use of choral music of the highest quality is also the key to a solution of many other problems faced by the school choral conductor. In a Bach cantata, singers must constantly think of the phrase; voice quality has an opportunity to develop through the long melodic lines of a Schubert Mass; the ear can be trained by a mind which is forced to recognize the intervals in a 12 tone piece; a sectional independence is developed through diLasso's compositions; choral grace grows out of work with the Brahm's Liebeslieder Waltzes; sight reading is greatly improved . . . the list is almost endless. In short, I find the quickest avenue to vocal development of any age group to be through the use of quality literature.

In addition to these immediate benefits, there are numerous long-term gains as well. Since students become so familiar with and learn to love music of the highest quality, they are inclined to insist on that type of music in their church choirs and community choruses; they choose items of permanent value for their record collections; they investigate literary works by authors whose words they have sung . . . a whole new world is opened to them, both now, and in later life.

"Education" and "Training"

Both "learning to know" and "learning to do" are necessary objectives of the choral music program which expects to achieve permanent success. The director has a compelling obligation to the students, the parents, the school, the community, and to himself and his chosen profession to maintain a proper balance of these two important ingredients. He must keep from merely *talking* about music (while listening to someone else perform it) as well as resist the temptation to organize an elaborate performance schedule of "learned-by-rote" music (which only *he* may understand).

Students (whose minds are quite open) are capable of grasping musical sounds and compositional techniques which many adults (whose minds and ears are full of the 19th Century Romantic concert repertoire) consider incomprehensible. The director must continue to both train and educate, even in the face of what may sometimes seem like *everyone* (students, parents, administrators, townspeople) paradoxically clamoring for him to spend class time in an educational institution working on what are really distasteful "ditties", while he ignores the exciting literature of our great music heritage.

These comments, from an end-of-the-year, anonymous evaluation Princeton High School students were asked to write, illustrate a gradual, but eventual, acceptance of quality.

> "When we first began singing *Les Noces* it just seemed like a bunch of notes without much meaning or feeling."

> "I usually don't care for Stravinsky, but I liked this one and I think it's only because I had worked on it."

> "Bach teaches us more about music than a Broadway tune."

> "Music like Webern's or Schoenberg's is a part of our musical education which very few of us would ever have become acquainted with otherwise."

> "My parents were dead set against it and I had to drag them to the concert, but they admitted they liked it."

Public Relations

Too many times administrators (whose association with music has been little more than sharing a stage with the chorus at commencement) or students (who have heard only the radio and TV choral groups) or parents (who remember the extra-curricular "fun" type "Glee Club" popular when they attended high school) or even the choral director himself (whose musical growth may have been stunted by the limited repertoire of his college choir) develop the mistaken conviction that "souped-up" arrangements of popular songs will "really *sell* the program." They fail to realize that this music wears so poorly that they are actually creating a public image of shallowness, expediency, and the most temporary of educational objectives.

On the contrary, the choral director who is enough of a professional educator to resist the first inclinations of a musically uninformed population as he goes about the task to which he has dedicated his life (the musical education of our young people) will create the best possible public image: one that is based only on the best literature, chosen from a musical heritage spanning the entire aesthetic history of mankind.

THE MUSIC CURRICULUM

Based on "music for education, not light entertainment," an instructional program should be designed to provide students with a basic music literacy which enables them to sample, in depth, music of quality from every period.

Princeton High School maintains a 4 year program consisting of 7 periods of 50 minutes duration per day. As an integral part of the curriculum (not co-curricular or extra-curricular) we offer classes in Beginning, Intermediate, and Advanced Vocal Techniques. Theory and Harmony I and II are also available, but only a few of those in the Advanced Vocal Technique Class (the select choir, actually) are able to work it into their schedules.

We find that sometimes students are unable to schedule advanced music work because of special considerations, such as preparation for college work in another area. We always respect this decision. On the other hand, we also find some students giving up advanced work in other academic areas for the advanced vocal technique class.

In addition to these classes, there is a chorus, meeting once or twice a week during the activity period, which is open to all students who cannot enroll in the regular classes the current year because of scheduling problems. About 75% of these students have already had at least one year of instruction in vocal technique classes.

A summer program of chorus rehearsals and semi-private instruction is offered. The purpose is not to prepare a final concert for the school or community, but rather to allow students an opportunity to improve themselves individually, thus increasing their chances of being selected for the advanced choir the following year. About 10% of the students take private voice lessons which are available in the community.

VOCAL TECHNIQUE CLASSES

Before students can be expected to gain an understanding of the world's great literature they must first understand and be able to speak the language in which it is written. This seems perfectly obvious and insultingly elementary to mention, when high school teachers and administrators are discussing the content of English and American Literature courses whose prerequisites are many years of intensive, daily, formal, and informal instruction in the mother tongue. Of course, no math teacher would ever attempt to teach algebra to high school students who could not add, subtract, multiply, and divide.

Still, choral directors, for a number of reasons (among them the holdover of the "activity" concept) often rehearse a group of students whose ages span at least 4 years, and whose native ability, musical background, technical capability, and previous training are even more widely separated. It is a sort of musical one-room schoolhouse, in which students spend from 3–4 years (depending on the school grade plan), singing music which is constantly diluted by the addition of inexperienced students. An organized system in which students actually learn and can progress to advanced levels must be developed.

THE BEGINNING VOCAL TECHNIQUE CLASS

Princeton High School freshmen boys and girls meet separately 3 times per week to gain basic music literacy, vocal technique, and some familiarity with choral literature. The class participates in 2 performances per year, being incorporated into 1 or 2 choruses of a Bach cantata, for instance, presented by the advanced classes.

We have a printed course outline, but rather than follow it methodically (which often holds one back) I try to cover as fast as possible, those things which are necessary for our ultimate goal (see Fig. 13–1, Freshman Theory Exam).

1. Identify the following intervals:

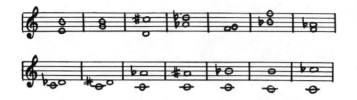

2. Add the note needed (above the given pitch) to complete the interval:

P5	M2	P4	M3	M6	m3	M7	M6	P5

3. Place the proper key signature on both the treble and bass staves:

G	B♭	C♭	A	E♭	F	D

Fig. 13-1

**Princeton High School Beginning Vocal Techniques
(Freshman) Theory Exam**

THE INTERMEDIATE VOCAL TECHNIQUE CLASS

Like the beginning class, separate soprano/alto and tenor/bass sessions are held 3 times per week; although, were it not for our own particular scheduling problems, the class would not be divided after the ninth grade. Work on basic literacy continues, but in greater depth. As the students gain more and more technique, more time is spent on literature and there are more performances.

THE ADVANCED VOCAL TECHNIQUE CLASS

This is the select high school choir. It meets every day. Although work with intervals, ear-training, solfeggio, etc. is still pursued, the major concentration is on the finest choral literature.

The first 5 to 10 minutes are spent in warm-up. Scale vocal exercises are used with girls and boys singing both together and separately. I will ask for chords to be sung in root position, beginning

Fig. 13-2

The Girl's Section of the Vocal Technique Class Conducted at Princeton (N.J.) High School by Mr. Hilbish

with A major, for example; then I will say, "perfect 4th higher," and all voices will jump up that interval to a D major chord. After that I might say, "minor 3rd lower," and they will all move to B major. This type of exercise repeated daily, using different intervals which are called out quickly, has probably helped the members of the group more than anything else; since their minds, ears, and voices must react so quickly.

Other Ear Training Devices

Bach duets are often used in the vocal technique classes. When preparing a cantata, I sometimes ask the students to *solfeg* a chorus the first time. In this way they are constantly reminded of the technique.

Both melodic and rhythmic types of dictation are given by means of recordings so that I am free to circulate throughout the room to note where students are making errors and thus improve the quality of the instruction.

Although I have no strong objection to the "movable do" system, I am more comfortable with "fixed do," and began teaching it mostly because my own training had been in this system. One day 1 came across a little group of girls who were holding their ears and singing. Their excited greeting, "This 'fixed do' helps so much that everytime you give us a new piece of music we get together and solfeg it," made me realize the special value of this system, particularly in reading 12 tone music.

Tryouts and Placement

At the end of each school year tryouts are held and the level each student has attained is determined. Most students spend their freshman year in the Beginning Technique Class, and their sophomore year in the Intermediate class where they remain until selected for the Advanced Technique Class (the choir), although occasionally an outstanding student may be taken in directly from the beginning group.

The membership of the top group, which is subject to continual tryouts, is held to between 50 and 60 voices. Those students who are not selected may remain in the intermediate class where they work to achieve an acceptable level of proficiency. Even though some never advance to the choir, they feel the vocal training and choral literature offered in the intermediate class to be valuable and therefore usually remain in the program.

Every choral conductor who has developed his own concept of the qualities he feels members of his organizations must possess will be able to recognize students with ability very quickly. I do not use any standardized achievement scale or musical aptitude test when auditioning students, but I look for those who can sight read in tune with good, easy, vocal production. When faced with a choice of "wonderful sound—poor reader" versus "average sound—excellent reader," I will always select the latter, since training the vocal production apparatus is a much faster process than training the ear.

OTHER IMPORTANT CONSIDERATIONS

Promotion of the choral music program is always necessary in one way or another, since each new student and each new parent must be convinced, each year that the study of good music deserves top priority and will directly influence the conductor's every thought and action. Some new teachers may find it necessary according to their individual taste and talents, to make the program a little more "exciting" in the beginning, but some programs remain all excitement, without ever becoming musical.

Organization of students into an assisting executive committee with appointment of various chairmen for robes, library, etc. can be a great help to the director, and allow him to spend most of his time teaching music of quality.

Choosing music from the vast lists in every publisher's catalogue is an extremely difficult task, and one that requires constant study and investigation. With the advanced choir I use many of the larger forms, rather than the shorter, individual pieces which require a shift in style after a relatively brief period. In either the *Jesu Meine Freude* or the *Missa Brevis in F*, for example, it is possible to investigate Bach and Mozart in depth.

Regular rehearsals should be scheduled on school time—as part of the curriculum. If the school administration feels that music is important enough to hire a specialist to teach it, classes should be held during regular school hours, and students should have before and after school hours to themselves.

Attracting top students is an important part of the director's job. Many a program has collapsed because the conductor, in answer to the insistent, "Can't we sing—," or "Let's sing—," has allowed musically uneducated students, parents, or administrators to choose music lacking in permanent value. Soon the intelligensia tire of it, drop out of the program, and leave the director still merely catering to those mediocre students who want to sing trash, rather than guiding the entire student body through a deeply satisfying and thorough investigation of the best musical literature.

Outside appearances of the group should be limited to those organizations who are sincerely interested in music of quality. We refuse invitations which seem to be inspired by the need to fill time on a very light, purely entertaining program, rather than an honest desire to hear the very best we can offer in the field of music education.

Departmental harmony must be maintained. No one facet of the music program can achieve permanent success if it is at the expense of the others. When a member of the choir informs us that in order to round out his high school musical education he wants to play in both band and orchestra one year, and thus cannot also schedule choir, we respect this decision.

Parent organizations formed to provide needed support for the director's program, sometimes undermine it through an attempt by some members to usurp the director's decision making powers. Choral directors are hired because they are professionals: the reigns of leadership must remain in their hands. Parents must be kept well informed, however. We have a "back-to-school" night once a year where the entire choral music program is explained.

Report card grades in Princeton are the result of an end of the marking period session in which the advanced choir is divided into quartets. Each group sings certain measures, picked at random. The beginning and intermediate classes sing in duets for their grades.

Small ensembles should be organized and supervised by the director. Not only is there a wealth of fine literature available in this medium, but there is a great deal of satisfaction and valuable training in the vocal independence required.

The choral director in establishing a truly permanent successful program must consider that elementary and junior high general music programs have a great effect on the background of the student who presents himself for training in high school. Elementary students are capble of many activities heretofore reserved for later years. We are now conducting monthly "interval bees" (like spelling bees) in the second grade. Some fourth graders are composing, individually. Much additional study and experimentation is required in this field as the resources of students in this important age group are not commonly understood and have not been fully developed.

PERMANENT SUCCESS

The choral music program which provides the best possible musical education for the students must be called "successful," regardless of the number of students enrolled, the number of out-of-town trips, or the length of the applause at a civic club luncheon.

The patient, dedicated director who uses his ability and energy to establish a bona fide instructional program, not just a flashy chorus, may not be accepted immediately by all, but the members of the community will ultimately understand that their young people are receiving a quality education under the tutelage of a professional musician-educator, and their recognition of his work, when it comes, will be of a more sincere, understanding, and permanent nature.

The skillful teacher can encourage the community to grow in understanding as he develops his program, but this takes time. In the first 3–4 years he may experience difficulties which would never occur in the 7th or 8th year, because then, people begin to realize what a director believes after a number of firm stands based on a consistent philosophy.

Quality music education (like all true education) has a tendency to spread out, often almost imperceptibly, and to permeate the atmosphere with its enlightening effects. Since *educators* must educate rather than merely entertain, and *musicians* must seek the highest of musical standards, we who call ourselves *professional music educators* must never surrender control and direction of music programs to non-professionals, by giving the public only what they seem to want at the time. Rather, it is our obligation to introduce them (both directly and through their young people) to the very best our art can offer.

This struggle for integrity, loyalty to the profession, adherence to one's intellectual instincts and aesthetic convictions is a battle which must be fought and won over and over again. Each new school year brings new students who represent new families; each new concert is a new challenge. If the conductor feels the compulsion to teach students the best music he knows, recognizes the fact that he himself can (and *must*) continue to learn, and has the will to create an educational program in the face of a clamor for mere light entertainment; he can establish and maintain a choral music program of permanent value. It has been done, it is being done—throughout the country, in large cities, in farm communities, in slums, and in private academies—by choral directors of vision who have great faith in the ability of teen-agers, and who are developing a serious musical curriculum which can keep pace with the tremendous advancements in all areas of academic achievement.[1]

[1] *Editor's note*: The choral music program created by Mr. Hilbish in Princeton is tangible evidence of the validity of this conviction. Eric Salzman wrote, in the *New York Times,* "Only a few years ago, the choral music of Anton Webern was considered to be virtually impossible to sing accurately. Yesterday the Princeton High School Choir sang the two Webern Cantatas accurately and with musical understanding. Hearing the notes, singing them, putting them together into lines and harmony, making them expressive and meaningful, is a challenge that few professionals today seem to be willing or able to meet. That these boys and girls could do it so magnificently is one of the happiest and healthiest signs that our musical culture has the potentialities of growth and renewal."

Index